Digging Deeper

Digging Deeper

Issues in the Miners' Strike

Edited by Huw Beynon

Verso

**British Library
Cataloguing in Publication Data**

Digging deeper: issues in the miners strike.
   1. Strikes and lockouts — Coal mining —
Great Britain —
   History — 20th century
   I. Beynon, Huw
   331.89'2822'334   HD5365.M6152 1984

First published 1985

© Verso and the authors

Verso
15 Greek Street London W1V 5LF

Filmset by PRG Graphics Ltd, Redhill, Surrey
Printed in Great Britain by Thetford Press Ltd, Thetford, Norfolk
ISBN 0 86091 820 3 (Paperback)
     0 86091 113 6 (Hardback)

Contents

Contributors

Huw Beynon is Reader in Sociology at the University of Durham. He is the author of a number of books including *Working for Ford*. He has been closely involved with the NUM as a lecturer and researcher in Durham and South Wales.

Dave Feickert was a founder member of the Work and Environment Research Group at Bradford University. He is currently an Industrial Relations Research Officer for the NUM.

Alan Fountain is Commissioning Editor for Independent Film and Video at Channel 4 Television.

Bob Fryer is Principal of Northern College, Barnsley. He is closely involved with trade unionism in the public sector and is the author of several books and pamphlets on redundancy and unemployment.

David Howell is Senior Lecturer in Government at the University of Manchester. He is the author of *British Social Democracy* and *British Workers and the Independent Labour Party*.

Kim Howells is a Research Officer for the South Wales NUM. He contributed to the *South Wales Miners' History Project*.

Ray Hudson is Senior Lecturer in Geography at the University of Durham. He is the author of various books and articles on regional problems including *Regions in Crisis*.

Chris Jones is Senior Lecturer in Social Policy at Preston Polytechnic. He is co-editor of the *Bulletin of Social Policy* and author of *Social Work and the Working Class*.

Loretta Loach is a member of the *Spare Rib* Collective.

Doreen Massey is Professor of Geography at the Open University. She is the author of *The Spatial Division of Labour* and *The Anatomy of Job Loss*.

John McIlroy teaches Industrial Relations in the Extra Mural Department of Manchester University. He is the author of *Strike!*

Peter McMylor teaches Sociology part-time at Sunderland Polytechnic and is a member of the editorial board of *Critique*.

David Sadler is a Research Assistant in the Department of Geography, University of Durham. He is the joint author of a major report on unemployment in Consett.

Bill Schwarz teaches Cultural Studies at North East London Polytechnic. He is currently writing a history of the Conservative Party.

Colin Sweet is Director of the Centre for Energy Studies at the Polytechnic of the South Bank, the author of *The Plight of Nuclear Power* and the editor of *The Fast Breeder Reactor*. He was a witness at the Sizewell and Windscale Inquiries.

Hilary Wainwright is an Economic Adviser in the Popular Planning Unit of the GLC. She is co-author of *The Workers' Report on Vickers*, *The Lucas Plan* and *Beyond the Fragments*. She is Chairperson of the Socialist Society.

Jonathon Winterton teaches at the University of Bradford. He is convenor of the Work and Environment Research Group which initiated research into the MINOS computer system at the NCB.

Acknowledgements

A lot of people have helped in very many ways in putting this collection together.

The people who have written the articles did so very quickly, and to impossible deadlines, when they had many other things to do. They have my thanks for that. I have talked with them all about the book, and I hope that they are pleased with the result. The idea for the book came from Colin Robinson and Neil Belton at Verso, who, along with Misha Glenny, were an enormous help in getting the materials together and working the final collection into shape.

Many people have given me their advice and generous support over the past month, and I would particularly like to thank Dewi Beynon, Pat Beynon, Greg Philo, Geoff Shears, Mark Berry, Ann Suddick, Hannah Roberts and Ross Forbes. Bob Fryer was extremely helpful in discussing the overall structure of the book and Bill Schwarz gave tremendous assistance in its later stages. Thanks also to Kim Howells and Hywel Francis in South Wales (good friends who I have worked closely with over the past four years and learned a lot in the process) and in the North East to Billy Etherington and his 'communist lackeys'. One way or the other we have kept each other going. Above all my thanks go to the people in the mining communities who I have known for many years and the many others that I met during 1984. This book barely touches upon their experiences (which they themselves must document in 1985): it has been written for them and I hope that it helps in some way.

Huw Beynon, January 1985

Royalties and proceeds from Digging Deeper will be donated to a trust fund to relieve hardship resulting from the strike amongst miners and their families.

Preface

Eric S. Heffer MP

In February 1972, following the successful miners' strike which lead to a substantial increase in wages, A. J. P. Taylor wrote in *The Times*: 'Fifty years ago the miners were driven back to the pits by the lash of hunger. Successive governments combined indifference and brutality . . . Now the miners have avenged the defeats of 1921 and 1926'.

In 1974 the miners again went on strike. Their action led to the defeat of Edward Heath's Government at the polls and the election of a Labour Government. The ruling class, especially that section which looked to the 'radical right' as the answer to Britain's problems, never forgot or forgave this. Once the Conservatives regained political office, this time under Mrs Thatcher, they determined to bring the miners to heel and, if possible, inflict a major defeat on the entire trade union and labour movement. They prepared well for this struggle; *Digging Deeper* clearly outlines their strategy. The Ridley Plan, leaked to the *Economist* in 1978, was followed to the letter: coal stocks, in Britain and abroad, were built up: power stations were converted to oil use; Ian MacGregor, an industrial hatchet man first brought in to butcher the steel industry, was appointed Chairman of the Coal Board to employ his US union-busting techniques to the full.

In considering the 1984/5 dispute, which is basically about the fight to save jobs, one is bound to look back to 1926 to contrast the situation then and now. In 1926, as today, the miners were fighting for the entire trade union and labour movement. John Wheatley, the Catholic left-wing Glasgow socialist put it well when he wrote at the time: 'The miners are fighting alone, but they are fighting the battle of the whole nation. If they lose we all lose'.

Time proved Wheatley correct. The defeat of the miners after the collapse of the General Strike became a defeat for the whole working class. Not until after the Second World War, when the demand for a skilled work-force restored the confidence and strength of workers, did the movement begin to make the real gains that were reflected in the electoral victory of the first ever Labour Government in 1945.

Despite different circumstances, the similarities between 1926 and the present strike are remarkable. First, there was the breakaway of some Nottinghamshire miners and the establishment of the 'Spencer Union'. Secondly, Baldwin, the then prime minister, constantly referred to the miners' action as 'Cook's strike', just as Tory politicians today refer to 'Scargill's strike'. Both make the mistake of suggesting that one individual, acting alone, can determine when or how a strike occurs. Of course, one should not dismiss altogether the role of the individual in history. Cook and Scargill share remarkable qualities of strength and determination and Scargill is undoubtedly one of the most class-conscious leaders the miners have ever had. That is why the Tories and the media fear and revile him. But both leaders were only able to take the stand they did because of the strength and courage of their membership.

But there are significant differences between 1926 and 1984. Not the least of these is that whilst in 1926 there were one million miners, 200,000 in South Wales alone, today the entire work-force numbers only 180,000. Another change is that, unlike 1926, the TUC General Council this time round have not been closely involved with the dispute. The miners' leaders, undoubtedly conscious of the 1920s sell out and the much more recent problems encountered by ASLEF and the NGA, have decided to call on support from the movement as a whole without handing over their affairs to people who were known to be hostile to the miners' dispute, or more precisely, *any* industrial dispute.

One of the tragedies of the strike has been the lack of all-out support from the majority of trade union leaders. Unfortunately they have set the tone for those workers at grass-roots level who have failed to respond to the strike in the way they did to Heath's 1971 Industrial Relations Act when the 'Pentonville Five' dockers were imprisoned. Partly, of course, the lack of response by sections of the rank and file has resulted from fear induced by appalling levels of unemployment. But more importantly it has stemmed from a failure of the leadership to give a clear and unequivocal lead. Apart from Bill Keys, Jimmy Knapp, Ray Buckton, Rodney Bickerstaffe, Ken Cameron, Ken Gill and a few others, most trade union leaders have given the clear impression that they wish the strike would go away because it embarrasses them. Some, like Bill Sirs, Frank

Chappell and Eric Hammond, have been downright hostile to the miners, hoping that by appearing 'responsible' the class enemy will be kind to them. Never mind that when the movement falls to its knees the enemy pushes home its advantage, just as long as they get their 'sweets' — seats in the House of Lords.

The miners' union, although not one of the first trade unions to affiliate to the Labour Party, has always been central to Labour politics. In January 1887, *The Miner: A Journal for Underground Workers* was first published with Keir Hardie as its editor. Hardie, at the time, was secretary of the Ayrshire Miners Union and secretary of the Scottish Miners' National Federation. In the first issue he argued that workers must fight for their rights: 'Let them make war against the present system till it is abolished and not only will they strengthen their own manhood by so doing, but they will gain the respect of the community at large'.

He also wrote in the same article, 'There is something more desirable than the return of working men to Parliament, and that is to give working men a definite programme to fight for when they get there and to warn them that if they haven't the courage to stand up in the House of Commons and say what they would say at a miners' meeting, they must make room for someone who will'. This could be one of the first statements on re-selection ever issued.

It is a crucial point that industrial struggle cannot be divorced from political struggle. Leaders like Keir Hardie knew this well. Strikes may embarrass leaders but they will not go away. To pretend other wise is disastrous for the movement. It is impossible to say to workers, 'Stop industrial action, stop fighting the employers, stop the class struggle . . . wait for the next election and then vote in a Labour Government'. For the truth is that if workers fail to organize and fight they will become demoralized and that results in a lack of political response not, as some hope, a turn to left-wing politics.

One thing is clear, once the miners' strike is over, whatever the outcome, the situation of the working class will never be the same again. The role of the state in British society has been clearly revealed. The state apparatus, the police, the law, the judges, the Civil Service and the media have all been used against the workers. Those involved in the strike have learned its lessons by bitter experience and will never put their trust in the organizations of the establishment as they currently exist. They expect and demand a more class-orientated trade union movement and Labour Party.

This book argues the case for coal. It also argues the case for the miners. It outlines the activities of those women who have joined the front rank of the strike, of the youngsters who have become militant trade unionists, of those who have come to understand that the government are involved in this struggle so that, at its end, they can privatize the best pits. It explains the move towards a National Police Force, the use of the welfare state as a political tool, and the rise of a new kind of politics in the mining communities. Finally, it draws out the implications of this epic struggle for the Labour Party and for socialism in general.

I am delighted to have been asked to write this preface to *Digging Deeper*, particularly as I was chairman of the Labour Party in 1984, the year the strike began. The Labour Party, as a whole, did a good job during that year. According to Arthur Scargill, it raised more money than any other section of the movement. The NEC has given its unqualified support and has been right behind the miners from the very beginning. That is something of which I am proud. That is why I must take issue with one of the contributors to the pages which follow who says that 'Labour parliamentarians accepted the orthodoxy that such a (national ballot) counted as the ultimate in demo cratic procedures'. Not all Parliamentarians accepted that. We understand that when a majority of workers take industrial action for a just cause, they have to be supported. We know this from our past experience of industrial struggles. To do anything other than give our full and unconditional support is to undermine the fight. Labour, through its NEC and party conference has given that support wholeheartedly. It will continue to do so.

Introduction

Huw Beynon

The miners' strike of 1984–5 is a landmark in the political and economic development of post-war Britain. In the breadth of the issues involved, and in the drama of its action, it stands out — even to the casual observer — as a major social and political event. In its compass it is quite staggering. Initiated by a threat to cut capacity and jobs in the coal industry it is the first major strike of any duration to be fought over the question of employment. Viewed in the context of the near calamitous decline of jobs in manufacturing industry, and the sharp rise in unemployment, the strike stands like a beacon. In the sincerity of the people involved — women and men — as they talk about the threat to mining villages, to 'whole communities' and to the futures of their children, the strike evokes a deeply human response. Since March 1984 this response has been forthcoming from supporters, in groups and as individuals, throughout Britain and Europe. The yellow stickers of the NUM ('Dig Deep . . . ', 'Coal not Dole') have spread far beyond the coalfields.

The Experience of the Strike

There are many things to say about this strike. Most important, perhaps, is what it has meant for the people who have been directly involved; the miners, their wives and their families. To capture this experience in a few words is a simple impossibility. It would take a book, and more. When people stop and reflect over the months of the dispute they astonish themselves with just how much has happened. A lot of people say that they've never experienced anything like it. Ever. It has been the major event in their lives. None of them will forget it.

In one sense the strike has been full of confusion and contradiction. In a strike over 'jobs' many men made it clear that they had no desire 'to go back down that stinking hole'. Still, those people, at the beginning of the strike at least, talked of that hole as '*our* pit'. *Our* pit and *our* village. It was a national strike but not a national strike. A strike characterized in the media by 'violence' yet one in which wives, girlfriends and children became deeply involved; in many places these people were at its very centre.

The strike has been full of pathos. In Durham, support groups met to discuss the county's 'Boot and Shoe fund'. In Sunderland the 'Mayor's fund' was discussed, again in the context of children's shoes and clothes. On waste heaps and railway lines, men crawled on their hands and knees 'picking coal'. Children who wouldn't believe that 'Father Christmas was on strike' were equally convinced that 'things will be alright when my dad's back at work.' Across Britain union officials played Father Christmas in welfare halls; not a few of them were close to tears at times.

In spite of the hardship, the deep problems of survival, there has also been a lot of humour. On a picket line in Nottingham men were told that it was an offence to shout 'scab' and 'bastard' (when they asked what *was* permissible to shout they were told 'bounder'). One group split into two and stood on different sides of the road — one lot shouted 'bas' the other 'tards'. At a court case in St Helens the prosecuting lawyer described how Durham miners were shouting 'Hya we gow; Hya we gow . . . ' Local miners shouted in that accent for weeks. On that coalfield when it looked as if the deputies might possibly be called out on strike a wag pointed to the personal column of the *Sunderland Echo*, it read:

'**NACODS** Wearmouth Branch. General Meeting. Sunday October 21, Barbary Coast Club, 20.30 a.m.

SUICIDE, despair! Day or night talk to the Samaritans in complete confidence.'

Throughout the strike, miners and their supporters collected food and money outside local supermarkets. In Mountain Ash a group stood with their collecting bucket and a trolley full of tins of food. An old lady approached them and asked 'For the miners is it bach?' and reached into her purse for a ten pence piece. She placed the money in the bucket and took a tin of corned beef from the trolley. Peter Evans, one of the collectors, commented: 'I hope she doesn't tell everybody!'

Humour and pathos built around the need to survive, as for month after month miners and their families, with no strike pay and little or no help from the DHSS, held out on strike. Viewed in terms of endurance alone it is an extraordinary achievement. To Mrs Thatcher, who expressed the view that she would personally find it quite unbearable to be in a situation without a regular income, it must have been an experience quite beyond comprehension. But it has happened, and in its happening, for all the worries and the hardships, some extraordinary things have occurred. In village after village across the coalfields the story is the same. Miners' welfare halls, clubs and school halls have been taken over. Women, with men as helpers, pack tins of food, potatoes, sugar and breakfast cereals into boxes or polythene bags — 'the parcels'. This is the food supply. Canteens have been set up to provide hot meals; stalls are set out with clothes for the children. Everywhere co-operative effort and an incredible depth of organizational ability has been put to the task of survival. And they have survived — with good grace and often with a smile. They have gone through Christmas, and many of them insist that it was a *good* Christmas, 'better than normal because we're all together more.' The women say they would never have thought that they could have done what they have done; never have believed that it was possible; it would never have occurred to them that they would have the kind of experiences they've been through in 1984/85. It has been quite extraordinary. And as one young man put it, and this was in a *very* gloomy moment, 'one thing we can say, we can take a lot of pride from what we've done in 1984. A lot of pride.'

I mention this man's gloom because the strike, for those involved in and affected by it, has been an incredibly emotional and all-consuming event. One miner registered for a part-time university course found it impossible to do his preparatory essays through the summer: 'It's impossible, I can't get down to it, I just can't stop thinking about the strike.' Women became avid watchers of the news, and video recorders taped the documentaries which covered the strike and every one of Arthur Scargill's interviews. And they were all discussed intensely.

Little surprise, therefore, that for many of these people the strike has been an educative process. They learned a lot; about the miners, the union, the coal board — about how political power operates. They learned a lot about the industry too: Durham miners will proudly tell you that they have picketed in every coalfield in the country except South Wales. Often the extent of their awareness has taken people by surprise. James Fox, for example, visited South Wales in December and produced an evocative account of the way the people there lived and organized. He begins his story at the Bruce

Hotel in Mountain Ash in 'a bar of picturesque shabbiness': 'It is, in fact, more like a shebeen than a bar, and is known to its customers as "The Shed". The discovery I made at the Bruce might surprise Mrs Margaret Thatcher and Mr Peter Walker . . . as much as it surprises me. Its customers are striking miners . . . many of them I soon learned knew the contents or had their own grubby photocopies of the *Economist's* leaked version of the Ridley Report — the Tory Party study drawn up in 1978, which mapped out its policy to dismantle the nationalized industries . . . Given the vulnerability of the South Wales Coalfield (this document) meant one thing to them: an attempt to destroy their church, the National Union of Mineworkers.'[1]

Fox registered his surprise. Others have expressed similar feelings as they have listened to men and women from the coalfields talk at meetings about subjects as diverse as the production of coal, the need for an energy policy, the threat of nuclear, the power of the press, and their fear of the police and the rise of a national force.

It was the police force which occupied people's minds most vividly in 1984. For all that the Deputy Chief Constable of Yorkshire complained that the 'trouble makers' were not 'true miners', hundreds and thousands of just such 'real miners' have described in detail and talked endlessly about the unfairness of their treatment at the hands of the police and the magistrates' courts. Visitors to mining villages in the summer and autumn have been regaled with stories of unfairness and injustice, all told with intensity and conviction. Many of those villages have experienced 'police occupation'. At Easington in Co. Durham, for example, the police referred to the colliery offices as the 'command centre'. In South Yorkshire, keen observers described a state of near 'civil war'.

In 1984 almost nine thousand miners were arrested. Two miners were killed on picket lines. The leader of the Kent miners spent ten days in jail for picketing. The South Wales area had all its funds sequestered. The National Union was taken over by a Tory Councillor from North Derbyshire who, on the instruction of the courts, declared 'I am the NUM'.

It's hard to register the horror, the dismay and disbelief which overcomes people when they mull over facts like these. Ironically, mining communities are, and have been for a long time, self-regulated, orderly places. Within them life has a pattern of its own, people know the rules and transgressions are dealt with in one way or another. In these places, people will tell you that 'we know each other'. They know each other and they know where they come from; they also know where they belong. These are the people who march together in parades and galas, the same people whose banners have been captured, evocatively, in television news broadcasts and documentaries. These are also the people who risk their lives in what is still the most dangerous of jobs and who appear as heroes in stories of mining accidents and tragedies. It is the same people who have steadfastly refused to return to work in spite of the orchestrated blandishments of money from the NCB. It is these same people who have been described as 'the mob' by Mrs Thatcher and other members of the cabinet. 'The mob' and 'the enemy within'. The transformation in images is quite incredible and to many in the mining communities it is an unspeakable violation of themselves, their lives and all that they stand for. It has made them angry and very, very bitter.

In all these ways the miners strike has been an astonishing event. And its complexities don't end there. As a major struggle for jobs and employment undertaken by a union in the teeth of an offensive from the most right-wing Tory administration in living memory it would seem, on the face of it, to have all the makings of a *unifying* force within the British labour movement. Yet almost the opposite has happened. Within the NUM itself, areas refused to join the strike, and as time passed this division increasingly raised the spectre of a permanent split in the organization of the miners. For all the show of solidarity and support at the TUC conference, many union leaders were soon to admit privately that they 'couldn't deliver' the support of their members in strike action. To many it seemed that they had not tried very hard. At that conference, predictably, the electricians and the power station engineers registered their opposition to the strike and the leadership of the NUM. The Labour Party leader, speaking at the TUC and later at the Labour Party conference in Blackpool supported the miners while, by implication, criticizing them. These are the most telling of ironies and they deeply affected the viability of the miners' struggle.

Perhaps the most significant conflict, in human terms, took place within the mining communities themselves. From the beginning the coalfields in the Midlands were divided by the dispute. Nottingham and Staffordshire were split quite decisively while in Leicester and South Derbyshire only a handful of men joined the strike. In Leicester they called themselves the 'Dirty Thirty' and were deter-mined to hold out until the end. In South Derbyshire the strikers were spread in ones and twos across the coalfield. Isolated but politically convinced of the justice of their action, they cast a badge of their own. Distinctively shaped, it carried the motto 'Time — the Avenger'.

Pickets who entered these areas in the early months of the strike were surprised, sometimes shocked, by the lack of response they found from the men who continued to work: 'How could they pass through picket lines?', 'How can they drive past and see us penned in by police — like animals?' These questions, allied to ideas of solidarity and bound up in words like 'scab', were asked repeatedly. They drew from Roy Hattersley the admission that, were he a Notts miner, he would be on strike. They became more and more painful as the NCB pressed to break the solidarity and divide the miners in the strike-bound coalfields. The scale of the anguish as families divided against each other and life-long friends broke irrevocably was enormous. It became a moral and political struggle *within* the working-class movement. A struggle over the legitimacy of action — in which the men who worked, who defied the picket lines, the 'scabs', made repeated references to 'the ballot'.

The Question of the Ballot

Throughout the year of the dispute, a view persisted that the strike was, in some way, tainted by the absence of a national ballot. Certainly this was one of the sticks used, and used persistently, by members of the Tory Government to attack the NUM and its leadership. If that was the extent and limit of the criticism it could be dismissed as simple prejudice. However, similar criticisms (always accompanied by suitable caveats recording support for the miners) have also persisted within the labour movement. Few Labour Party or union branch meetings which discussed the strike have not raised the issue of 'the ballot' at some time or another. At their best these criticisms turned around a real worry that perhaps the union leadership had been involved in a bending of the rules and that this would rebound upon the miners in their attempts to build support both within the NUM itself and thereafter from other sections of the labour movement. At worst the persistent reference to the ballot has conjured up images of an unscrupulous union leadership, manipulating, even coercing miners to act against their better judgement and interests.

In considering these views it is important to recognize that they are not entirely ill founded. Wrong they may be, even malicious, but there is some substance to them which needs to be dealt with. For example, it *is* the case that in South Wales most of the lodges were reluctant to strike and that the miners there joined the strike largely as a result of picketing by striking miners from other parts of the area. Equally, in Durham, while the men at the two pits, Herrington and Sacriston, seriously threatened with closure voted to strike, men in the other pits agreed to join the dispute only so long as there would be a confirming national ballot within the foreseeable future. In that area, most people anticipated that the national executive committee would be calling a national ballot in May or June, certainly after the special delegate conference decided to reduce the necessary vote for strike action from fifty-five per cent to a bare majority.

With hindsight, the decision *not* to hold a ballot at that time might be seen as a tactical mistake. One man — totally loyal to the union and deeply committed to the strike — noted how: 'On looking back now I think we should have had a ballot then. It would have taken a lot of pressure off us. It has been like a monkey on our backs. Everywhere we've gone we've had to answer the question of the ballot: not the strike and the issue of jobs and nuclear power — the ballot. And I think we would have won it. I think we would have won it at fifty-five per cent let alone fifty per cent.'

There is some support for this view, certainly on the likely result of a ballot. In areas which *had* voted (mostly those least likely to support the strike), the 'swing' since the last ballot in March 1983 was around ten per cent. Yorkshire had polled a poor vote for a strike in that ballot; in 1984, with a Yorkshire pit directly affected, a call for strike action could have been expected to receive strong support in this, the biggest area of the NUM. One of the features of the dispute (and to reflect upon this is to ask quite a different series of worrying questions) has been that public opinion polls have rarely tested opinion amongst the miners. Where it has been done (by MORI for 'Weekend World', by the *South Wales Echo* in South Wales, and by the *Liverpool Echo* in Lancashire and North Wales), the results have shown a support for the strike which was deeply set and surprisingly strong. To have called a national ballot could well have been to poll a vote for victory. To an important extent this is 'water under the bridge'. The man quoted earlier ended his comments with just this phrase, and *everyone*, even those in the striking coalfields who spoke out forcefully for a ballot in March, agreed that subsequently it became an academic issue. It is something that history will have to judge, and with an eye on this it is important to add a few more points, to try to understand *why* there was no ballot.

The more even-handed of journalistic commentators admit

8

that 'the right' whilst in power in the NUM were particularly adept at manipulating things in their direction. They also concede that 'the left's' experience of the antics of Joe Gormley, the 'Battered Cherub', goes a long way to explain many of their present attitudes. Attitudes which are captured in comments to the effect that 'we have the presidency now'. However, it is less than adequate to move from this to a view of the strike which is simply Machiavellian as Michael Crick does, for example. He describes how 'Arthur Scargill simply outmanoeuvred the right with a move that Joe Gormley would have been proud of . . . In the course of five weeks Scargill and the left had pulled off a brilliant piece of political footwork. They had been able to call a national strike but without holding a national ballot'.[2]

There is no doubt that there are 'left' and 'right' factions within the NUM, nor that these factions meet occasionally in caucus; nor even need it be contested that there are people on the left and right who understand the union as a machine whose levers of power require firm manipulation by those in control. But to see the NUM entirely in these terms and to interpret the present dispute simply at the level of manipulation and backstage meetings is to miss a lot; maybe the most important things. To begin with, the left and right factions are nothing like as homogeneous within the union as they were in the 1970s. The rank and file NEC representation from Durham, and the election of Bill Etherington as general secretary of the Durham Mechanics (a union which, to quote the *Financial Times*, was once 'a byword for extreme moderation') were important events which reflected more than 'left organization'. They were part of a process whereby miners and their families were reacting to the issue of pit closures and the future of employment in the North. This point is verified by the role played by Sid Vincent ('El Sid' as he was described in the *Daily Star*) in Lancashire. Steadfastly of the 'old right' he remembers the pit-closure programme of the 1960s and, almost in spite of himself, has recognized that the 1980s represent a crisis of a similar order for the NUM and regions like Lancashire.

The issue of pit closures, its nature and its consequence, deeply affected the options open to the NUM. In this it has been held firmly in the grip of its past.

The idea that the NCB intended to close pits at a faster rate could have taken no-one active in the mining industry by surprise. Arthur Scargill fought his presidential campaign on precisely this question. In meeting after meeting, in every coalfield, repeatedly, he hammered out his speech: The government was out to attack the industry; there was no getting away from it; nuclear challenged coal

. . . again and again. And always with the same ending: 'If you want someone who will prostitute his principles for office get someone else because I'm not interested . . . I'm sick to death of leaders who say one thing and do another. I will not compromise . . . ' Again and again and always tumultuous applause; always packed meeting halls; always the young miners smiling, laughing, joking: 'Newcastle have got Keegan — we've got Arthur Scargill'. He won that election with the highest percentage of the vote ever recorded in an NUM national election. Normally tight-fought affairs, this one was a landslide: seventy per cent of the miners voted for Scargill. He swept through area after area. Chadburn and Bell were not in the frame. These are important points to remember. A general public whose access to the strike, to Scargill and to the miners is limited by the inadequacies of our national media probably lack any sense of the rapport which Scargill built up with NUM activists during the early 1980s. For them, his meetings (for all the grimness of his predictions) were something of a liberation. He voiced their feelings about the board. His humour — always deeply mocking and iconoclastic (Hobart House, NCB Headquarters, was regularly pilloried as 'that big loss-maker in London', 'the only pit they've been near is a pulpit'), relying heavily upon mimicry and detailed accounts of 'private' meetings — was quite revelatory. Scargill was different from the old left. He had a kind of star quality. He was certainly different from the old right.

Many people thought that he'd change — that office would change him, of necessity. For his part he has been singularly determined to remain the same — King Arthur. The first two years of office explored this tension. In July 1982, in the County Hotel in Durham, he'd never been better. He'd just returned from the NUM Annual Conference in Inverness. At that conference 'the left' had swept the board. It wasn't so much that 'the right' was in disarray, they simply hadn't fielded a side. Speakers at the conference repeatedly supported the progressive approach of the new leadership. Scargill commented, 'It's going so well I'm just waiting for something to go wrong.'

It started to go wrong in November 1982 with the negotiations over the pay round. The coal board insisted during these negotiations that the rate of colliery closure would have to increase. A special delegate conference decided that the membership be balloted in a way which combined the two issues. Miners were to be asked to vote against both the wage increase and the threat to collieries. Clearly the two issues were linked. Certainly they were linked in the mind of the coal board: they were prepared to greatly increase the wages of men in the super-pits on condition that the loss-making pits close. Equally certain is the fact that many members of the union objected to the way the issues were combined on the ballot paper: 'It might be wrong, but the way a lot of people look at it is that there were two issues on the ballot paper and they only had one vote. A lot of men objected to that, "It's my vote", that's the way they think. And a lot of genuine lads felt that. The other thing of course is that it give "the shit" a let out. The sort of people who are always looking for a way out of doing anything; them sort of people were able to say "I would have voted for the pits but I only had one vote and I wanted the wage increase".'

Whatever the reason the ballot saw the union's recommendation defeated heavily. The scale of this defeat had a severe effect upon the thinking of miners and union officials in the South Wales and Scottish coalfields. Scotland virtually caved in when faced by a pit closure programme that can only be described as an all-out assault upon mining employment in the area. South Wales, on the verge of a path-breaking 'investment strike' overwhelmingly supported by a ballot vote, stopped at the brink. The fear of isolation in these threatened areas was intense. It was matched only by the deep feeling of frustration induced by the increasingly assertive approach of the coal board, and the almost desperate state of local employment in the mining villages.

In March 1983 a group of men 'sat down' underground at the threatened Lewis Merthyr Colliery in South Wales. 'Sit downs' are emotive issues in the South Wales area, and hark back to the desperate struggles of the 1930s when members of the Miners' Federation struggled against company unionism. In the spring of 1983 the men of Lewis Merthyr obtained support across the coalfields of South Wales. The NEC supported the strike, and called for a national ballot. At that moment the South Wales area took a bold and imaginative decision. Miners from the area would visit every lodge and pit in the country to explain the case on pit closures. Buses left for Scotland, Durham, Lancashire, for Yorkshire and Nottingham; across the Midlands and for Kent; two thousand Welsh miners attempted to explain the case for saving Lewis Merthyr and assuring the security of mining in the 'peripheral coalfields'. This phrase was used a lot as miner met with miner and talked about the issues. Everywhere, they said, the reception was good. Many of them learned a lot about different things, especially wages: 'Some of the places we stayed in Nottingham were like palaces — miners' houses worth £60,000 or something like that. I stayed with a Nottingham miner and he was telling me the bonus that they earn at his pit was £24 a shift. We don't get that in a month at our pit.' They felt they were given the PR treatment by the Nottingham area. 'I think a lot of it was guilt money. They made promises and they treated us well but I don't think they really went out to argue our case for us. They said they would, but I don't think they did.'

These events need more detailed study and reflection than is possible here. Whether the Welsh strike was tactically right or not is something which still divides people. What unites them is an understanding that the union faced an increasingly difficult, even traumatic, period.

Again just thirty-nine per cent had voted for the strike and again the main source of opposition to the strike was certain groups, like COSA, the white-collar section, and areas like Nottingham and Leicestershire. The scale of this defeat forced miners in South Wales and some of the other threatened areas to ask deep questions about strategy. In doing so they looked at the ballot upsets of November and March and came to a number of conclusions. In March only fifteen per cent of COSA and nineteen per cent of Nottingham members voted 'Yes'. In Leicester the percentage was eighteen per cent; in South Derbyshire twelve per cent. Notts and the Midlands, so many people argued, would *never* support threatened miners in South Wales, Scotland and the North East. The March ballot vote was seen to condemn them almost out of hand — 'only twenty per cent of the fuckers would vote to help save the job of another man — that's fucking disgraceful that. It is mind. It's disgraceful.'

In this way the March vote was a truly decisive event, a marker. It produced a deep feeling amongst miners in the threatened areas that they were on their own. To some, this meant that they were finished: 'I think I know how the coal board are thinking now. All their investment will be going into the central areas such as Yorkshire and Nottingham and before long there'll be no pits left in Durham, in South Wales and Scotland. It will all be grassed over. It will be as if there never were any mines in these places.' Others, and at times this included the majority of the active union members in those areas, felt that there was now nothing left to lose. 'Over the top' was one phrase used. Another was 'backs to the wall', and 'it's us or them'. One man from South Wales reflected that the ballot vote itself was wrong. South Wales had come out on strike, constitutionally and in defence of jobs. The NEC had recognized the area's right to fight. The NEC should have left it at that. South Wales should have been allowed to fight on — alone if need be. At the time it was argued that South Wales pickets could have built on the contacts they had made and carried the idea of the strike into the other areas. 'Everything that was done up to the ballot was done right. It was the ballot that was wrong. The NEC should have left South Wales to carry on the fight for jobs.'

A number of things are important here. To begin with it's a matter of record that those things *were* being said and that they had an influence upon the thinking of leaders of the NUM. In 1983 the Scottish area was given permission, under rule 41 which allows areas to take strike action on their own, to pursue its defence of the Monkton Hall Colliery in the manner that it felt most able. More complex is the question of the structure of the NUM and the issue of colliery closures. Jimmy Reid, for example, has been a harsh critic of the NUM's conduct of the dispute and a strong advocate for a national ballot. Along with his supporters he has contrasted his own experiences with the UCS occupation and the idea that the unity achieved there and the support obtained from outside was linked to a ballot vote. What Reid and others have underplayed, however, is the way in which workplaces — like UCS — were allowed, under the constitution of the confederation of unions involved in the shipyards, to fight their own fight. Reid was not obliged to obtain a national ballot vote for a strike amongst all shipyard or engineering unions. In this, and many other ways, the situations are not similar.

The NUM is an *industrial* union and is the clearest example of this form of organization in Britain. Industrial unionism has been seen by the syndicalists, and other supporters of a strategically operated and militant trade unionism, as the most appropriate form of organization for dealing with modern industry. To an extent that is true. It does however have drawbacks. General unions can develop strike funds which allow members on strike to be supported by members not involved in the dispute; this is more difficult in an industrial union when all the members are likely to be on strike together. But in terms of formulating a policy and strategy for an industrial sector — formally at least — it has some powerful advantages. The NUM, however, is also a *federated* union, and the extent to which federalism — the independence and separateness of areas and groups — dominates the industrial logic of the union, affects its veracity as a powerful national body. The organization of the industry means that regional office staff (in COSA) rarely meet to discuss issues with miners on a day to day basis; miners in Nottingham never meet with miners in Kent. The structure of the union has done little to help break down these barriers of experience. Since the introduction of area incentive payment schemes in 1977, this separateness has increased to the extent that, in the 1980s, thoughtful union activists concede that 'we are a national union in name only.' Worries of this kind induced Jack Taylor's remark to the effect that he 'didn't really trust' the Nottingham area. The feeling had grown (rightly or wrongly, but out of experience, and the struture of the union, not out of malice) that Nottingham would *never* vote for strike action, and that on an issue which didn't directly affect them, like colliery closures, they could not be relied on to adhere to a national decision.

If the issue at stake in March 1984 had been a wage increase or cut there would not have been a strike. The issue was colliery closures and unemployment. It is for those reasons that Peter Heathfield has argued passionately and with great conviction that 'it cannot be right for one man to vote another man out of a job'; that a ballot on wages is a ballot which everyone enters on an equal basis and everyone is affected by equally; on jobs it is a different matter, especially when the jobs are at risk in some areas and not others. A political parallel with Ulster might be helpful: clearly an individual ballot vote taken throughout Ulster on the future of the Catholic housing estates would not be seen as democratic, and it has been accepted that built-in safeguards for minorities which go beyond the ballot box are an essential adjunct to the democratic process however defined. The miners' union faced precisely such a problem in 1984. The jobs issue cut deeply into its very bowels and there was no easy solution. Arthur Scargill put it well at the Barbary Coast Club in Sunderland on the critical weekend at the beginning of the strike: 'members of this union are at the cross roads and there are no easy options.'

Picketing and Politics

There is now little doubt that the Tory Government, aided by clear and long-term tendencies within the British State which are anything but benign, prepared carefully for a confrontation with the miners. Part One of this book explores the dimensions of this preparedness, and it shows how the Tories were able to view the development of the dispute with confidence. In 1974 a Tory Government had gone to the country in the middle of a coal strike; in 1981 the Thatcher Government had back-pedalled rapidly in the face of such an escalation. *Private Eye* carried a front cover with Heath

smirking at Thatcher's discomfort. In 1984, there was no possibility
of either course being followed. It was going to be a long strike or
nothing.

In June, while attending a Conservative student lunch at the Three
Tuns Hotel in Durham City, the Home Secretary, Leon Brittan, was
gently barracked by a group of miners from the Horden Colliery,
along with women from other pit villages in the area and their
visitors from Nottingham. He agreed to meet a deputation of six
people. They went in to talk with him; when they left their emotions
were running high. One of the men had wanted to explain to Brittan
about picketing and to ask the Minister why he had made such
provocative statements on the subject: 'I tried to explain to him what
it was like to live in this area and how we were all dependent upon the
pit in the village. I tried to get him to understand what it was like
from the standpoint of the ordinary working man; the ordinary
working fella . . . But he didn't want to know. He just didn't want
to know.' One of the Nottingham women was deeply upset. 'All he
said to us that I can remember is "You can't win". I kept saying
"We're going to win". For him though it was a question of winning
and we couldn't win.'

Given the scale of the coal-stocks, the pattern of voting in previous
ballots, and the kind of preparedness which ran right through the
state, Brittan's confidence was perhaps well-founded. Certainly the
way it was flaunted was characteristic of the new Tory style. Given
this it might be asked — and many have — why did the NUM strike
in such forbidding circumstances? The idea that the NUM was out of
its mind to strike at the end of winter, and wilfully wrong to provoke
the power of the Thatcher state, held a great deal of currency
amongst political activists on the left and centre of British politics.
Often in discussions with engineering workers there was a sense of
admiration (which trade union in Europe could sustain a strike this
long under these conditions?), but also of disbelief (how could the
NUM win against these kinds of odds?). Time and time again, in car
plants, engineering workshops and textile mills there had been campaigns against closures but never with success. Almost always they
ended in bitterness. But now, so late on, the NUM was standing out.
How was it possible?

These points need answering; and again they need to be treated
with some care. To understand the 1984 miners' strike as a provocative, offensive strike by a vanguard section of the working class is
to miss the point — almost completely. In terms of *its* strategy, the
NUM leadership wanted to fight in 1982. The stocks were low, it was

the beginning of winter and the writing was clearly on the wall for pit closures. (On that ballot, Joe Gormley broke with all established NUM protocol and procedure and wrote an article in the *Daily Express* which deeply undermined the position taken by the NEC. That too is water under the bridge.) Any plan the leadership had for 1984 rested with the overtime ban. Such a ban, which did not require a national ballot, was seen as an effective way of cutting back production. It was introduced in November, and in January Scargill seemed content to keep it in force for the whole of 1984.

During this period, Peter Heathfield was involved in his election campaign for the position of general secretary. In January the over- time ban was causing all kinds of problems for the union but, at bottom, he felt that 'it was better than a strike'. The NUM leadership was not spoiling for a fight in 1984. The election result for the general secretary (when the left's senior figure, Peter Heathfield, barely scraped home against John Walsh, a union agent from North Yorkshire) confirmed the feeling of caution. It was the widely leaked NCB plan for colliery closures which affected the situation decisively. The strategy being followed by the NUM was a defensive strategy, and the strike, when it came, was a defensive strike.

In March 1984 the union was placed in a difficult position. On 6 March, the NCB announced to the joint representatives of the con- stituent unions, the NUM, NACODS and BACM, that there was to be a cut in capacity of four million tonnes and that a third of this was to come out of the North East area. (In Durham the blatant unfairness of this was often raised and people would ask 'why?'. The answer often given 'because they think we're a soft touch' says a lot about people's attitudes and feelings at the time.) The four million tonnes reduction was to be on the *actual* production totals for 1983/4. This total was four million tonnes below output targets because of the overtime ban. The cutback to 97.5 million tonnes represented a *capacity* cut of eight million tonnes. As far as the NCB was concerned, this was not a negotiable situation. The cuts were a *fait accompli*. As if to make this clear the Yorkshire area announced the imminent closure of Cortonwood Colliery. Located in an area of high un- employment, the pit had an established life of over five years. Men who had been transferred to the pit within the previous fortnight had been promised a secure spell there before it closed. The announce- ment of closure broke all procedures established in the industry for dealing with questions of capacity reduction and colliery perfor- mance. It was a deeply provocative act.

In the period which followed the 'successful' strike of 1981, when the NCB last announced a pit closure programme and were forced to withdraw it, the NCB proceeded to close pits at an accelerating rate. In 1982 they broke the back of the Scottish area with the closure of Kinneil. What followed, in what has always been thought of as a 'hard core' area for the union militants, was a year of union frailty in the face of the tough approach of its crew-cut area Chairman, Albert Wheeler. Commenting on his approach the *Scotsman* noted that 'viewed dispassionately as an exercise in aggressive management (his) tactics and record in directing the Scottish coalfield command a certain kind of black admiration. In just thirteen months he has slashed the number of Scottish pits from fifteen to nine with only one new colliery being opened up in the future.'[3]

At least, in Scotland they had *one* new pit. In the North East and Wales there was no such consolation. The South Wales area headed by Philip Weekes (the boyhood idol of Neil Kinnock and a man who had been closely involved in the Welsh Labour History Society conferences of Llafur) had taken a softer line. There, of course, the board had burned its fingers in 1981 and in 1983. Also the specialized coals found in that coalfield acted as a check upon the narrowly financial enthusiasm of the NCB. This enthusiasm ran unchecked in the North East, however, where another aggressive Scotsman, David Archibald, had, in his tight-lipped no-nonsense style, slashed the area dramatically in the year that followed the 1981 dispute. Houghton, Blackhall, Boldon, Marley Hill, South Hetton, all closed; other collieries on the way down. All of this, looked at from the standpoint of the board, was plain sailing. South Wales demoralized, Scotland finished. The North East — with its history of moderation — not really a starter were it to come to a showdown. All that was left was Yorkshire.

In 1981, when Scargill was president, the Yorkshire area ran a campaign against pit closures. It organized an area ballot in which Yorkshire miners were asked to agree that the area would strike immediately a pit in the area was threatened with closure outside the framework of agreement laid down in the pit review procedure. Yorkshire miners insist that the eighty-three per cent vote in support of that resolution saved pits and jobs in Yorkshire. They also insist, and with sound logic, that the Cortonwood closure was a *political* decision, (i.e. more to do with the balance of power than the economic or geological logic of coal production), aimed at isolating the Yorkshire area and finishing off opposition for good and all.

To an extent, of course, this is speculation. However it isn't *wild* speculation. The NCB, under MacGregor, was clearly set upon a course of action in relation to pit closures. Scargill, equally clearly, represented a focus for opposition when the powerful Yorkshire union (over sixty-thousand miners and his home base) could be the muscle needed at a crucial moment. To get Yorkshire out on strike and isolated at a bad moment could be the finishing touch of MacGregor's strategy and provide the basis for an unhindered move towards profitability and privatization.

The Tory Government had clearly prepared for this dispute, but it is most unlikely that they anticipated or prepared for a strike that would last a year and demand such intensive and costly counter-measures. They had planned to defeat the NUM quickly. They didn't succeed.

But the NUM, for its part, was fighting on a different terrain from that which brought it victory in 1972 and 1974. In the early 1970s unemployment was still under one million, at the beginning of 1984 it was nearer four. British manufacturing industry has virtually collapsed — nowhere more dramatically than in the West Midlands, the scene of the mass picket at the Saltley Coke Works. Ten years ago shipyard workers and miners were able to call upon the support and loyalty of engineering workers at picket lines and also at rallies and parades. Today many of these workers have either been forced to change jobs (via the sack or 'redundancy') or they are out of work. Those in work are increasingly oppressed and frightened by the threat of closure and redundancy. While many workers have refused solidarity action because 'the miners can't get their own members out', equal numbers have hesitated because of the vulnerability of their own jobs and the companies they work for. The way in which this fear in the minds of, say, steel unions and the oil-fired power station workers links into the question of the legitimacy and nature of the NUM's tactics during the dispute is an issue of central importance.

The NUM's strategy for a successful strike rested largely on two assumptions: that Nottingham could be involved in the dispute and that the Triple Alliance, so carefully developed in the early 1980s, would produce the muscle necessary to throttle the coal economy. However, both came unstuck. The kind of police presence exercised at Warrington for the NGA picket in November 1983 was a clear signal that picketing in 1984 was going to be a lot different from 1972. With the closure of exit points on the M6, the use of police in riot gear, the stories of direct and unprovoked attacks by police on pickets, and the destruction of the NGA's communication van, the writing was clearly on the wall, and with hindsight was written in very big letters indeed. To cope with the scale of the police organization the union would have had to mount its own military-style operation. And in spite of repeated statements from the Home Office ministers to the effect that the NUM was organizing a national conspiracy, the structure of the union precluded the emergence of such a command network. Within the union each area was responsible for its own picketing operations. Pickets were paid a daily subsistence fee and this came out of area funds. Although a national co-ordinating committee was set up at Sheffield, it was never able to take the strike by the scruff of the neck and direct it. The only 'national' event, as such, was the mass picket at the Orgreave coke works. That event was significant for the fact that the police force allowed the buses of miners to arrive in Sheffield, and then confronted them with the immense power of an organized military operation — something which no one who witnessed it will ever forget. What emerged was a series of more or less *ad hoc* arrangements built up around area autonomy. One such arrangement found the Yorkshire area mostly responsible for picketing in Nottingham, and as a strategy for halting the movement of coal this failed. However much its extent and significance was played down, it was clear that if bridges couldn't be built with the Nottinghamshire miners the production of coal there would continue to be a problem for the union. It untied the knot of support with the NUR and ASLEF whose members supported miners in the striking areas while moving coal to power stations in the Midlands.

Not quite as damaging, but damaging enough, was the link with the third party to the Alliance — the steelworkers. Within the logic of the Alliance, these workers should have agreed to limit their intake of coal; they should have cut production and supported miners on strike. It didn't work out like that. With good cause the miners in the striking coalfields (and *all* the coking coalfields were on strike, *no* coking coal being produced from the deep mines) felt disgruntled. They could point to the ways in which they had supported the steelworkers during their confrontation over wages in 1980. Perhaps however, and with hindsight again, this was predictable enough. For although steelworkers and miners live in the same areas (Scotland, South Wales, the North East and Yorkshire), they tend to live in separate worlds. The steel plants are all on the coast and three of them are linked to deep port facilities for the importation of coal, coke and iron ore. The Triple Alliance, (for all its formal statements and undertakings), had organized few meetings which actually brought together workers from the pits and the steel mills to thrash out a common understanding. Local agreements had been built up between areas of the NUM and the ISTC and the variations between them became quite critical during the strike. The steelworkers, remember, had already been savaged by the cutbacks in capacity imposed under MacGregor's chairmanship. Of the five supermills that remained open, rumours persisted that one, or even two, might have to close. As one miner put it: 'the steelworkers are shell-shocked after what has happened to them.' So shell-shocked were they, in fact, that the threat by BSC of catastrophic damage and plant closures was enough to weaken any resolve that existed for a fight in support of the coal industry. Certainly there is no excusing the lack of integrity shown by ISTC leader Bill Sirs, but as one man put it at a meeting in the North East 'it's like asking for a blood transfusion from a corpse.'

With this two–pronged strategy in tatters, the NUM's prosecution of the strike was in severe difficulties. If the strike was not going to be a knock-out blow for the NCB, neither was the NUM going to get a quick victory. For the NUM to place a tourniquet upon the flow of coal, it needed something better than the Triple Alliance. Best of all, of course, would have been an Energy Alliance which linked miners with workers in the oil and gas industries and the power stations. Such an alliance however, while clearly expressing the new *economics* of coal, cut against the historical and political grain of the NUM and other unions in the TUC. Without such a link the NUM was deeply vulnerable. The more so given its isolated position within the international coal mining unions. While Belgian and Australian miners and dockers gave support to the NUM, deliveries of coal from Poland, West Germany and the USA escalated. Coal flooded up the Humber and the Trent (where the hedgerows and verges were blackened with coal dust) and to virtually every unregistered port from Inverness southward along the east and south coasts. In this respect the contrast between the NUM and, for example, the union organization at Ford is quite startling. At Ford, the international structure of the company produced a form of trade unionism which, when necessary, could seal off imports from Europe. Ford workers, however, almost certainly lack the community forms of organization necessary to sustain a strike for as long as a year.

By the late summer the strike had become a war of attrition. As a strategic exercise in controlling the movement of coal it had almost ceased to exist. In the strike-bound areas coal stockpiled at pit heads and on open-cast sites stayed put; elsewhere it moved more or less freely, and 700,000 tonnes a week were delivered to the power stations in the Midlands. In this period, the pickets were pushed back on the gates of their own pits or diverted to the task of organizing support meetings and collections, and speaking at rallies across Britain and Europe. Many of them had been bound over or were free on bail conditions which severely limited their movements. The strike had become a test of endurance; it also became increasingly political. As John Lloyd put it, the issues were 'basic, fundamental, ideological and apparently unbridgeable.'[4]

Put in this way, the main features of the strike can be reassessed. A defensive strike fought under difficult conditions by a union which, unlike all other national unions, had not been savagely cut back as the recession bit in the late 1970s, the strike represented not so much the front line as the last ditch. In its continuation and strength it rested to an enormous extent upon the will-power, imagination and organizing abilities of the people who live in the mining villages. This 'community' strength and loyalty was the NUM's ace; a card that represented years of historical experience of struggle and strikes, reflection and story-telling. Throughout the 1984 strike the people of the mining communities young and old, men and women, talked about other struggles and about how this strike differed from 1972 and 1974. They asked questions about 1926: How long did it last? When did it start? In all this they gained a strength from the fact that they, or their parents and grandparents, had been through such a struggle before. It could be done again.

The Politics of Unemployment and Change

Margaret Thatcher was right about one thing. This has been no ordinary strike. If the right to strike for jobs causes problems for union ballots, so too does conflict over jobs and the survival of communities raise questions which go to the heart of our political system.

Harold Macmillan, Lord Stockton, described the miners as 'wonderful men . . . they'll never give in'. The strike, he said, was breaking his heart. More ironic perhaps were the views of Enoch Powell. Speaking to Manchester Conservatives in November he expounded his theme, talking of a deeply dangerous society caught in the grip of 'gloomy resignation and passive acceptance of inevitable catastrophe', of resentment building up 'at the apparent wilful blindness and ignorance of those in authority'.[5] If the action of the miners and their families in defence of their stricken communities touches

chords in the old Toryism of the right (a form of politics now
blocked by the ascendancy of the Thatcher group) it is truly ironic
that sympathetic developments have been so limited on the left of the
political spectrum. Here, all too often, the view of history is dominated by technological imperatives. This was the case in the 1960s
and the modernizing period of Harold Wilson. Today the talk is of a
post-industrial society. In his article in *The Spectator*, Jimmy Reid
wrote that: 'the labour movement must come to terms with the new
technological revolution. It must see it as a means of liberating
workers from dirty and dangerous jobs. The right to work must
mean shortened working hours for everyone. In the long term this
cannot be achieved by claiming a person's right to work at a specific
job for the rest of his or her life. This would freeze the division of
labour and would preclude any economic or technical progress. If
jobs had been frozen two hundred years ago, we would still have
thousands of stage-coach drivers in Britain today, presumably
driving stage coaches. By the end of this century I would hope that
modern technology, among many other things, will have ended the
need for human beings to work like moles in the bowels of the earth.
To envisage people working down the pits for evermore is not just
Luddite, in the worst sense of that word, but thoroughly reactionary.'[6]

This view of technology as a neutral, and essentially liberating
force, echoes the statements made by Peter Walker that the future is
one of an 'Athens without slaves', and represents a shared understanding of what is happening inside the British economy and where
it will end. Reid recognizes that in the late 1970s 'things started to go
wrong', but he seems convinced that in the late 1980s 'the world
capitalist economy' will get things right again. However, this view
is not shared by many of the people who live in the threatened
coalfields. The extent to which the strike, for all its problems and
hardship, has retained support is related to the attachment which
miners and their families feel towards the places where they live, and
to their assessment of the likelihood of continuous employment in
the mines *or elsewhere*. In the coalfields of the North East, the
valleys of South Wales, and the dense mining areas of Yorkshire,
there is no sign of new technology providing a basis for new and
expanding employment. Workers can look to Ebbw Vale, to
Consett, or to Sheffield and see the aftermath of steel closures, a
reality which makes fantasy of Reid's predictions. New technology,
where it has penetrated mining regions, has been tied to low-waged
work for women; routine, demanding work performed for em-

ployers antagonistic or at best lukewarm towards independent trade unionism. If BSC Industries had little success in invigorating the economies of these towns, what hope for the belated, and under-funded, NCB Enterprises?

All of this was confirmed by the Tory Chancellor when he ex-plained that: 'We must not be seduced by the wonders of high-tech into overlooking the fact that many of the jobs of the future will be in the labour-intensive service industries which are not so much low-tech as no-tech.'[7] Such qualifications were well made given the fact that Britain's trade deficit in electronic products quadrupled between 1979 and 1983. It has to be said clearly, and in the strongest terms, that for many of the people who live in the stricken coal-mining regions, the future (in the wake of a defeated strike) looks grim indeed. That is why they asked, throughout 1984, 'are we winning?'

The argument doesn't stop there. It may well seem 'reactionary' to stand in the way of beneficial developments in science and tech-nology, but to see 'technology' as an independent source of progress displays naivety. Certainly the development of technologies which utilize the energy of coal as it lies in the seam are to be welcomed — in human terms alone the benefits would be enormous. Whether this is the kind of development that will take place in the British energy sector is quite another matter. The likelihood is that under the policies outlined by this government we will be saddled with nuclear power stations as a source of electricity (and warheads) and with the sterilization of countless millions of tonnes of precious fossil fuel.

The leadership of the Labour Party, even in its own electoral terms, has missed the boat in 1984. The revelation, by John Torode, that the outpourings of James Reid were little less than the private thoughts of Neil Kinnock was disturbing enough. More worrying perhaps was an attitude highlighted by the comment of one political correspondent to the effect that the Labour leadership was looking at the miners' strike 'through the rear view mirror.' The strike was seen as a re-enactment of the 1926 confrontation, with the ending pre-ordained. (Kinnock's reference to Gallipoli was revealing in this context.) But history never repeats itself except as farce — and this strike was no farce. It was clearly serious, with many people's lives hanging on the result. To many of them the failure of the Labour Party to initiate action in support of their cause; to point vigorously to questions of unemployment and energy policy; to raise clearly important issues about civil rights and the workings of the police force and the legal system, was not simply treacherous, it was incomprehensible.

The unhappiness felt about Neil Kinnock's leadership amongst the miners who have been most active in the strike is hard to exaggerate. One man put it like this: 'I worked hard in our constituency to get Kinnock nominated. Most of the people in our branch wanted Hattersley. I really thought that Kinnock would do a decent job like. Particularly as he represented a mining constituency. But he has done nothing to help us. He's hindered us really. The way I look at it, he'd have been better off saying nowt than the tripe he's come out with. I didn't think I'd ever say this, but I feel now that I'd rather have Hattersley as leader. At least he says what he means; you know where you are with him'

In July, Kinnock spoke at a national rally organized in Durham. It replaced the annual gala which the miners have held in the city since 1869, and which has become a central part of the Labour calendar. Kinnock had the difficult task of speaking last after Scargill, Heathfield and Skinner. During his speech the normally attentive Durham audience thinned noticeably. There was no heckling. People walked quietly away, some shaking their heads. That the executive of the Durham Miners' Association (the union which ranks above all others in its loyalty to the Labour Party) should be discussing in January 1985 a letter requesting that the union withhold an invitation to the July Gala from the party's leader is the most telling evidence of how deeply let down the miners feel.

This sense of disappointment is made all the more galling by the fact that the strike made possible a new approach to political thinking and struggle. Jimmy Reid is quite wrong to suggest that the miners and their union are 'Luddite', with no policy for technical progress and development. The NUM has argued strongly for a new approach to technology in the mines, one which takes account of the needs of people as workers and the needs of local communities. In its opposition to nuclear power, in the links it has built between coalfields and between miners and other groups of supporters in the cities and abroad, the miners' strike presented the possibility of organizing a new kind of radical alliance around energy, peace, and urban decay. It can be argued that much more could have been made of these issues by the union as the strike progressed, certainly as it became clear that no simple form of words was going to unlock the dispute. The NUM was involved in a political struggle, and in Europe, in the Northern countries especially, this was seen clearly and the strike fired an imaginative response within trade unions and progressive parties. For one thing the struggle for jobs, and for communities, along with a demand for an ecologically sound approach to the extraction of coal and the use of energy, fitted well into the 'green' politics which are of growing significance in Europe. For another, many people are increasingly aware of the deeply intertwined nature of the capitalist states and the economic crisis which affects them. One German reporter, visiting the North East, put it this way: 'People understand that Mrs Thatcher and her monetarist policies are an *international* phenomenon. They affect all the industrial states in the West. Mrs Thatcher is seen as the leading advocate of those policies and to many people in Germany and in Scandinavia the miners are involved in a struggle that will affect everyone by its outcome. That's why everyone watches it so closely.'

This assessment of the critical significance of the miners' dispute is revealed by the scale of international support received by the NUM. The international picture is a mirror image of Britain. Workers in threatened industries, organized in unions unaccustomed to taking risks or to entering a political dialogue with their members, have been reluctant to strike in solidarity. However, the mobilization of support beyond the work-place — through collections of money, food and clothing, through exchange visits, and through regular and sincere messages of support and solidarity 'against Mrs Thatcher and her policies' — was a major factor in keeping the strike going.

The NUM is the only trade union in Europe that could have entered a strike of this kind, and sustained it for so long. The particular nature of the coal industry, a nationalized industry based in labourist areas and interconnected communities, meshed with the scale of the British crisis and the determination of the NUM leadership to produce a unique event. It has shown up a lot of things for what they are. Without any doubt, it has been a turning point for us all.

This collection was put together, very hurriedly, during December 1984 and January 1985. At the time the 'drift back to work' strategy was underway and the national media was performing herculean tasks as a PR organ for the NCB. At that time everybody involved in the book felt that the themes and issues which ran deeply through the strike were being masked behind the shallowest of interpretations. So much was this the case that the union's leaders, both nationally and in the regions, felt strongly that the political lessons and the implications of the strike had barely touched the wider audience of workers and their families. As such we felt that a book which attempted to bring together some of the social and political research relevant to the dispute would be both useful and an important act of solidarity. This is our attempt at it.

Before saying what it is that we are trying to do in this book, it is important to make clear what we have not done. This is in no sense a definitive account of the strike or an evaluation of the countless experiences which have gone into its making. Such accounts will be produced in time and they will be based upon the amazing range of insights and understandings which the people at the centre of the strike have developed for themselves. It is their story and we shall have to wait for them to tell it.

The book is organized into three parts. *Part One* focuses upon the way in which the strike served to highlight important political questions about the state and the organization of power in our society. It raises questions about the role of the police and the law courts. Clearly these are burning issues in the dispute. Less well understood is the way in which the nationalized industries and the Welfare State have been turned as a weapon against miners on strike. In these ways, the strike can be seen to raise fundamental questions about how trade unions organize, now and in the future.

In *Part Two* the book shifts more directly to the experiences of people in the dispute, and offers an initial assessment of their impact on the development of politics in the future. The strike has, in all sorts of ways, pointed to real weaknesses and inadequacies in what Gavin Laird referred to in Brighton as 'this great movement of ours.' The theme of this part is that 'the movement', if assessed from the standpoint of the TUC or Labour Party headquarters, is in pretty bad shape. However, and the keen optimism of these chapters is important, another 'movement' may have been brought to life and been tapped by the strike. It has a future.

Part Three turns to the mining industry and the question of energy. Its main theme is that coal mining and the coal-mining regions could play a significant part in the future development of Britain, but they are under real threat. This threat can be seen in the use of nuclear power, the use made by the NCB of new technology, the expansion of open-cast operations, privatization, soaring unemployment, and the sterilization of valuable coal reserves. The starkness of this threat contrasts with the hopes and possibilities presented by an environmentally sound energy policy and a political understanding of how production can be organized not for profit but for the common good.

Notes

1. *The Observer*, 16 September 1984.
2. Michael Crick, *Scargill and the Miners*, Harmondsworth 1985, pp. 106–7.
3. *The Scotsman*, 7 February 1984.
4. *Financial Times*, 29 July 1984.
5. *The Times*, 10 November 1984.
6. *The Spectator*, 13 October 1984.
7. *The Guardian*, 26 October 1984.

PART ONE
An Irreconcilable Foe:
The Tories and the Strike

1
Decisive Power
The New Tory State Against the Miners

Huw Beynon and Peter McMylor

'. . . this programme of revolution in the hands of Reaction turns into a satire on the revolutionary strivings involved, and thus into the deadliest weapon in the hands of an irreconcilable Foe.'

Engels on Bismarck

'It's a hell of a thing this — the state; it's a hell of a thing. A powerful thing'. As the lodge Secretary of one of the big North Eastern pits spoke, police massed behind him with riot shields and helmets, blocking off the main gateway to the mine. His thoughts were shared by many others. One, a theoretically inclined electrician, put it like this: 'I've thought that something like this would happen. In fact we've talked about it. We've talked about what the state would do and what this government would do with the state when it was pushed. But theorizing about it and experiencing it — coming face to face with it — is a different thing. Emotionally it's different. I can't say that I'm surprised because I expected something like this. But I am shocked. It has affected me.' Many people were both surprised and shocked. Many people 'never expected things to be pushed this far'. But they've adapted to it; they've learned about the new situation. That's why they all talk of being changed deeply by the strike. But what *has* changed?

The Thatcher Government is now in its second term, and it is clearly engaged in a more radical break with the past than once seemed possible. This break has been seen by some influential analysts as an essentially *ideological* one — rooted in the processes by which British public opinion has taken on increasingly authoritarian, racist and individualist forms.[1] Without underestimating the importance of these factors it is possible to *overemphasize* their significance and the pace of change in people's thinking. The Tories were, after all, re-elected on a reduced vote that represented barely a third of the public. Equally, the stress upon ideas and upon the 'way people think' can divert attention from the changes which this government is making to the structure of the economy and the operation of the state.[2] And here there is much more involved than 'monetarism'.[3] The Thatcher Government's economic strategy is predicated upon fundamental changes in social and political relationships. The miners' strike can be seen as a critical moment in this process of change, as the most recent chapter in the state-led restructuring of British capital — a process which gains in intensity with the accelerating decline of British manufacturing industry and the deepening international recession.

In this way the miners' strike of 1984 can be related to the advent of the 1964 Labour Government with its promise of economic recovery through technology and science. *That* government's politics also turned on the closure of coal-mines. It was in the 1960s that 'shake-out' replaced 'unemployment' in our vocabulary and people 'took' their redundancy rather than 'got' the sack. Alastair MacIntyre commented bitterly on this in an article entitled 'The Strange Death of Social Democratic England'[4], written in 1968 at a time when unemployment had gone over half a million – the highest June figure since the war. To this MacIntyre added 'another fact', that 'this unemployment has been deliberately created by the government'; in his view 'We ought all of us surely to be a little more astonished and appalled than we are. Every previous Labour Government regarded rising unemployment as a defeat, as a sign that its policy was not working or that it had chosen the wrong policy. This is the first Labour Government which must regard rising unemployment as a victory for its policies, as a sign that they are working'. So the nominal party of the working class abandoned a central part of the post-war settlement — full employment — in what MacIntyre termed the effective disenfranchisement of the working class from the political system. The Chancellor of the time was Roy Jenkins.

With much posturing and not a little hypocrisy the Wilson Government singularly failed in its efforts to engineer state-led modernization of the British economy. Increasingly its attempts to deal with the central economic problem, capital-labour relations, placed it alongside the interests of capital. It was here, with legislation aimed at outlawing unofficial strikes and compelling the balloting of union members before strikes could be held, that the Wilson Government foundered. The unions proved too strong and Wilson had to retreat.

In 1970 Heath was elected at the head of the most right-wing government since the war. 'Selsdon Man' committed the Conservative Party to many of the ideas of the new right. Heath's strategy was fairly straightforward — get Britain into the EEC in the hope of reinvigorating British industrial capital; prevent a sterling crisis by floating the pound; dismantle the instruments of state intervention; and shift the burden of taxation away from companies and the richer tax payers on to the working class.[5] Leys summarizes well when he says: ' . . . the next decade is the story of how at first Selsdon Man was defeated, because the consensus had not yet been weakened enough, and of how from 1974 to 1979 the consensus was then further eroded in a second unsuccessful attempt by Wilson and his successor, James Callaghan, to rescue Britain's competitive position without challenging the balance of power between capital and labour.'[6]

The consensus which Leys refers to here was based upon that classic political settlement of 1945. This settlement — one of class compromise — saw the emergence of social welfare policies, nationalized industries and a series of tripartite arrangements in economic policies which brought capital and organized labour together within the committees of the state. This compromise also extended to civil society as collective forms of activity — in welfare, education, employment — became accepted within the life of the working class and key sections of the middle classes. It is this consensus that Thatcher proudly claims to oppose, which ultimately brought down Heath, and which Wilson and Callaghan attempted to reconstruct. The background to all of this has been one of deepening economic crisis.

In this way, the Heath Government can be seen as 'premature Thatcherism'. Like Thatcher, Heath sought to break the consensus through refashioning the state. Unlike Thatcher he attempted the move at a time when the collective powers of the trade unions were relatively strong, and before the economic recession began to bite with real savagery. A sense of the level of conflict which resulted can be gained from the fact that a State of Emergency was declared on no less than five occasions between 1970 and 1974 (the Emergency Powers Act passed in 1920 has only ever been used on twelve occasions). However, it was the miners' strike which most clearly demonstrated the confrontation between the state and the organied working class. The closure of Saltley coke depot — when massed pickets of fifteen thousand miners, engineering workers and their supporters outmanoeuvred less than a thousand police — sent shock waves through the Establishment. Jeffrey and Hennesey, in their outstanding account of the British Government's role in strike breaking since 1917, see this event as a critical moment. 'The effectiveness of the miners' secondary picketing enabled them to control power supplies with the passive support of their union colleagues, which meant that one union in the 1970s could do what both the Triple Alliance and the General Strike had failed to do in the 1920s. It is a demon still to be exorcised in the contingency planning community.'[7] The impact of this action is illustrated in the words of the 1972 special adviser to the Chancellor of the Exchequer, Brendan Sevill: 'At the time many of those in positions of influence looked into the abyss and saw only a few days away the possibility of the country being plunged into a state of chaos not so very far removed from that which might prevail after a minor nuclear attack. If that sounds melodramatic I need only say that — with the prospects of the breakdown of power supplies, food supplies, sewerage — it was the analogy that was being used at the time. This is the power that exists to hold the country to ransom: it was fear of that abyss which had an important effect on subsequent policy.'[8]

This policy initiative was set in train under Heath by Lord Jellicoe, the Lord Privy Seal. The result was a refashioning of the Civil Contingencies Unit (CCU), located in the cabinet office and having the status of a standing cabinet committee. It became established as the main government instrument for dealing with serious strikes. While Wilson used the Secret Service to tail members of the National Union of Seamen in 1966, in the 1970s he and his successor had a more elaborate armoury at their disposal. The 'efficiency' with which the Callaghan Government dealt with the Fire Brigades' Union strike in 1978 owed no small thanks to the presence of the cabinet office's operations centre, known in Whitehall as COBRA (Cabinet Office Briefing Room). This 'is fitted with a large table around which CCU ministers and officials sit. A cluster of microphones drop out of the ceiling and enable the Home Secretary, who chairs the committee whenever ministers are present, to speak directly with Chief Constables and Major-Generals in the military districts up and down the country.'[9]

The Callaghan Government, faced with a deteriorating economic situation, tried desperately to rework the old theme of corporatism and with it the reform of class compromise within the state which had been the hallmark of the 1945 settlement. In the new conditions this could no longer work. The economic room for manoeuvre had disappeared — IMF loan conditions, imposed in June 1976, tied the government to deflationary policies, higher unemployment and wages control. Both materially and ideologically the recession of the second half of the 1970s saw the erosion of the post-war settlement. In the context of a still relatively well–organized working-class, revolt was inevitable. Some of the most poorly-paid workers in the public services went on strike and brought into sharp relief the financial neglect of public welfare. Against this background coal remained relatively secure within the tripartite arrangement of the *Plan for Coal*. It was a security which kept the miners' union separate from the critical struggles at the end of the Callaghan years. However, these struggles were the life-blood of the Tory opposition. As Stuart Hall wrote in 1977: 'On the other side of the Parliamentary scene we can observe the Thatcher leadership preparing for power and constructing an authoritarian popular consensus, in part by attempting to 'represent' capital (anachronistically, but no less effectively) in the "venerable disguise and borrowed language", the "names slogans and costumes", of a disappearing class fraction — the small shop-keeper.'[10] From the beginning Thatcher had been anxious to break the old consensus; this became her boast. The old class compromises were not for her, neither were collective forms of life, and relationships. With all *corporate* forms apparently in crisis, the powerful articulation of *individualism* was made to seem both fresh and plausible. In this way of thinking the phrase 'right to work' became deflected from its original social–democratic meaning of a *public* commitment to full employment, towards a citizen's right to sell unhindered one's labour as an *individual* in the market-place.[11]

Individualism and the market economy represented one strand of Conservative thinking while in opposition. The other involved the mechanisms necessary to achieve those political ends. It related to the Tory Party (and the danger that the old guard might get cold feet), and the state. In the ways in which she has controlled her cabinet, Thatcher has effectively neutered the threat from within her own party. In this process — one of increasingly personal rule — she has relied centrally upon the effectiveness of a state machine which she has successfully captured. This process, and the resultant state form, has been described by commentators like Adam Raphael as 'Boadicean autocracy' and its significance was made clear early in the strike. After heavy picketing and 'disturbance' in Nottingham the *Financial Times* on 16 March 1984 noted that 'The Prime Minister is understood to be angered by the failure of the police to prevent the disturbances. She is believed to have banged the table while making critical remarks about some Chief Constables during a meeting with Tory back-benchers.'

In his detailed account of the assumptions behind the new, free-market Toryism, Gamble has explained how 'if the economy is to remain free, the state has to become strong, and nowhere stronger than in the dealings with organized labour'. While this approach excuses trade unionism from direct responsibility for inflation (this being laid at the door of the money supply), all other economic problems can be seen to have their roots in the *collective* association and organization of workers: 'they are made directly responsible for . . . unemployment, stagnation and disruption and so the strongest measures can be justified against them in the public interest.'[12]

Unlike that of Heath, Thatcher's Government did not set up special courts to deal with the trade unions. The reverse card was played. Rather than bring the unions before a 'Tory court', the law would be arranged so that trade unions were 'no longer immune'. The immunities they enjoyed, as collective bodies, would be removed and their organizations would become as 'Everyman' before the law. The appeal of this populist gambit can not be underestimated; neither should its dangers. For behind the gradual secretion of employment law into the statute books, a process achieved with remarkably little organized opposition, lay a more direct strategy for coping with trade unions and trade unionists who stepped out of line.

Again, the 1974 defeat weighs heavily in this process. Without doubt the power of the miners and their union burned deep into the psyche of those directly involved in that Tory administration. Walker and Thatcher ('wet' and 'dry' in the cabinet) share equally in feelings of hostility and anger towards the power of organized labour generally, but especially when coherently organized against government and state. In opposition this 'problem' was one of overriding concern for the newly-elected leadership. Sure that their turn would come again they were equally convinced that next time they would not easily be brought to their knees.

Carrington had been the Energy Minister under Heath and his first task under the new Tory leadership was to provide a detailed report on the lessons to be drawn from the confrontation with the miners in 1973 and 1974. The document, based upon highly confidential discussion with businessmen and former civil servants, was a deeply sobering one for senior Conservatives. It dispelled the widely held view that the debacle could be explained in terms of the personal frailties of Heath's inner circle. Instead it pointed to the enormous potential power available to workers in key industries if organized in strong trade unions. The report drew particular attention to the effects of advanced technology in the fuel and power industry, the economic dependence upon electricity in a modern society, and the central role played by coal in the British economy. The argument was simple: the balance of power in society was uneasily weighted between the state and relatively small, strategically-located groups of workers. In relation to the power workers, Carrington's words were most pointed. Armed forces' personnel did not possess the skills necessary to take over the running of the giant coal and oil-fired boilers and turbines that make up a modern power station. A power workers' strike could be totally decisive.

It was against this background that Thatcher pressed Nicholas Ridley to produce a further strategic document. This report — widely leaked in 1978 — made plain the intentions of any future Tory Government. It represented a sophisticated political strategy for dealing with the critical issues raised by Carrington. Attuned to the prospect of a 'political threat' within a critical industry with the support of 'the full force of communist disrupters', it drew up a five point strategy for dealing with such an eventuality. These points deserve to be reprinted here in full:

1. Return on capital figures should be rigged so that an above–average wage claim can be paid to the 'vulnerable' industries.

2. The eventual battle should be on ground chosen by the Tories, in a field they think could be won (railways, British Leyland, the Civil Service or steel).

3. Every precaution should be taken against a challenge in electricity or gas. Anyway, redundancies in those industries are unlikely to be required. The group believes that the most likely battleground will be the coal industry. They would like a Thatcher government to: a) build up maximum coal-stocks, particularly in the power stations; b) make continengency plans for the import of coal; c) encourage the recruit-ment of non-union lorry drivers by haulage companies to help move coal where necessary; d) introduce dual coal/oil-firing in all power stations as quickly as possible.

4. The group believes that the greatest deterrent to any strike would be "to cut off the money supply to the strikers, and make the union finance them".

5. There should be a large, mobile squad of police equipped and prepared to uphold the law against violent picketing. "Good non-union

drivers", should be recruited to cross picket lines with police protection.[13]

The extent to which this report has been followed as a blueprint by the Thatcher Government is vital to an understanding of the 1984 miners' strike: it contrasts graphically with the near-chronic lack of preparation by the trade union and labour movement. The 1984 TUC Congress had a trance-like quality at times as trade-union officials recognized the threat but failed to register its nature, scale and significance. During the debate on the miners' strike, (when 'oil' was not mentioned on one occasion), a visiting miner from South Wales interrupted a speech by John Lyons of the Electrical Engineering Union: 'Nicholas Ridley made it clear — to buy you off; he's bought you all off'. Mostly the faces reflected non-comprehension and puzzlement. Yet during the Thatcher years, the real price of coal remained relatively constant whilst the profitability of the CEGB was enhanced and with it the wages and conditions of its workers. At all costs, it seems, disruption in the electricity power sector had to be circumvented; at all costs, the potential alliance of coal-miners and power workers had to be undermined. Ridley's report was clear: 'every precaution should be taken against a challenge in electricity or gas'. It was also clear that there was bound to be a 'battle', and that this 'should be on ground chosen by the Tories'. This bears some examination.

In 1981, at a time when Thatcher's popularity was at its lowest ebb, NCB Chairman Derek Ezra announced a dramatic pit-closure programme. As the list of pits was confirmed at area level the South Wales miners came out on strike and were joined by spontaneous strikes at threatened pits in Durham and other areas. The immediate reaction of the Tory Cabinet was to retreat. *Coronation Street* was interrupted with the news that the closure list had been withdrawn and Joe Gormley, the union's president, quickly claimed a victory and demanded a return to work. Here was a moment of critical historical importance. And it was made clear by John Biffen in his interview with Brian Walden on *Weekend World*. Frankly, he admitted that he didn't 'come into politics to be a kamikaze pilot', and that to take on the miners at this time would be just such a suicide mission. Equally frank was his assertion that the business of good government was to ensure that groups did not use their 'decisive power'. In the following three years — and with the increased political strength of a victory abroad in the South Atlantic and at home in the General Election —the Thatcher Government followed that course, and with it one which built up the powers of the state for its major battle. Increasingly it became clear that the battle would be with the miners, and the sheer scale of the government's prepared-ness is testament to this.

On the eve of the 1981 strike, coal-stocks stood at thirty-seven million tonnes. Three years later they had risen to fifty-seven million. In part this increase was a simple product of market forces — 'too much coal being produced'; it was also part of a deliberate, and strategic, approach to stockpiling.

In 1982 Glyn England found that his contract as head of the CEGB was not renewed. His departure was widely interpreted as the sack. In the same year (as coal-stocks increased rapidly) oil *imports* in-creased by 3.1 million tonnes to 12.5 million tonnes. England had been directly instructed to substitute oil for coal in the power stations to accumulate coal-stocks ready for the impending battle. He was reported to think this view 'hysterical'. In his place Thatcher appointed Sir Walter Marshall. If England's sensibilities were in-clined towards coal, Marshall — the key ideologist of the nuclear power industry — was as steadfast in his antagonism. Repeatedly in those early weeks he proclaimed the view that 'seventy per cent dependency upon coal is excessive', repeatedly he talked of the 'monopoly power of the miners'. In Marshall, Thatcher had a prota-gonist who shared her political inclinations. MacGregor at the NCB was a similar appointment. Here were men who were willing partners in the task of operating the Ridley plan — which, ulti-mately, involved a deeply political and strategic approach both to energy and the state-owned industries.

The scale of the Tory preparations — as well as the interrelation-ships between an authoritarian state and the ideology of indivi-dualism — can be seen in the development of the strike.

The nationalized industries are viewed by Thatcher and her government as a major block to capital accumulation in Britain. The declared policy is one of privatization and this has been widely accomplished. However, the power monopolies of gas and elec-tricity remain firmly in the state sector, as do coal, steel and the railways. Owned by the state, these industries — an 'economic burden' according to one view — are also amenable to centralized control. During the miners' dipute this control was increasingly exercised directly. Take the case of the CEGB. Electricity supply had been identified by COBRA as a key strategic area in the British state. Here the recommendations of Ridley and the operating criteria of the state meshed decisively. Electricity supply had to be protected. The build up in stocks was one part of this process. Another was the retention, in 'mothballs', of the big oil-fired generating stations on the south coast, and the introduction of dual-firing facilities into the major coal-fired stations. Drax, for example, is listed as a coal-fired station, yet it has one oil turbine. In the 1970s, a hydrogen pipe-line was laid into the nearby Ferrybridge 'C' power station, and oil and chemical storage facilities were developed on site. David Smith, the GMBTU convenor explains: 'During the previous miners' strikes, hydrogen was a problem so they installed a hydrogen line. Oil was a problem. But they have now raised the capacity for oil here. We are now fairly self-sufficient.' Tommy Rhodes, the engineering workers' convenor, put it like this: 'We are of the opinion that the government engineered this over a long period. There is no other explanation for these changes at the station.' All the major power stations are much more self-sufficient than they were previously; they also have greater flexibility in their use of fuel. The scale of these changes is dramatic.

In 1983 the CEGB used 108 million tonnes of coal or coal-equivalent in its generation of electricity. This was made up of 81 million tonnes of coal, 8 million tonnes of oil, 16 million tonnes of nuclear and 2 million tonnes from hydro–electric plants. Coal thus fuelled seventy-six per cent of electricity generation. The transformation during the strike has been near complete, with oil substituting for coal as the major source of electricity supply. While in the winter of 1983, oil was used only at peak hours, in 1984 it took over as the fuel for the industries baseload. In November 1984, it was estimated that the CEGB was burning oil at the rate of one million tonnes a week. The *Financial Times* commented: 'The government is also believed to have been surprised by the amount of oil which the Central Electricity Generating Board was using in place of coal. It was assumed in Whitehall that the CEGB would be unable to burn more than 700,000 tonnes of coal equivalent of oil in a week. The CEGB is using slightly more oil in six weeks than throughout the whole of 1983. Even when demand reaches its winter peak, power stations will still be burning up to thirty per cent less coal than oil . . . Oil is being burned not only in large oil-fired stations such as Isle of Grain and Littlebrook on the Thames . . . but also in coal fired stations.'[14]

Didcot was such a coal-fired station and in November its 2,000 megawatt capacity was reduced to 1,160 with oil used as a baseload. The cost of this operation has been enormous. Oil sells at £25 a tonne more than coal. On 5 September the Electricity Council was informed that these extra costs were in the order of £20 million a week. It has been estimated that the total costs — until the end of January — amounted to £1,500 million. This is a staggering amount, and it is one which no private capitalist firm could bear. If we add to this the £130 million lost in freight charges by British Rail, the point is reinforced. Private employers would, if placed in the position of BR or the CEGB, have pressured the NCB to settle. As state industries, with their losses covered, they have been able to combine in an attempt to break the strike; sometimes inertly, at other times through more direct action.

At Didcot, for example, the manual workers at the power station had refused for seven months to co-operate with the delivery of coal. Didcot was one of thirteen stations where workers had voted not to handle fresh supplies of coal in solidarity with the strike. On 25 November, this policy changed. Each of the workers received a letter from the manager of the power station. The letter made a number of points: 'It said that refusal to handle coal supplies constituted a breach of the workers' contracts of employment; that national unions' advice not to handle coal did not represent an instruction; that a refusal to handle coal strongly affected the whole 450-strong workforce and damaged morale; and finally that the coal being delivered was coming from the normal source of Leicester and the Midlands coalfields.'[15] This direct involvement by management in the decisions and decision-making processes of trade unions is a critical part of the 'new industrial relations'. Reminiscent of the 'paper warfare' practiced by the Ford Motor Company in the 1960s (and dismissed by many industrial relations experts as 'American'), it is a further indication of the changes taking place within the nationalized industries. The NCB, and its' conduct of the dispute, is the most telling evidence of these fundamental transformations. MacGregor's appointment may be seen as central to this process. In the coalfields the news that he was moving across from BSC to the NCB was clearly understood as a political appointment and a decisive challenge. One man, in the North East, put it like this: 'If I think I had to put a date or a time on when I decided that Scargill was right it was when Thatcher appointed MacGregor. Let's face it, we *knew* then. It was obvious we were either going to have one hell of a fight or go the way of the steelworkers.'

The number of steelworkers had been reduced by a half under MacGregor's chairmanship and a similar reduction had taken place among the workers employed at BL while he served on the board there. People were therefore clear about MacGregor's brief — he was appointed to close pits and reduce capacity and few miners were surprised by the announcement made on 6 March 1984. What they were less prepared for was the scale of the attack upon the political and social fabric of arrangements within the NCB. With the benefit of hindsight Michael Eaton commented: 'I think the government brought in Mr MacGregor because he thought all of us at the Coal Board were a cosy set of buggers and we'd got too cosy.'

The NCB came into existence in 1947. Above all institutions, it was representative of the post-war settlement of the Attlee Government. This settlement got rid of the coal-owners (the overwhelming political necessity), and established in their place a state corporate structure within which the newly-formed NUM had a central role. The union was reorganized, it sat on a range of committees, and it was from its official ranks that the first welfare and industrial relations departments were staffed. The first director of industrial relations for the NCB was Ebby Edwards, the man who was also the first general secretary of the NUM. 'The Board', as it was universally known, was based upon class collaboration. When the industry was last in line for pruning, Macmillan appointed an ex-Labour cabinet minister as chairman. 'Us' and 'them' never disappeared — both miners and managers will tell you that — but in its area organization, in its promotion structure, and in its plethora of committees and local activities it became a uniquely 'labourist' part of the coalfields and British society. This is the 'cosiness' Eaton refers to. It was a cosiness built around coal. All deputies and managers in the NCB are qualified in the technical and legal aspects of mining and few of them have worked in any other industry. The contrast with other parts of the economy are quite graphic. In the American transnational ITT, for example, managers are frequently moved from one branch of the corporation to another. One of them explained it like this: 'If you're responsible for only one product — like cars or hotels — you get emotionally involved; you get to like them too much.' As the company's critical biographer comments: 'ITT executives are taught not to make things but to make money (engineers, with their hopeless pride in perfection, are their villains)'.

While the parallels aren't complete they are real. The last chairmen of the board — Ezra and Siddel — were internal appointments. When Ezra gave the Industry Lecture at the University of Durham in 1979 he was introduced by Sir William Reid, ex-Chairman of the Northern Region and of the University Council, who spoke of him as a man who 'loves coal'. MacGregor — for all his mining background in the USA — could never be described in those terms.

MacGregor's appointment is of a man from outside. When addressing a seminar of Harvard 'old boys' in Paris in November, MacGregor spoke of the problem of obtaining loyalty from managers and employees. In his view 'the quick method is to chop heads off. Otherwise it takes longer.'[16] As at British Shipbuilders and British Steel, the personnel with the requirements necessary to cut through the social relationships that have become the hallmark of the state and the 'traditional' sector of British industry are from *outside*, more than this they are *foreigners*.

The importance of this point, which is not a xenophobic one, should not be lost for it indicates the deeply *social* nature of class relationships in Britain and the equally social character of the politics which locked the class compromise of the post-war period into place. The extent to which these arrangements permeated all aspects of life — and gave meaning to the pattern of life in certain localities — underlines the way in which economic depression verges on social crisis in places like the North, Scotland and South Wales.

This is revealed in a number of ways. The crisis in the NCB has been referred to. The sacking of Geoffrey Kirk and the resignation of Ned Smith are seen as evidence of communication problems and a certain intolerance and capacity for bungling of the new chairman. We suspect that the crisis runs much deeper. Kirk is a good example of a 'board man'. He began work in the North Derbyshire area as a clerk at the age of fourteen. Successive promotions took him to Hobart House and head of public relations. MacGregor, however, increasingly relied for his public-relations advice upon men who he had taken onto the board on a part-time basis. The contrast is complete. Tim Bell is a director of Saatchi and Saatchi, the advertising company used extensively by Mrs Thatcher and the Tory Party in election campaigns and for the public 'image-making' of the Prime Minister. David Hart is a free-lance journalist and, in his own words, a 'public relations executive'. Hart is especially close to MacGregor and (as the *Daily Mirror* revealed) one of the important influences upon the Nottingham Working Miners' Committee in the early months of the strike. Tommy Thompson of Opinion Research and Communications provides the new chairman with advice based upon regular polling of miners' attitudes and public opinion.

MacGregor's track record speaks for itself. In the USA, as head of AMAX, he established a mining company with a clear anti-union reputation. The *United Mineworker of America* described it in this way: 'We all know AMAX for what it is — a leader of anti-union activity throughout the nation and especially in the West'. It is salutary to remember that MacGregor's first introduction to a state-owned industry in Britain, BL, was at the behest of Eric Varley (now of Coalite). Under the Tories he has been an effective instrument of job cutting and of repoliticizing the structures of the nationalized industries.

This repoliticization was clearly seen in the deep and concerted effort made by the NCB to break the solidarity of the strike. In the North East, eleven of the fourteen pit managers were, according to some accounts, deeply unhappy about the instruction they received which obliged them to send letters to each miner at their pit inviting a return to work. These letters, sent on 7 July 1984, began 'Dear Colleague' and read: 'You are probably as frustrated as I am by the failure to end the present dispute. The longer it goes on, the worse it becomes, and the worse hardship is caused to men and their families. The tragedy is, that all this is unnecessary for there's nothing for anyone to win — but certainly more to lose . . . Your colliery is open for work and transport will be available from Monday July 9th.'

On that day no–one returned, but in the run up to Christmas the knife was turned. The policy practiced in North Derbyshire was extended as workers were identified and encouraged to return to work, to break the strike. 'Arrangement would be made', 'at pick-up points', with the police, and the return to work would be co-ordinated. This was the context of the account, which begins this article, of trade-union activists — experienced in dealing with the NCB over a period of years under the 'normal arrangements' — who found the way to their union office barred by a policeman; who found it impossible to talk to their 'members' as they were ushered through the gates in police vans; who found — on the single occas-sion it was attempted — that talking with the manager involved a police escort and police surveillance in the office block. It repre-sented an enormous change. In other cases managers entered into the process of breaking the strike with enthusiasm. In November managers in the Doncaster area were reported to be 'going for gold' in their determination to keep the daily total of 'non-strikers' rising. As their spokesman put it: 'Yorkshire was always going to be a tough nut to crack but we are looking to punch a psychological "hole" next week.' He added that men who defy their union, the men who were called scabs, 'Have equal rights and their jobs will be protected. We will not sack them. We are going to stand by our word.'[17]

Within all this bravado, however, there is a sense of unease. While some managers relish the cut and thrust and would dearly like to break the union in the mines, others, and this is probably the majority, recognize the seriousness of the break that is under way. The general secretary of the manager's union, BACM, complained to MacGregor about the treatment of Mr Kirk. His approach was overwhelmingly one of self interest, complaining about the 'inexcusable' treatment of senior members of management. He added this however: 'The industry will get back to work again, I was going to say normality but I can't honestly say it will be normality. There is a lot of work to be done: reconciliation, recovery; and management is going to be right in the thick and the brunt of that.'[18]

As it is spoken, however, so it rings false, because things won't be 'normal' again. This strike represents a breaking of 'normality' — perhaps finally — a breaking (within the citadel) of the corporatist pattern of compromise which has been the hallmark of post-war British society. It reveals clearly how state power, accumulated over a period of dealing with the relative strength of organized labour, has united with the determined control of the Tory Party and the transactions and prejudices of class in a concerted assault upon the collectivity of labour. The scale and the power of the assault is quite awesome. As one union official puts it: 'They have learned their lessons from their mistakes and they corrected them; they consolidated their forces. We — because we were successful in 1972 and 1974 — didn't go through this examination. They were better prepared than we were. There's no doubt about that.' But this man also believes with considerable vehemence that 'the battle' is by no means over. 'They have set the terms; they have said it's winner take all and that's the way it's going to be now. We are not defeated and we're not going to lie down and give in'.

At the heart of the Thatcher strategy there is an enormous *risk*. In breaking with the past so clearly and so provocatively, in cutting loose, so single-mindedly, the plethora of social arrangements that formed both the basis of resistance *and* the (often conservative) bedrock of stability, she puts at risk the very basis of arrangements that make production (and profits) possible. At a meeting of miners in Sunderland it was pointed out that it would take months to put the pits right — even with good will. The response from the audience was clear: 'there'll be nee good will'.

In its challenge to workers in the nationalized industries (via privatization and the autocratic direction of those industries that

44

remain under state ownership), the Thatcher Government raised important questions for the workers' movement about future *socialist* strategy. In this context the classic pamphlet published by the Unofficial Reform Committee in South Wales in 1912 bears careful reading. In its pages *The Miners' Next Step* calls for a movement which would produce the emancipation of workers and a democratic socialist society. Nationalization, it insists, is not the way forward, rather it 'simply makes a National Trust with all the force of the government behind it.' This view was expanded by the Welsh syndicalist leader, Noah Ablett, in that same year. Speaking in the Rhondda he argued that nationalization would 'simply place an important section of the working class in the hands of a state servile to capitalists' interests, who would use their opportunity to increase the servility we abhor.' The miners have seen the truth of this in 1984. The task now, for all of us, is to go beyond the servile state and to build the conditions where, to quote Ablett again, 'knowledge, discipline, solidarity are all blended to make possible the capture of society.' For in this strike, miners have seen the world change. They could now be in a position to change it again. To change it for themselves.

Notes

1. Stuart Hall, 'The Great Moving Right Show', in Hall & Jacques, *The Politics of Thatcherism*, London, 1983. Some of the most thoughtful criticism of this view has come, improbably enough, from staff members of the *Financial Times*, see Malcolm Rutherford's review in *Marxism Today*, and Peter Riddell, *The Thatcher Government*, Oxford, 1983, p. 19, where he writes 'These Marxist commentators have conferred on Thatcherism greater coherence and consistency than it has had in practice. Many actions taken since 1979 — ranging from the increased aid to British Steel to the tighter Whitehall controls on local authorities — were much more a response to the failures of earlier policies and to short-term pressure than the implementation of a carefully worked out blueprint'.

2. See Abercrombie, Hill and Turner, *The Dominant Ideology Thesis*, Longon, 1980; the best critique of Hall *et al* to have appeared from the left is Bob Jessop *et al*, 'Authoritarian Populism, Two Nations and Thatcherism', in *New Left Review*, no. 147, which concentrates on a more political and institutional analysis, and reflects some of our own concerns here.

3. For a valuable overview of the nature of Thatcherism and the failure of Keynsianism which led to its widespread adoption, see F.A.E. Smith, 'The Bourgeois Economic Theory of the Crisis' in *Critique 16*, Glasgow. The phenomenon of monetarism is, of course, international. For an interesting political/historical analysis of the economic crisis of the 1970s see Part II of Alan Wolfe, *The Limits of Legitimacy — Political Contradiction of Contemporary Capitalism*, New York, 1977.

4. See D. Widgerey (ed.), *The Left in Britain 1956–68*, Harmondsworth, 1976.

5. For an account of this, and the extent to which this economic redistribution was allowed, see Colin Leys, *Politics in Britain*, London, 1983.

6. See Leys, p. 79.

7. Jeffrey and P. Hennesey, *State of Emergency: British Governments and Strike Breaking Since 1919*, London, 1983, p. 235.

8. *Ibid*.

9. *Ibid*.

10. S. Hall, in A. Hunt (ed.), *Class and Class Structure*, London, 1977, p. 57.

11. This is of course premised on the separation of the economic sphere and the political sphere in a capitalist society. This is crucial because it allows a person to be both a worker and a citizen, with formal equality before the law and real subordination while at work. It is the delicate balance at the heart of all capitalist democracy that grants real political freedom whilst guaranteeing the 'efficient' working of the labour market without too much interference, see A. Giddens *A Contemporary Critique of Historical Materialism*, London, 1981, p. 125–127.

12. A. Gamble, 'The Free Economy and the Strong State', in R. Miliband and J. Saville (eds.), *The Socialist Register*, London, 1979.

13. Reprinted from 'Appomattox or Civil War?' *The Economist*, 27 May 1978. The Ridley Report also had far reaching proposals for the conduct of the nationalized industries as we shall see later.

14. *Financial Times*, 28 November 1984.

15. *The Guardian*, 10 November 1984.

16. *Financial Times*, 25 November 1984.

17. *The Guardian*, 10 November 1984.

18. *The Guardian*, 3 November 1984.

19. Quoted in R. J. Holton, 'Syndicalist Theories of the State', *Sociological Review*, 1981.

2
Let Them Eat Coal *

The Conservative Party and the Strike

Bill Schwarz

> Sound and honest investment requires as its first
> essential a resolute reduction of public expenditure
> Winston Churchill

> You have been fighting the legions of hell
> Arthur Cook

The Conservative Party is in its own way a close-knit community
held together by wealth, patronage and a concomitant set of
customs, values and taboos. Even to this day there exists an extraordinary symbiosis between the dominant political institutions of the
land and the social institutions of the wealthy which does much to
enhance a compact sense of identity and self-recognition for those
who join its ranks. To others excluded from this community, its
values often appear to be little more than inbred, inculcated bigotry
and prejudice. But like any community it also produces a conception
of its own history which is critical in delineating its collective identity. Memories of past victories and catastrophes, an ebullient
heroism mingling with the stark humiliations of defeat, play an active
role in articulating and making sense of Conservatism for its contemporary believers. This imagined, mythological history depends
less on an unencumbered chronology than on the epic moments of
danger and trauma when the very existence of cherished values
seemed most in peril. 1926, 1972 and 1974 can form the backbone of
this history too. Out of this evocation of the past arises a very
particular demonology in which the miners play the leading part.

Now it is true that in some respects the election of Mrs Thatcher to
the leadership of the Conservative Party in 1975 did much to unsettle

---

* with thanks to James Dunkerley, *compañero*

the clubbable, patrician values of the Tory elite, prompting one senior colleague (generally believed to be Julian Critchley) to describe it as a second peasants' revolt. It is also the case that Thatcher's second term of office, since June 1983, has been widely viewed as a story of continuing incompetence and internal dissension. A community, of course, can turn in on itself. In July 1984 the *Economist* warned that 'Mrs Thatcher's second government is stepping out to become Britain's most inept since the war'. There has been the long-running division between the 'dries' and the 'wets'. At the end of 1984 there developed a noisy crescendo of backbench rebellion in which two leading cabinet figures, Sir Keith Joseph and Patrick Jenkin, were badly mauled in quick succession.

Divisions inside the party are clearly more than a journalistic mirage. They are vital for understanding the shifting profile of the Conservative Party since the beginning of the miners' strike. A revealing episode occurred four months into the strike. Francis Pym, a card-carrying wet sacked from the Foreign Office by Mrs Thatcher, published his personal manifesto, *The Politics of Consent*, devised as a philosophical and strategic alternative to Thatcherism.[2] Pym obviously believed this would be a provocative and controversial intervention. This it did not prove to be. The sense of occasion arose more from the spectacle of discord and insubordination in senior Tory ranks than from any decisive political regroupment.

However, *The Times* was quick to move, fulfilling its role not merely as a close ally of the Thatcher Government but also as a superior political force always ready to set the pace and, when necessary, remind Mrs Thatcher of her own first principles. Under the title 'They cannot forgive her' a brutal editorial — the style and content strongly suggest the hand of the editor — marked the publication of Pym's book. Its author took hold of Pym's call for a new Conservatism which would 'improve the bad', claiming the phrase 'epitomizes a kind of Conservatism which has carried out an elegant, concerned but essentially defensive operation against collectivism for the last forty years. The kind of Conservatism which prefers to improve the bad than to eliminate it has in consequence avoided most of the painful decisions which now have to be taken . . . If a city is under prolonged siege the defenders at some stage have to make a decision to carry on defending an ever contracting perimeter or to break out and take the opposing forces into their flank or rear in order to lift the siege. One can imagine the anguished arguments in the citadel when the risks of such a course are weighed . . . Such are the arguments in the Tory citadel.' Predictably, *The Times* lauded the Thatcher endeavour to break out from the encirclement of collectivism and social democracy, exulting in her initiative in launching after four decades the long-awaited counter-attack.[3] From this perspective Pym and his epigones appear to be no more than the waverers, politicians of low calibre ever content to appease the opposing forces.

Partisan though it may be *The Times'* description of the long-term Thatcherite programme pitted against collectivism and the more cautious objectives of the Conservative dissidents is undoubtedly accurate. There can be no question of the political seriousness of this divide. But it is worth asking, if this division runs so deep through the party then how has the position represented by Pym become so effectively marginalized by the leadership?

Time and again the substance of the public arguments of the dissident wets comes down to little more than a plea for greater flexibility and pragmatism in place of dogma and ideology. This is clear in *The Politics of Consent*. Behind these beliefs lies the fear that the SDP is usurping from the Conservatives the middle ground. In an article promoting his book (and given the title of 'SDP, the only smart party' by a calculating but cheeky *Times* sub-editor), Pym made this explicit and advocated a policy which 'demands a sensitivity to the emotional element of the middle ground'.[4] Put like this, this is a case which leads to neither incisive thinking nor a determined politics. Indeed, the arguments themselves are too frequently terribly weak, proposing little more than a slow crawl back to an already discredited system. The response, far from generating the outcry he had expected, slowly transmuted into predictions about the extinction of the wets as an identifiable and influential grouping within the Conservative Party.

Secondly, the wets have refrained from the merest hint of elementary political organization. Whether this has been due to a gentlemanly sense of loyalty, downright ineptitude, or to the fear induced by the elaborate, autocratic system of surveillance and control set up by the Prime Minister, it is too early yet to judge. But even by the end of 1981, after the reshuffle of September, the wets had lost the political initiative and were in disarray.

The third reason is the most revealing. Quite simply, on many immediate issues the wets endorse the short-term objectives of the leadership, even if they despise the autocracy of the means. Most of all they want the miners beaten. On this Pym can speak for himself: 'There is a myth about the miners' strike, usually propagated by the Labour Party, that a ready compromise lurks somewhere in the wings. It is hinted that only the Government's intransigence prevents a solution, and that others more flexible — even more flexible Conservatives — would end the strike in no time. This is nonsense. However it is dressed up, the final outcome will be a defeat for one side or the other. For the sake of us all, let us hope it is a defeat for Arthur Scargill.'[5] Note how this is put — not a settlement for the coal industry but the greater objective of defeating Scargill.

It might have been supposed that ten months of the coal strike would have exacerbated the splits inside the Conservative Party: at the time of writing all the evidence suggests the contrary. The Conservative Party is united in its desire to destroy what it labels 'Scargillism'. Indeed, it could be said that following exactly the trajectory of the Falklands/Malvinas War, the mining dispute has once more made unity possible inside the Conservative Party. The real worry for the dissidents, as Pym implied in a speech in Cambridge shortly before the party conference, was that Thatcher — so deeply dedicated to a policy of frontal assault — might blow it. On other, lesser issues back-bench revolts have taken place which, although tactically awkward for the whips, have not as yet unduly damaged the long-term authority of the government. On the essential objective the fight is to the kill, the demonology of the miners common across all positions in the party, and the memories of 1972 and 1974 overpowering.

Thus in the aftermath of his summertime farrago Pym himself was perfectly correct to describe as 'silly' the idea that he was plotting a coup, pointing out that to have succumbed to such fantasy, the source of these rumours — the Prime Minister's secretariat was prominent — must have been badly rattled. The very midsummer of madness.

The unity of the party on the issue of the strike is perhaps made even clearer by the case of Peter Walker. Walker has aligned himself with the wets, even if he has never been so bold in his posturing as Pym or Sir Ian Gilmour. As Secretary of State for Energy he has been positioned in the forefront of the campaign against the miners. This may well have been an astute move by Thatcher, not only putting him in the front line, but also drawing from his experience as Secretary of State for Industry at the end of the Heath regime, when he was responsible for government dealings with the miners — hoping, presumably, he would have learnt from his mistakes. But there has been little indication that Walker has diverged from Thatcher on the issue of the strike or that he has desired anything but an unflinching fight to the finish.

It is the case, however, that in the second Macmillan lecture in November he did distance himself from the full-blown Thatcher economic programme, returning for guidance to the proto-social-democratic texts of the young Harold Macmillan. The press immediately announced this as Walker's repudiation of Thatcher. It was nothing of the sort. At no stage in the speech did he directly criticize the government's policies. What he did attempt, though, was to put a marker down for his place in the battle for the Tory succession. He was hardly in the position to transform himself, even overnight for an occasion as removed from the political stage as this, into the figure of aspirant general leading the pronunciamento portrayed by the pundits.

On the other hand no-one inside the Conservative Party suffers any illusion that if Mrs Thatcher were to fail in her objective of breaking the miners, she would fast be ejected from the leadership. The risks are high, and getting higher. Her closest lieutenants are most certainly keeping a sideways watch on their colleagues, assessing at every moment the shifting balance of forces in anticipation of what moves to make were this eventuality to come about. But this is secondary. The full force of the government, and pre-eminently of Thatcher herself, is to ensure that the party does not fail.

The Budget and the 'Last Battle'

Breaking the miners holds a central place in the overall strategy of Thatcherism — the dismantling of key areas of the public sector, the expansion of the free market, and the imposition of a strong state. The Conservatives' progress along this road has been much slower than the leading ideologues originally supposed and wish. In the first administration several links in the chain of social democracy had been severely weakened. The job of the second administration, it was argued, was to inflict a blow at the basis of collectivism sufficient to prevent the left ever again being able to reverse the policies implemented by Thatcher. To achieve this it was thought necessary to confront and beat the Labour Party and the labour movement on a decisive issue, and what better than settling old scores with the miners?

There are two parts to this process. The first is to weaken the organized, defensive powers of the labour movement sufficiently so as to be able to generalize the implantation of Thatcherite ideals. That much is clear. But second, there is also the hope of reasserting the proper domain of constitutional politics; this requires not the destruction of the NUM as such, but the uprooting of a politicized unionism in which the springs of syndicalist action lift trade-union struggles into opposition to the state and the existing political order. This is the importance of the personalization and vilification of Scargill. It is precisely the refusal to hold fast to the distinction between the properly designated objectives of trade unionism and the constitutional and political objectives of parliamentary parties which the government sees as so dangerous. It is the NUM as presently constituted that it is so desperate to break, in search of the chimera of a pure and simple trade unionism ever obedient to the overriding diktat of the market.

Confirmation of this in its most extreme form came from Mrs Thatcher's principal aide, Norman Tebbit, at the Conservative Party conference in October 1984. Undoubtedly the abiding memory of Tebbit at the conference has been formed by the grisly picture of his being pulled free from the rubble in the aftermath of the bomb attack on the Grand Hotel. But two days earlier with millennarial fervour he was speaking his mind at a party fringe meeting. Here he insisted that the fight with the miners could be 'the last battle' in the attempt to break the 'shackles' of trade unionism in Britain. For Tebbit, the trade unions in recent years have acquired such power that the whole edifice needs to be confronted. 'Unless the ball and chain, the irons and the handcuffs of traditional trades-union attitudes are struck off we will continue to be handicapped in the race for markets, customers, orders and jobs.'

Andrew Gamble has demonstrated in a careful analysis that this strategy was in effect codified in Lawson's budget in March 1984, which proclaimed the continuation of tight monetary and fiscal controls, the determination to hold inflation below five per cent, sweetened by the promise of a boom in tax cuts for those still in work. The budget was premissed on the idea that unemployment would remain high and that, politically, the unemployed could be written off. In turn, this assumed the continued war of attrition against the institutions of social democracy and intensification of the fight against its foremost defensive bulwarks, the trade unions. The inexorable logic of these assumptions led the Conservatives to the conclusion that their old class enemies, the NUM, would be in the front line. At the same time this emphasized the government's determined rejection of any long-term plan for the revitalization of Britain's traditional manufacturing base.[6] Thus 'profitability' became the overriding concern for the government, and the mines the critical test case. Thereafter the struggle could be extended. In the wake of the budget the stock-market was jubilant. But by then the strike in the coalfields had already begun.

Preparing the Ground

'The Government now wandering vainly over battlefield looking for someone to surrender to — and being massacred all the time.'[7] So ran the entry in Douglas Hurd's diary for 11 February 1972. Hurd was Heath's political secretary; the date, the day following Saltley. Within the week, under the cover of the Wilberforce Report, the government caved in and an award was won by the NUM which amounted to nearly thirty per cent.

Almost two years later, in 1973, the NUM Executive voted for an overtime ban to start on 12 November. Within a day of the ban starting the government ordered a state of emergency: amongst other measures street lighting was curtailed and television programmes stopped at 10.30 p.m. Rumours of petrol rationing spread quickly. This was followed by the government announcement that the three-day working week would be introduced in the new year. Patrick Jenkin, the eager new Minister for Energy (a job he was to hold down for all of seven weeks), helpfully reminded the population that they could brush their teeth in the dark. Despite this, the pressure on Heath mounted. On 4 February the NUM ballot revealed that eighty-one per cent of the membership supported strike action. Three days later Heath gave in and it was announced that an election would be held on 28 February. Labour gained a four seat majority over the Conservatives, and after Heath's abortive dalliance with the Liberal Party, Labour took office.

The combined experience of 1972 and 1974 was critical in activating the disillusionment in the Conservative Keynesian camp which eventually was to deliver a number of prominent former Heathites straight into the hands of the radical right. Between 1975 and 1979, with the unequivocal support of the new boss, Mrs Thatcher, and her leading henchman of the time, Sir Keith Joseph, the terms of political debate were increasingly cast according to the agenda of the party's new right. After the debacle of the Heath administration, policy for the nationalized industries, and for coal above all, was regarded as urgent.

The first indication of a sharp shift in orientation was a policy document drafted by Nicholas Ridley. This was leaked in May 1978, the *Economist* predicting that it was 'likely to cause a humdinger of a row'. (Needless to say it didn't; the affair quickly blew over as these things do.) The detailed implications of this for the coal strike of 1984 have been discussed in the previous chapter. However, the report also attempted to develop a more general strategy for the nationalized industries as a whole. The basis of Ridley's proposal was that the criterion of the market-place should determine the workings of the industries which had been nationalized. Each nationalized industry should achieve a set rate of return on 'capital employed', and this rate of return, once decided, should be 'totally inflexible'. Thus the government would be able to extricate itself from the day to day running of the nationalized concerns — leaving it all to strong, localized managements which would receive government support only for so long as they could achieve results within these limits. The objective was, simply, that 'management should manage'. This assumed two consequences: first that the issue of wages in the public sector would be taken out of the orbit of direct state regulation; and second, that it was necessary to create a new, professionalized managerial cadre for the nationalized industries. This 1978 document provided the framework for the government during the coal strike in 1984.

In addition Ridley assessed the possibilities for denationalization. His proposals suggested that as an alternative to outright privatization — which carried with it unknown political risks — a future Conservative Government should consider fragmenting the industries, destroying them as conglomerate entities (and thereby also undermining the power of the large unions), even allowing the possibility for the development of worker cooperatives in the pits.[8] This, too, was to reverberate in 1984.

Under the threat of an NUM strike in February 1981 the Conservative government stepped back from confrontation, conceding a number of issues. Both David Howell, who was then Secretary of State for Energy, and Thatcher herself have claimed that the reason was because the ground was not yet properly prepared. When pressed later about Howell's direct involvement in the issue, contravening the government policy of non-intervention, Mrs Thatcher's reply was coy and ambiguous: 'It took us time to get it right'.[9] After this climb-down, preparations intensified. On the Prime Minister's instructions and in the strictest secrecy the Civil Contingencies Unit set up a committee, MISC 57, chaired by Robert Wade-Gery, a civil servant, and drawing on the skills of the unit's secretary, Brigadier Tony Budd. Their first task was to examine the files on 1973/4 and prevent the vulnerability arising from low coal-stocks.

The Plan Complete

There was one crucial ingredient still to be added: the reorganization of the Coal Board. The whole conception of the government's preparations depended on there being a strong, indeed an unbeatable, management at the NCB. This would make possible the fiction of the government's non-participation in what could be represented simply as an internal dispute between the board and its employees. This approach reversed the tactics of 1972 and 1974 when the government was all too visible as a contender in the struggle, Heath even staking the election on the choice between the government and the miners. Thatcher proposed to follow more closely the campaign of 1926 when to all intents and purposes Stanley Baldwin, after an initial radio broadcast, simply closed up shop, waiting for the trade unions to come to him and surrender.

The final move was made on 1 September 1983 when Ian Mac-Gregor was formally transferred as chairman from British Steel to the NCB — an appointment made by Nigel Lawson, then Secretary of State for Energy. *The Times* for 1 September gives an insight into the moment and conjuncture of forces which underpinned Mac-Gregor's appointment. Mrs Thatcher had just given one of her characteristic speeches in which, brim-full of confidence and a sense of her own place in the march of history, she reiterated the type of society she hoped for — organized around private enterprise, tax boons and the 'ladder of incentive' — and declared she was following in the footsteps of Churchill, Home and Macmillan (but Churchill most of all, naturally). Playfully she closed by expressing the hope that in future years Conservative leaders in their turn would boast of following 'in Mrs Thatcher's footsteps'. Alongside this — easing the ladder into place — reports were carried of the closure of Brynlliw Colliery and plans for the completion of the privatization of British Telecom. And a letter from David Howell, denouncing those critics on *The Times* who supposed the government's initiative had started to falter, defended the Conservative Party's 'brisk start' on privatization under Thatcher and continued: 'There is a great deal more to be done to free and unravel the old centralized state sector of the British economy, and I do hope that the momentum built up in some areas from 1979 is not going to be allowed to slacken'. He need not have worried.

Shortly after, on 1 October, the NCB announced its offer of 5.2 per cent and gave notice of a rapid scheme of pit closures. Arthur Scargill went on record as 'detecting the hand of the government'. The Prime Minister was quick to respond: 'Mr Scargill has a vivid imagination. There has been no contact with Mrs Thatcher or the government'. The NUM declared its overtime ban on the 23 October. The following day the headline in *The Times* read: 'Mac-Gregor set for showdown'.

The Strike: the First Phase

There is still a good deal of contention about whether the Coal Board's decision to announce, on 1 March, the imminent closure of Cortonwood Colliery was deliberately provocative. Given the extensive preparations it is unlikely, although not impossible, that between them the government and the NCB would have blundered into such a move. But whether intended or not, it was the detonator for the strike.

What is more curious, however, is that the government's initial stance remained so cautious. This first phase of the strike lasted until about the middle of May. So far as it is possible to deduce, the government had two immediate objectives, first, to peddle the fiction of its non-involvement; second, to prevent another Saltley, a recurrence of a situation in which the government were seen to surrender to force its numbers. Ministers assumed that if they were to succeed in these objectives they would be able to sit out the strike.

Coal stocks were high and the summer ahead. A cabinet sub-committee, MISC 101, was immediately set up, embarked on its twice-weekly meetings and functioned according to plan. It was chaired by the Prime Minister, and composed of Leon Brittan (Home Secretary), Nigel Lawson (Chancellor), Walker, Norman Tebbit (Industry), Tom King (Employment), Ridley (Transport) and Sir Michael Havers (Attorney-General), with Brigadier Budd and David Goodall of the Civil Contingencies Unit in attendance. The policing, too, went according to plan, and there were no immediate flashpoints which threatened the government on the scale of Saltley. In the first weeks of the strike David Hall, the Chief Constable of Humberside who was also directing the National Reporting Centre at New Scotland Yard, took time out to reassure Conservative back-benchers that all was in order. At the end of March a journalist could comment: 'The first difference between

Saltley in 1972 and Nottinghamshire in 1984 was the quality and robustness of the policing', anticipating that the miners had finally been nailed.[10]

The government's public stance was explained by Walker in the Commons on 12 March. Refusing to be goaded by his back-benchers, Walker delivered the well-rehearsed line: 'I am not going to intervene in what is basically a clear-cut managerial position of a management that wishes to invest more in economic mines and cut out the burden of uneconomic mines and do it in a civilized and generous way.' Coupled with this, MacGregor received full ministerial support. At the beginning of April the Prime Minister repeated this position on *Panorama* — not forgetting to chip in with a quick eulogy to the 'very, very great achievement' of the police. Thereafter both Walker and Thatcher were entirely predictable in their Commons answers, parroting the familiar themes of managerial rights, generous government subsidies, and the brutalities of picketing. Their case was set.

This policy did not suit all the anti-NUM forces. Tory back-benchers in particular hoped for a more vigorous campaign. For example, Anthony Beaumont-Dark, something of a liberal in the party, despairingly asked Walker (12 March) whether 'it isn't time MacGregor stopped his softly-softly approach?' David Owen, with all the acumen of the renegade, saw the need for an early debate on law and order so as to dish Labour's mounting criticism of the police, and pressed Thatcher to go ahead. He too got his chance to indulge in mystical reveries about the unique qualities of the British police. But there also occurred unbelievable blunders from two of the leading personnel, keen presumably to raise the stakes.

First, Tebbit advocated the denationalization of the NCB at a press gallery luncheon. He later had to apologize to the cabinet for his 'off the cuff' remark, suggesting that 'on reflection' he 'felt his remark had been silly'. (It wasn't. It was later revealed that a secret cabinet sub-committee was actively investigating, not denationalization of the NCB as such, but a system in which its profitable pits could be developed by private companies. Tebbit had simply jumped the gun.) Second, at the same moment that Tebbit was making public his apology, MacGregor started blowing hot and cold about the need to engage troops to transport coal. The next day, courtesy of the *Jimmy Young Programme*, he did his level best to retract the idea, and the NCB found it necessary to issue a statement declaring that such a suggestion 'did not come under his purview under any circumstances'. Even the best laid plans . . .

However, none of the government's tactics amounted to any more than a defensive operation, hoping to contain the strike and prevent public humiliation. It may be that even at this stage the cabinet felt unsure of the ground ahead and fearful of the risks involved. At the start of the strike Mrs Thatcher was locked into confrontation with the chairman of the 1922 Committee, Edward du Cann, over the matter of her 'presidential' style of governing; and for the first time since the Falklands/Malvinas War, Labour was ahead in the opinion polls. These may have acted as restraining forces. But much more important, it seems most unlikely that the government had even an inkling, at this stage, of the determination of the strikers.

The Strike Transformed

Towards the middle of May the conflict began to take a radically new turn and the leading cabinet ministers were jolted out of their entrenched position, unwillingly forced to adopt a more offensive, interventionist style. Four events account for this change. First, the increasing seriousness of the situation on the picket lines, from the Mansfield rally on 14 May to the escalating confrontations at Orgreave and elsewhere, threatened to undermine the early successes achieved by militarized saturation policing. Second, in early June the *Mirror* published documents which proved conclusively that the government had recently been actively involved in public sector pay deals, thus demonstrating the mendacity of a written parliamentary answer supplied by Nicholas Ridley, the Minister of Transport, on 9 April. Third, MacGregor's letter delivered to every member of the NUM at the end of June, attempting to win hearts and minds but failing to elicit a positive response on any scale, heightened the frustration of ministers and the bad feeling between the cabinet and the NCB, and convinced the government of the necessity for switching to a harder line. Fourth and most significant, the onset of the first dock strike, from 9 July to 21 July, greatly increased pressure on the government and looked as if it was about to make the political dimensions of the situation the urgent and inescapable business of the day. This was exactly the escalation which government tactics had sought to avoid.

In early July the press was steaming with reports of anonymous senior ministers anxious about the government's unwillingness to be more actively involved. *The Times* categorically reversed its earlier endorsement of Mrs Thatcher's policy of non-intervention, publishing on 16 July a call for an immediate state of emergency and — with history unshakably on its side — an authoritative account of the normality of an active military presence in twentieth-century British civil society.

Simultaneously the ideological work of the government began to change tack, emphasizing now above all the politicization of the strike by NUM leaders. The hope was to isolate Scargill and incessantly drill away at Kinnock in an effort to push him either into unequivocal support for the NUM leadership (in which case he carried the virus of 'repulsive thuggery' into the very sanctuary of the constitution), or into its denunciation (in which case the labour movement as a political and leading force was split wide open). Walker, Brittan and MacGregor initiated this switch at the beginning of June.

At this point the demons were beginning to come to life before the very eyes of the party leaders. The leadership was now prepared to make the running with the tabloids and *The Times*. Earlier backbench interventions — Geoffrey Dickens' analysis of Scargill as a 'confessed Marxist surrounded by communist aides and advisors' and his belief that 'much more serious support for him is coming from the Kremlin' (3 April); Cranley Onslow's frequent suggestions that unidentified figures were 'controlling and directing riotous mobs'; Anthony Marlow's wish that Scargill would 'be arrested for organizing a private army' (19 June) — now came to settle on the front-bench as reasonable contributions to serious and intelligent political conduct.

The climax came on 18, 19 and 20 July. Thatcher finally broke loose — her speech to the 1922 Committee savouring her description of 'the enemy within' and drawing on all the political capital which had been accruing since her great, symbolic imperialist adventure. Walker, Brittan and Lawson were recruited to gang up on Kinnock. Indeed Walker seemed to have undergone a grotesque transmutation — if we can believe what we read — in which he boasted of his father's activities as a shop-steward and flaunted the fact that he was whiling away his leisure moments immersed in *Marxism Today* and *New Left Review*. What is more *The Times* was by now lagging behind. On 20 July its leader proclaimed 'There is a war on'. There was no need for *The Times* to tell us this: it was merely a gratuitous gesture, for everyone already understood.

The Enemy Within

The ideological construction of 'the moderate' and 'the extremist' has a critical place in British history, stretching back at least as far as the years preceding the Great Strike of 1926. It forms the very syntax of the political language of modern constitutionalism and can be highly effective in assembling discursive fortifications when public order is about to be threatened. As if by a natural process of selection, moderate men of reason, people like 'us', line up on one side; the dupes and the red manipulators, the 'jack-boot' pickets, in short, the violent extremist minority, are lined up on the other. For the extremists — for 'them' — the full coercive powers of the state are all that can fairly be expected; or as Leon Brittan put it on 11 September (an ominous date for such talk), they are 'the criminals whom the police will unearth'.

This ideological work flourished after the lead given in July by the senior cabinet ministers. Again and again — in the closing speech of the Conservative Party conference, at the Free Enterprise Awards Ceremony (the judges were unanimous: the top prize went to Eddie Shah), in the Guildhall speech — Mrs Thatcher reiterated her condemnation of 'violence': an abstract, dehistorized, fluid rendering, providing the means by which the stigma of 'extremist' could be transmitted this way and that, bringing together all those who dared to step outside the Thatcher consensus. At the Guildhall in November she pronounced upon 'the ruthless leadership of the NUM' and continued: 'We are drawing to the end of a year in which our people have seen violence and intimidation in our midst: the cruelty of the terrorists; the violence of the picket-line; the deliberate flouting of the law of the land'.

From the logic of this division between moderate and violent extremist there follows precisely the idea of a deeply malevolent phenomenon known as Scargillism, dedicated to the wholesale destruction of British society. Arthur Scargill himself is an enormously controversial figure, capable of arousing volleys of passionate criticism from the left let alone the right. But that is not exactly to the point. The idea of Scargillism is a poor explanation for the fact that one hundred thousand and more miners and their families have sustained a terrible exhausting strike for the best part of a year. Yet it is precisely this idea of Scargillism which has been propagated most consistently by the governing classes since the summer of 1984, conforming closely to any number of previous red scares, but still able to shock and inflict a dreadful bashing on the British polity.

This was a product of the *grand peur* of the July days, which did so much to set the agenda for the subsequent campaign when the government was forced into the realization that the strike simply was not going to evaporate out of existence.

When the government was losing the initiative, as it clearly looked to be on a number of occasions in the autumn, it fell back on the tried and tested tactics of conjuring up the demons. Day by day through August and September Walker was getting visibly more angry and impatient. Ministers were frequently furious with MacGregor, especially over his determination to shoot the ball hard and fast back into his own net. Whenever there was even a glimmer of a peace initiative the Prime Minister or her colleagues welcomed it on the one hand while consolidating their intransigence on the other. On the eve of the Conservative Party conference slightly more than half of Tory voters thought the government was handling the strike poorly. But the last thing that Thatcher could do at this stage was to be seen contemplating a compromise.

The Hidden Hand

At this point we must switch attention away from the public manifestations of Conservative policy and assess briefly the covert activities of Conservatives and their agents, particularly in relation to the various Working Miners' Committees.

It was in the *Mirror* that the activities of one David Hart were first published. Hart, a wealthy property developer, has in the past established himself as an unofficial adviser to the Prime Minister; in August his varied skills were directed to briefing MacGregor; and on a number of occasions he has been given space in *The Times* to air his very eccentric and none too pleasant views on the miners. At a moment when the working miners in Nottinghamshire were intensifying their struggle against Ray Chadburn and other NUM officials who supported the strike, Hart described for the benefit of *Times* readers an NUM meeting he had witnessed. He suggested, first, that the officials had deliberately provisioned plentiful supplies of beer in the hope of intoxicating those NUM members present; his keen eye spotted 'directionless young militants' along with the inevitable 'skilled agitators', while Scargill appeared as the 'messiah'. His sense of smell was equally alert on the day for he detected 'in the air the unmistakable stench of fascism'. With such an enemy at large, he concluded, it is necessary not only for a defeat to be inflicted in the body politic: 'These men will have to be defeated in the soul politic too'.[11]

For Hart, the soul politic had a very precise location — the Castle Donnington Guest House. It was here that on 19 August he attended the conspiratorial launch of the National Working Miners' Committee. He regularly attended further meetings, generously dipping into his pockets for handfuls of bankrolls.[12] None of his activities in organizing this campaign he thought sufficiently worthy of mention in his columns in *The Times*. The whole activity remained resolutely undercover.

The significance of Hart is primarily due to his connections with Downing Street and the NCB. It is not at all clear how seriously either of these bodies regard him, although there can be no doubt that every effort to organize the working miners would be welcomed. It is probable that there have been other, better concealed, attempts emanating directly from the government and the Coal Board aimed at sabotaging the strike, not to mention the role of the various intelligence departments of the police. Even the *Telegraph* felt free to admit that MacGregor himself was closely involved in the appointment of the sequestrators and the receiver in the bid to gain control of the NUM's funds.[13]

Much of this is to be expected, and so too the funding of such initiatives by private enterprise, and the involvement of Conservative journalists, lawyers and publicity men. The extended network of provincial business and Conservative associations has clearly come into its own. But none of this can mean very much politically unless it wins substantial sections of the NUM, and evidence of effective links between Working Miners' Committees and union-busting Conservative organizations is extremely slender.

To suppose that the working miners have all been gripped by the truth of Thatcherism is rubbish. The declaration of the first Nottinghamshire Working Miners' Committee was emphatic in its rejection of any attempt to break with the NUM. For many, the issue of the ballot has been predominant. The commitment of the working miners to the overtime ban, for example, suggests that in Nottinghamshire and elsewhere, their views do not conform to any recognizable anti-union Conservatism. The chances of the working committees becoming *focos* for Toryism do not look high.

This is not at all to underestimate the very great seriousness of the organized return-to-work campaigns, especially in Nottingham-shire. They undoubtedly form the weakest link in the strike. What is manifest here is a shift in a whole culture of trade unionism, which remains proletarian, even remains committed to the collectivist principles of the trade-union ideal, but can no longer readily sub-scribe to the historic alliance of labourism which has been held in place since the 1920s. The erosion of this alliance forms the current crisis of Labour and underlines the successes of the new right. Electorally, miners' constituencies now contribute to the dominance of Thatcherism. In April 1977 in the Ashfield by-election the Con-servative Party overturned a Labour majority of 23,000; Mansfield is now a marginal seat; the new constituency of Sherwood, containing one of the highest concentrations of miners in the country, has had from June 1983 a Tory representative.[14] However, these electoral shifts, crucial though they are, do not necessarily mean a complete abandonment of working-class instincts for solidarity and collec-tivism, a collapse into the possessive individualism of Thatcherism. They represent more, perhaps, the absolute end-point of the long tradition of labourism and the inability of its representatives — union and party leaders — to speak, automatically, for their members and constituents. It signifies, as much as anything, the ground which must be won, and future work in formulating an adequate set of ideals for the labour movement of the 1980s.

For these reasons, the situation in Nottinghamshire today cannot be understood simply as a reassertion of Spencerism — of a union premissed on collaboration and the refusal to strike, which charac-terized Nottingham after the defeat of 1926. Spencerism was a clearly formulated break with the classic institutions of traditional labourism. Today, however, these institutions no longer have the roots they once had in working-class experience and the situation in Nottinghamshire reflects this. It is part of the much more general process of 'the forward march of labour halted'. Thus it is just at this point that the analogies with 1926, supposing the continuation of a labour movement of the 'classic' type, fall down. Objectively, there can be no doubt of the dreadful dangers resulting from the organized working miners' pressure groups. The job, however, is to win them back.

Also, there does exist, of course, the Thatcherite minority, the 'lions' of the Tory Party conference. Whether the redoubtable Silver Birch comes into this category is not immediately apparent. The secrecy and mystery of his persona, the quite ridiculous publicity and the cheap drama of his entry into the media all suggest that he has the plausibility of the pantomime wrestlers of Saturday afternoon television, on a par with a 'Skull Murphy' or 'Scrubber Daley'. But anyone who travels the country in the company of the industrial editor of the *Mail on Sunday* must be up to something and this makes all the protestations of a pained innocence a little hard to swallow.

The Enemy Draws Closer

The Conservative Government has found it necessary to fight on every front, looking also to its rear. This in part follows from the logic of the belief in the 'enemy within' for it can never be settled with certainty who at any particular time is wavering, shifting from friend to foe. It invites the rolling authoritarianism in which actions and opinions can be condemned as treasonable. Innocence can only be established by indulging in a perpetual litany of denunciation of others. A similar collapse in the norms of a civilized and democratic polity took place in the period before the General Strike of 1926, following a sustained red scare when a dozen Communist leaders were jailed — under the authority of the 1797 Incitement to Mutiny Act — because they refused to foresake their political beliefs. This gut politics recurred during the war with Argentina in 1982 when the most unlikely figures were accused of treasonable activities. Today, with the strike, when motions are seriously debated in Oxford colleges which call for the arrest of Scargill for treason, or for his mutilation, we are witnessing a vigilantism which carries us across the threshold of fascism. Perhaps *The Times* knew full well what it was about when it acknowledged that the 'dangerous counter-passions which lurk beneath the surface' of our society might be 'excited' if the strike were prolonged.[15]

Nowhere is this shift in the contemporary political culture more strongly evident than in the Conservative Party's relationship to the Anglican Church, the party's traditional spiritual homeland. True, Archbishop Davidson had a hard time of it in 1926, silenced on government orders for advocating reconciliation during the General Strike. But that was smartly patched up the moment the strike came to an end.

More recently it has been possible to detect an unbending hostility to the Church from those on the outer reaches of the Conservative Party — from Lord Salisbury, for example, who was curious to know whether the Anglican Church had become the fifth column of the international communist movement;[16] or Edward Norman who in 1977 was emphatic in his assertion that 'I have to add the Christian churches to the list of those whose social outlook now contributes to the subversion of capitalism'.[17] It wasn't until the Falklands/ Malvinas War however, when the Prime Minister deemed the episcopacy insufficiently patriotic, that such ideas coursed through the major arteries of Conservatism.

Thus when John Habgood, the Archbishop of York, suggested in April that the aims of the NUM could not be discounted out of hand, it was little surprise that Enoch Powell and *The Times* were quick to correct him, with strong hints that he had no right to say such things. But this was nothing to the embittered attacks on the Right Reverend David Jenkins, Bishop of Durham, who — having not long previously upset his colleagues by making comments on the virgin birth which were generally viewed as theologically suspect — calmly proposed that 'the miners must not be defeated', suggesting at the same time that we all might be better off without the services of 'an imported elderly American', by whom he meant Ian Mac-Gregor. The Tory response was immediate. John Carlisle MP hoped that 'the thunderbolt that struck York Minster might similarly strike Durham' and the irrepressible Nicholas Fairbairn argued that if the bishop 'wishes to worship earthly gods like Arthur Scargill let him foresake the post to which he has just been wrongly appointed'.[18] Norman St John-Stevas alone dispensed a little wisdom claiming the whole affair was no more than a 'hysterical brouhaha'.[19]

As if to fuel the spiritual fires yet more *The Times* then sought out the views of the Archbishop of Canterbury, Robert Runcie, publishing an extended interview on the eve of the Tory Party conference. In what seemed a supremely measured commentary Runcie expressed mild worries about the handling of the strike and complained also about people being treated 'as scum'. John Selwyn Gummer, Conservative Party chairman and member of the General Synod, expressed his dismay; Tebbit thought the whole thing 'woolly' and took the opportunity to rehearse his favourite parable — 'The characteristic of the Good Samaritan is that he had a wallet with the cash in it to pay the bill'; Anthony Beaumont-Dark thought it 'mindless'; and Nicholas Fairbairn, in a satanic mood, proposed that the Archbishop should, as penance, 'eat coal in public'.[20]

Despite this onslaught the bishops did not give up. They made public their intention to meet the leaders of the NUM in order to further the possibilities for compromise. Stung by this, Gummer attacked the Church in a sermon delivered in the University Church of Great St. Mary's in Cambridge — a more appropriate location, perhaps, to fight the battles of the 'soul politic' than the Donnington Castle Guest House. But anxious that the flock witnessing this battle might be rather sparse Gummer took the precaution of circulating the sermon in advance to the press, through Conservative Central Office.

The Politics of the Bunker

It is unclear, at the time of writing, whether Thatcher can hold together the Conservative Party, and the NCB, as she has done already, into — say — the winter of 1985/6. The government has blundered frequently and had no conceivable idea that the strike could possibly last so long. But each day, the government enters a situation in which the risks of failure are increasingly more difficult for ministers to contemplate.

Meanwhile the absurd, nightmarish circus continues. Walker blithely assured us on the last day of 1984 that 'there will be no power cuts in 1985', at the same time as which it was revealed that the strike is costing the taxpayer some £85 million each week. Enoch Powell has been stalking up and down calling for 'real' leadership.[21] The chairman of the NCB publicly advocates privatization of the industry over which he has charge,[22] and Professor Patrick Minford, a monetarist of the Jesuitical variety, has gone on record as saying that the strike is a 'good thing'.[23] Harold Macmillan, appearing now as Lord Stockton, has spoken with eloquence and compassion about the strike as a terrible disaster, paying tribute to the miners as 'the best men in the world'. And he issued, too, an oblique word of warning to those in his party: 'They beat the Kaiser's army and they beat Hitler's army. They never gave in'.[24] When a few days later, the erstwhile leader of the Labour Party, James Callaghan, tried to follow in his wake making a similar argument the opportunism could not have been plainer. Dr David Owen, the nearest thing we have to a proto-Mussolini figure, emerged as the *Spectator*'s parliamentarian of the year, a disturbing choice to say the least. Mrs Thatcher — determined to fulfil her Churchillian fantasies — echoed the master's refusal to indulge in 'a lot of defeatist trash' and provided a mystical *tour de force* with a paean to Runnymeade and the English Constitution in that famous 'workshop of democracy', the Carlton Club.[25]

But the last word should be left to Mr MacGregor, ready perhaps with his escape plans: 'I am not one of your local characters. I don't vote here. I vote in Florida'.[26]

Notes

1. *The Economist*, 7 July 1984.
2. F. Pym, *The Politics of Consent*, London, 1984.
3. *The Times*, 26 June 1984.
4. *The Times*, 23 June 1984.
5. *The Times*, 19 September 1984.
6. A. Gamble, 'Thatcherism Mark III', *Marxism Today*, June 1984.
7. Quoted in M. Crick, *Scargill and the Miners*, Harmondsworth, 1985, p. 62.
8. *The Economist*, 27 May 1978.
9. *The Times*, 1 June 1984.
10. P. Hennessy, *The Times*, 20 March 1984.
11. *The Times*, 2 May 1984; see too *The Times* of 6 July 1984, 3 August 1984 and 13 September 1984.
12. M. Hollingsworth, *New Statesman*, 14 December 1984.
13. *The Daily Telegraph*, 4 December 1984.
14. Crick, p. 118.
15. *The Times*, 24 September 1984.
16. Lord Salisbury, *Salisbury Review*, 1983, no. 2.
17. A. Kaletsky, *Financial Times*, 24 December 1984.
18. *The Times*, 22 September, 1984.
19. *The Times*, 27 September 1984.
20. *The Times*, 8 and 9 October 1984.
21. *The Times*, 22 September 1984.
22. *The Times*, 5 December 1984.
23. *The Guardian*, 7 December 1984.
24. *Hansard*, House of Lords, 13 November 1984, col. 240.
25. *Second Carlton Lecture*, 26 November 1984.
26. *The Times*, 12 June 1984.

3
Trade Unionism in Crisis
The Miners' Strike and the Challenge to Union Democracy

Bob Fryer

'In the present situation, the leaders of the miners must fight every inch of the way against all attempts to impose the burden of the new crisis upon the miners. They have a right to demand measures to prevent imports of oil from still further depressing the coal industry. They have a right to demand that the pits, essential for the life of the community, shall be maintained as long as possible. There are points where it is no longer possible to demand that a pit be kept in existence. A pit, like a man, has a specified life. And when it is finished there is nothing else to do but to let it die. But in the situation in Britain, when a pit dies, the village which has depended upon it dies as well, and so we face again the tragedy of the derelict mining areas which we remember from the thirties.

The nation has a responsibility to the youngsters who were persuaded to take up the hard life of a miner with promises that they would never be out of a job, that never again would fear of unemployment haunt their lives.'

From Arthur Horner, *Incorrigible Rebel*[1]

The miners' strike represents the most sustained industrial dispute in Britain since the General Strike of 1926. The issues involved — national energy policy, community organization, labour solidarity, civil rights and economic strategy — have provided new opportunities for socialists to advance solutions radically different to those of the Conservative Government. Yet, from the NUM's point of view, the dispute has been maintained in the most discouraging circumstances and some key political opportunities have been embarrassingly fumbled. The timing of the strike was determined not by the NUM but by pre-emptive NCB and Government initiatives. When the strike began, coal-stocks at power stations and pitheads stood at unprecedentedly high levels; despite numerous warnings from the NUM leadership about an NCB 'hit-list' and Government plans for an attack on the union, earlier national ballots for industrial action had failed to secure the necessary majorities; disputes in other sectors, which might have added to the Government's political problems alongside the coal strike, never materialized or were settled relatively swiftly. The great danger of divisions opening up within the NUM was evident from the outset: Nottinghamshire and the rest of the Midland coalfields were likely to be a problem and bitter memories of unsupported struggles in 1983 in South Wales and Scotland necessitated vigorous campaigns to secure widespread support for a strike.

Once begun, the dispute was harassed by a well-co-ordinated succession of determined police, legal and media attacks. Politicians of all parties, some trade unionists, and dissenting working miners, voiced loud public criticism of the NUM executive and particularly Arthur Scargill, for orchestrating a national strike without recourse to a new national ballot. Throughout the dispute, national co-ordination of the semi-autonomous areas has presented difficulties, especially where strikers were in the minority. It has at times seemed easier to mount large-scale demonstrations and confrontations than to restrict systematically the movement of coal and other fuels while the lack of support from the electricity supply unions has further weakened the potential impact of the strike.

For the Thatcher Government, an onslaught on the NUM promised a clutch of inviting triumphs. It provided an opportunity for Mrs Thatcher to demonstrate the effectiveness of her resolute style of government in dealing with the miners, in contrast to Heath's ignominious defeats of 1972 and 1974. The parliamentary Conservative party were thus furnished with a righteous cause likely to overcome the criticism and reservation of Tory back-benchers that has often appeared to threaten the Government more than opposition attacks. At the same time, the tardiness, confusion and division within the Labour Party leadership has served to bolster the image of a clear-sighted, strongly-led and united Conservatism. The conduct of the dispute, particularly the massive deployment of police (including the Special Branch) in the coalfields, has been a practical demonstration of the government's unswerving commitment to its own peculiar version of law and order, especially on the picket lines and later in the courts. The defiance of the working miners has been seized upon to promote the Tories' distorted conception of the 'right to work', exemplifying the Conservative protection of individual freedom against the alleged tyranny of collective intimidation from militants. As the strike unfolded, government ministers were able to take pains to associate striking miners with violence, criminality and subversion and the NUM with blatantly anti-democratic practices, especially in its refusal to sanction a national ballot on the dispute.

The NUM and its national leadership have been portrayed as characteristic of British trade unions — urgently in need of legal regulation and the enforcement of secret ballots to douse their 'unrepresentative' militancy. This latest political assault, combined with the cleverly drafted 1984 Trade Union Act to introduce compulsory strike ballots, individualize union electoral systems and impose limitations upon union political activities, constitutes a severe challenge to a movement already under siege.

On many fronts British unions face restrictions, decline and the threat of defeat. There is no doubting the significance of the miners' struggle for the trade-union movement as a whole, but while proposals of support are passed at union conferences the movement generally seems frozen in its response. Union leaders have had to admit that, much as they would like to, with the notable exception of ASLEF and the NUR, they cannot 'deliver' their members into the struggle to support the NUM. This fact alone points to the complexity of the present crisis. Clearly the attack on the miners' union is something which the Tory Party have prepared for and thought over long and hard in their years in opposition. But this is only one side of the story. Over the last twenty years or so, industry after industry has declined — or collapsed — in the face of a restructured international capitalism. No industry has been more decisively affected than coal. During this period governments — Conservative and Labour — have attempted to *manage* decline. In this the trade unions themselves have played a central part; they have been active agents in the politics of Britain over the past twenty years. Because of this the struggle in which the miners are involved is with more than a Tory conspiracy, it represents a deepening crisis within British society and one in which the institutions of the working class are centrally involved.

The Unions in the Crisis

The 'union question' has been central to economic and political strategy since before the election of Wilson's Labour Government in 1964. Fashions in industrial relations have come and gone with remarkable alacrity. Once upon a time, progress was to be achieved through productivity bargaining, then through the reform of payment systems, or by plant bargaining generally. The encouragement of local representation, and especially shop stewards, followed hard upon earlier reforms as did a focus upon industrial democracy, worker participation, and the creation of so-called 'quality circles'. It is less than ten years since the heady declaration of a new 'social contract' between unions and the state, when wary critics warned of the dangers of corporatism and the bureaucratization of rank-and-file opposition.[2]

This dazzling succession of remedies for the 'British diseases' of strikes, low productivity and falling profits was halted abruptly when Michael Edwardes at British Leyland, powerfully supported by co-director Ian MacGregor, swept aside established procedures in a determined reassertion of managerial power that set a new pattern for the future.[3]

It is not surprising that the inconsistencies of the economy and of government industrial relations policies over the past thirty years have been reflected in a lack of coherent strategies on the part of the trade unions. Nevertheless, the unions appear to have achieved a great deal. Despite the various changes — the expansion of the white-collar service industries, the growth of female employment and of part-time work — union membership not only held steady but, until 1980, actually increased both absolutely and as a percentage of the employed work-force (density). This gain resulted from an increase in the density of manual unionism in manufacturing and numerical and density increases in clerical and service industry trade unionism, particularly in the public sector. This was promoted by a combination of factors including managerial and governmental benevolence, closed-shop agreements, the 'check-off' of union subscriptions from earnings and successive government attempts at incomes policy. In a rapidly changing environment the unions had to run fast to stand still but nevertheless achieved more than might have been expected.

Behind the bland figures of maintaining or slightly improving overall membership, the situation varied greatly within and between unions. Single or near single-industry unions declined with the parent industry, especially where no attempt was made to modify the traditional 'closed' nature of membership eligibility. Some unions, like the NUM, simply shrank, while others amalgamated, often with a more 'open' general union where their fortunes varied according to their size and importance in the new conglomerate.

With the growth of the public services, NALGO and NUPE expanded to become two of the largest British unions.

But in these developments there were manifold paradoxes. While union membership was increasing and opportunities for union education expanding, opinion polls, surveys and, ultimately, elections revealed public ambivalence and even hostility towards the unions. The frequently observed (though little understood) contradiction between values based on concrete experience and those that are generalized or abstract may help to explain some of these responses. Public criticism of the trade unions by politicians, employers and the media has also contributed to their unpopularity. But these factors do not adequately explain why the trade unions, with so many members, a huge and recent expansion in educational work and apparent acceptance from employers and the state, should excite widespread critical responses to the point where only a minority of trade-union members voted Labour in the 1983 General Election and Thatcherite proposals for union 'reform' evoke considerable support from union members themselves.

Public Sector Militancy

One possible explanation, with obvious appeal to dyed-in-the-wool critics of unions, is the growth in union militancy in the public sector. To successive governments it has seemed more feasible to impose wage restrictions on the public sector than on the private sector, and these differentiated incomes policies have drawn public sector unions into bitter disputes with the government. Dustmen, postal workers, gasworkers, ancilliary health staff, teachers, civil servants, railway workers, fire brigades, social workers, doctors, ambulance staff, nurses, electricity supply workers, postal workers, steelworkers and, of course, the miners, have all challenged government policy not only on wages, but also in opposition to cuts in public spending and, more latterly, in fights against privatization. Many of these workers found themselves in the front line of strikes, or industrial action of any kind, for the first time and their disputes were part of the general shift in union activity from private to public sector, and from unofficial to official strikes.

As such — and with the growing scale of the *economic* crisis — these workers (while defending their legitimate interests) found themselves in the centre of major *political* disputes. Of necessity, much of this new public sector militancy required the exploration of new methods of organization to increase the impact and heighten public awareness of the dispute. Nevertheless, these unions were ill equipped to handle accusations that more damage had been inflicted upon innocent members of the public than upon employers or government.

A willingness to draw, perhaps unreflectively, on tactics and approaches to strikes forged in confrontations in manufacturing industry exposed the public-sector — particularly public-*service* — unions to a shrill chorus of public denigration, particularly in the aftermath of the 'winter of discontent' that immediately preceded Mrs. Thatcher's election to power.

If workers in public services were pilloried for their 'callous disregard' of other workers and their families, it was very likely that some criticism drew its strength from attacks upon public services that had been mounted throughout the 1970s. The public services had been portrayed as unproductive, inefficient and a drain upon the public purse. By contrast with private manufacturing industry, public services were seen as of secondary importance, almost a luxury and dependent upon the primacy of production. Nor were politicians and employers alone in encouraging such a perspective, for some trade-union leaders openly lent their voices to the onslaught. Although the public-service unions fought back, one possible reason for the skilled workers' flight from Labour in the 1979 General Election was the suspicion that public-service workers were somehow less deserving. In any case, it was felt by some skilled and traditionally better paid workers, that the public-service unions' pay campaigns of the 1970s had upset legitimate wage differentials. Such misgivings, added to the hostility to public service and to public-sector militancy, guaranteed the continuation of a fragmentation and sectionalism which has so often divided trade unionists among themselves. It pointed also to the ways in which trade unions — if they were effectively to defend their members' interests — would need to develop a campaigning style, think strategically about the dissemination of propaganda and information, and consider deeply their relationship to the media. In short they would need to look very critically indeed at the nature of their organization.

Members and Activists

The difficulties for the unions did not stop there. It was only in the ever more obvious and depressing circumstances of national and global capitalist restructuring that certain deep-seated trade-union problems began to constitute a serious threat to the well-being of the movement. Chief amongst these was the gulf that had opened up between the formal structures and machinery of government of the unions and the rank-and-file membership. Strangely, although there had long been plenty of evidence of this caesura, it had attracted little attention from trade unions, their supporters or even their critics.[4] Such an unholy alliance of silence can be understood only in the context of a common concentration upon work at plant level.

Trade unions had inherited local systems of organization, particularly the branch and district, that owed much to late nineteenth and early twentieth-century conditions of employment and collective bargaining. Typically geographical in basis, the union branch usually occupied a key position in the administrative, electoral, informational and governmental arrangements of the union. Equally typical was the situation where, exceptional circumstances aside, attendance at branch meetings was sparse and important decisions were made in the name of the branch by a few doughty and active members. There were very good reasons for poor turn-out. Remoteness from both home and place of work, timing, arcane procedures and archaic language, and a resentment by the loyal few at the sporadic yet vocal appearance of the many all contributed to low numbers at branch meetings. The contrasts with potentially lively workplace unionism were stark. At the branch, the rank-and-file were expected to be mostly passive, whilst leading lay members and full-time officials held forth. At work, particularly on the shop floor itself, there was always the chance of getting in on the act. Moreover, words and action at shop-floor level were more obviously related and union members could immediately translate their policies into practice rather than passing on resolutions, recommendations and votes to other levels of union organization. Employers, keen to distance themselves and their own labour force from the concerns of other employers covered by a given branch, also preferred the action to take place at workplace level. Where workplace organization did not already exist, it was sponsored by the unions and fostered by workplace collective-bargaining arrangements. Soon public policy (especially after the 'Donovan' Report in 1968) endorsed the focus upon the workplace, or more precisely, upon the shop steward, to the extent that even attempts to relocate the branch at workplace level (where that was practicable), failed to attract regular mass attendance. In any case, the model of workplace activity, drawn heavily if selectively from union practices in engineering, could not simply be forced on to every local union organization irrespective of local employment and membership circumstances. Even in the mining industry, where branch and lodge organization might have been closely integrated with the pit, the extension of 'bussing' miners into work from areas where faces and pits had been closed meant that lodge work fell increasingly to an activist minority.

'Today, every miner is a member of the union, and the term 'union man' is used to denote a union activist who attends his branch meetings regularly and argues the union's case in the pit, or sometimes more narrowly a member of the branch committee. 'Union men' act as intermediaries between the members of the union and their elected officials and committee. They take the feelings and opinions of the members to the general meetings of the branch, and take the decision of the branch back to the members. In the continual discussions underground on union policy, union men are expected to provide information on a countless number of issues, from compensation for industrial accidents to free gloves for men who work with metal sheeting, and from a national pay claim to the number of officials allowed to ride on the cage at knock-off. Though the men often look to the union man for leadership and advice in the endless disputes with management, they often hold him personally responsible for the sometimes unpopular decisions of the union branch, and many a heated argument in the pit terminates in a union man rounding on his opponent and telling him, "If you don't like it, get yourself along to the meetings, and do something about it!" '[5]

None of this is to say that the activists in the branch and the local representatives at the workplace (often the same people) did not perform honourable and sometimes herculean tasks. On the contrary, at intervals during the 1960s and 1970s, many of the advances registered by the unions were led by shop stewards' organizations. However, it was still an error to treat the activist minority as if they were simply conterminous with the membership at large. The very focus of education, information and representation upon the stewards and local officials always threatened to mark them out as less than typical members, even where extensive turnover appeared to ensure a degree of rotation of office that might spread experience. Leading local representatives appeared, often encouraged by local management and furnished with appropriate facilities. Branch and shop stewards' committees developed skills and procedures which, in their very effectiveness, ran the risk of being shown to be somewhat distanced from the understanding of the membership at large. Suspicion was also aroused that the relative absence of the membership from local representatives' initiatives was not always a matter of complete regret amongst the activist minority. Again, this was an understandable if ultimately grave shortcoming, for the leading activists were far more likely than the mass of the membership to grasp quickly the significance of managerial and governmental initiatives. That management itself soon appreciated this position was demonstrated by the practice made popular by the British Leyland Edwardes Plan of appealing directly to the members over the heads of the stewards and completely bypassing established channels of collective bargaining.

When both capital and the state moved to shift the terrain of struggle from workplace to company or national levels or, in the case of multi-national firms, to international levels, even the strongest workplace systems were found wanting. The more they attempted to recover the position by pointing out the massive threats posed by managerial and governmental strategy, the more were these latter able to castigate the local representatives as dangerous and irresponsible and to cash in on the caution and parochialism which rising unemployment understandably evoked from the membership. A popular phrase for both employers and politicians offering explanations for the ills being visited upon workers was that 'hot-headed workplace militancy', not the restructuring of capital in crisis, was actually at the root of the problem.[6] But when Labour Party activists suggested that international capital was to blame and added that the problems of the British economy could be tackled through an all-embracing 'Alternative Economic Strategy', they were greeted with incredulity on the doorsteps of the electorate.

By the time of the General Election of 1979, trade unionists and their families had other reasons for their ambivalence towards the unions. The social-contract period of the mid 1970s, whatever short-term gain it brought to certain groups of workers, was easily portrayed as an era of a cosy 'fix' between the Labour Government and certain trade-union leaders. It didn't demand much skill in public relations to turn such allegations to the political disadvantage of the unions. Nor were memories of the Wilson years of government between 1964 and 1970 any more encouraging. It was no longer easy to demonstrate that Labour was the natural choice of the rank-and-file working-class elector.

Women Workers

Worker ambivalence to the unions, and to Labour in general, also came from other sources. Despite the fact that many of the new union members were women, the unions appeared to be more willing to accept women's subscriptions than to discover whether union organization, methods and structure required revision to meet their needs. Although union meetings and conferences increasingly endorsed resolutions covering a wide range of women's social, political and economic demands, little thought was given to advancing them in a union movement dominated by men, reliant upon the language and practices of 'fraternity' and involved in patriarchal forms of collective bargaining and employment arrangements. In the coalfields, closure and redundancy was often associated with a simultaneous shift in the sexual division of labour. Mining communities, traditionally reliant on the paid employment of men, increasingly became dependent on women's earnings. Nor was capital slow to take advantage of the large numbers of women workers on low wages with little more than formal representation by the unions.[7] Yet even this nominal involvement meant more protection than that available to the unpaid sisters of women workers. The long-established base of the union movement in waged labour continued to exclude women performing vital domestic work, except perhaps at the odd social or as extra pairs of hands in a crisis.

Where women had joined unions, in common with so many of their male counterparts in the late 1960s and 1970s, membership rarely went beyond mere card-holding. Union organization was replaced by the completion of consent forms for new members' dues to be collected at source from their wages. The work of full-time officers and stewards left little time for developing the knowledge, understanding and commitment of members. Accordingly, during industrial action, methods and tactics were imported wholesale from incomparable unions or acquired from friends and the media although often inappropriate for the circumstances. Closed shop and union-membership agreements were secured to increase membership, exclude other unions and simplify managerial administration rather than to provide the basis for committed union solidarity against the employers. Once such arrangements proved unacceptable to capital, or met legal opposition, their fragility was cruelly exposed.

Back to the Conservative Government

The analysis so far suggests not so much a simple and long-standing conspiracy to smash the unions as the quickening revelation of a series of contradictions and weaknesses in British trade unionism which, once identified, facilitated an attack by the Conservative Government, especially after its re-election in 1983. Not even the Thatcher Government, however, could predict the exact course the struggle would take — during the past five years various unions and groups of members have responded quite differently to the attacks they have sustained. The unfolding events have demanded that tactical choices be made by the trade unions as well as the employers, government, courts or police. Nevertheless the framework for the attack was clearly laid out by the Conservative Government, first in its Green Paper *Democracy in Trade Unions* in January 1983 and subsequently in the 1984 Trade Union Act.

The starting point for the Conservative critique was clear enough. It linked together two assumptions: trade unions are privileged bodies which benefit from unusual legal immunities; trade unions should be demonstrably responsive to the express wishes of their members and to the satisfaction of the public. The trade unions' power to inflict damage, under legal protection, and the possibility that union leaderships and actions might be unrepresentative of the wider membership, were thus portrayed as proper areas for government concern. According to the Green Paper, this was especially true in cases where unions had obviously failed to initiate reforms to remedy their own shortcomings and weaknesses.

The Green Paper addressed itself to three key issues: secret ballots for union elections, ballots before strikes and trade unions' political activities. Running through the discussion of each issue were a number of common themes, skilfully seeking to contrast what the government presented as incontrovertibly democratic standards with the 'murky and unrepresentative' practices of the unions, or at least the majority of them. The simple device employed to highlight these stark differences was a series of chilling comparisons, each one intended to suggest the need for urgent intervention by the government. In places the device is transparent, presumably quite deliberately so, elsewhere the contrasts are more insidiously suggested by allusion, innuendo, nudges, winks and nods. At the heart of the Green Paper stands the comparison between an ideal of extensive membership participation in union affairs and the inference that in reality British trade unions are run by unrepresentative and unaccountable cliques and cabals. Votes taken by shows of hands in public suggest to the government not simply a regrettable lack of privacy but, more dangerously, the threat of pressure and even intimidation.[8] Implicitly, the Gadarene senselessness of the 'mob' is contrasted with the measured balance of the individual. Collectivism is thus equated with the oppression of the individual so that unions opposing secret ballots bring to mind opponents of reform of the parliamentary electoral system in the 1880s! From here it is an easy step to conclude that unions are potentially unrepresentative, manipulated and authoritarian, requiring, therefore, public regulation to bring them within the recognized (but unexplicated) canons of democratic behaviour. To secure the freedom of individual members within the unions, the Green Paper put forward a number of proposals. These centred upon making the secret ballot-box vote routine, possibly with the use of the postal vote. In the case of strikes and other disputes, ballots, subject to a membership 'trigger' or even conducted by employers, would be compulsory before legitimate industrial action — benefiting from immunities at law — could begin. At the time of the Green Paper's publication, the government invited responses to its arguments but, in the event, the legislation that was eventually enacted went much further than might have been expected. During the intervening period, the Conservative Government had been re-elected with a greatly increased parliamentary majority.

What is remarkable about the 1984 Trade Union Act, is its determinedly simplistic approach to union government. Not only is there no recognition of the essentially collective and corporate nature of union organization but, even more strikingly, no account is taken of the necessarily complex and varied systems of administration and decision-making in different unions and occupations. In fact, the legislation is predicated less upon the theory of government than upon one of mentality; the simple assumption is that the imposition of individualism and secrecy will lead to a diminution of union militancy.

Throughout the miners' strike, critics of the NUM have been able to make great political capital out of the executive's decision not to hold a national ballot on the dispute, insisting that this single procedure would conform with the canons of democratic decision-making. This 'superstitious worship of the ballot-box' as the Webbs called it, is full of political instruction; a moment's reflection indicates why governing bodies in all sorts of organizations (including governments and political parties) are unwilling to resort to referenda in decision-making, and why they would quickly be rendered ineffective by such a practice. As the Webbs said of trade-union experience in the nineteenth century: 'the attempt to secure the participation of every member in the management of his society was found to lead to instability in legislation, dangerous unsoundness of finance and general weakness of administration . . . The reliance of trade-union democrats on the Referendum resulted, in fact, in the virtual exclusion of the general body of members from all real share in the government.'[9] Ironically, it was the Durham coal-owners who were quick to appreciate this problem. 'The Durham Miners' Association, notwithstanding its closely concentrated sixty thousand members, fails to exercise any important influence on the Trade Union world, and even excites complaints from the employers as to "its internal weakness". The Durham coal-owners declare that, with the council overruling the executive, and the ballot vote reversing the decision of the council, they never know when they have arrived at a settlement, or how long that settlement will be enforced on a recalcitrant lodge.'[10]

Not that such a confused state has always been to the disadvantage of the employers or anti-radical groups within the unions. In the NUM in 1977 it was only thanks to clever manoeuvring between the court of appeal and the union's then leadership, that a confused response to the NCB's proposals for the introduction of an incentive scheme was possible. After decisive rejection of the scheme by a national ballot, individual areas were still able to proceed with the implementation of the scheme following a refusal by the President, Joe Gormley, to rule out of order such a procedure.[11] The court case taken by the South Wales area to prevent this course of action received the judgement that: 'the result of the ballot, nationally conducted, is not binding upon the NEC in using its powers in between conferences. It may serve to persuade the committee to take one action or another, or to refrain from action, but it has no great force or significance'.[12] This was also the view of the Webbs. 'Whatever advantages may be ascribed to the Referendum, it has the capital drawback of not providing the Executive with any policy.' In 1984/5 it is not the democratic procedures that are the root of the problem for the courts and the government — it is the *policy* of the NUM.

This recent Conservative legislation following on from the 1980 and 1982 Employment Acts is but the latest in a succession of government assaults upon organized labour in the related spheres of employment, working practices, earnings, job security and trade-union rights. During the NGA dispute and now the miners' strike, these incursions have been extended to include an apparent determination to 'criminalize' certain trade-union actions, especially mass picketing, and deliberately to associate the vigorous dissent of trade unionists with the menacing treachery of an 'enemy within'. This disposition accords well with government decisions to withdraw trade-union rights from certain groups of workers — GCHQ staff, for example, and with moves to limit the right to strike in essential public services.

The intention has been clear: to portray trade unionism as not only undemocratic but essentially anti-democratic; to represent trade-union policies not as legitimate demands within a democracy but as an essentially illegitimate challenge to democracy itself.

The Problem Restated

There is nothing, unsurprisingly, in the Conservative Government's approach to trade unionism intended to strengthen membership and invigorate participation in the organizational structures of British unions. Attrition and massive restructuring have already visited severe damage upon trade unionism, not least to membership numbers. The NUM is only one example amongst many where the former strength and extent of organization have been savagely diminished by shifts in economic policy. Such difficulties have been increased by changing employers' strategies, and also, it must be said, by deep-seated weaknesses in trade-union strategy. These weaknesses include endorsement of massive contractions over frighteningly short periods, focus only upon immediate demands and what resembles the voluntary self-exclusion of trade unions from the arenas of socialist debate in Britain for too many years.

A willingness to reduce the number of unions and facilitate mergers and amalgamations — called for repeatedly since the First World War — has not been lacking in the trade-union movement. On the contrary, the record in this field is impressive. More difficult to achieve has been the capacity for union structures and practices to benefit from the widespread shifts in class organization, composition and aspirations that have characterized twentieth-century British society. True enough, more women, more white-collar workers, more migrant labourers, more public-service employees and more workers from all sectors have been recruited into unions over the past forty years. But this new, and potentially heady, wine has perforce been decanted into some decidedly old bottles so that its vitality has been short-lived and found no ready outlet within the unions. The unions have been too content to struggle to match, as best they could, the constricting contours of a limping economy and the limitations of wage labour. Quite properly, the unions themselves have emphasized that the variety and complexity of their systems of government and organization are products of their development and collective-bargaining arrangements, and cannot simply be jettisoned in favour of externally imposed, supposedly more democratic, models. To outsiders, and to some trade unionists, the validity of this argument has led to a complacency about established structures, although a minority of unions have taken careful stock in recent years. The TUC's own publication, *Hands up for Democracy*, contains a wide range of powerful and important defences of union democracy and influence in Britain today, but its silence over problems still not recognized, let alone tackled, has left the field open for the Conservative Government.

Here is the root of the present crisis. In a period of rapidly changing social, economic and political conditions, when the character of labour, capital and the state is changing decisively, British trade unions have been exceedingly slow to modify their own structures. The fragility and, in some cases, the shallowness of union organization — so cruelly exposed in the crisis — was temporarily masked by state sponsorship and trade-union and employment rights promulgated under the social-democratic policies of the Labour Governments of 1964–70 and 1974–79. The current Conservative Government, however, has been able to draw heavily upon a rich legacy of anti-union rhetoric so often deployed in economic crises by politicians of all parties as well as by employers, newspaper publishers and representatives of international capital. It has been able to work this into the grain of much working-class experience. The Thatcher Government's projection of a highly selective conception of 'democracy' represents only the most energetic attempt to circumscribe public notions of the propriety of popular and accountable mechanisms of power within a pluralist society. However, in this present phase the challenge to trade unionism is facilitated by the powerful confluence of each of these aspects of British society within the panoply of a persistent and vibrant class structure in which employers, the police and courts have no need to conspire but only to play their proper parts with unrestrained enthusiasm.

The Miners' Strike

The difficult and embattled circumstances of the miners' strike have provided some hopeful examples of the possibilities for developing unionism into community and eventually class action. But these are fragile initiatives and, unnurtured, they may not survive the dispute, particularly if they are portrayed as supplementary to, rather than inherent features of, the fight against pit closures. Equally important, they provide opportunities for a widening of working–class democracy, built upon the initial collectivity of trade-union organization. The dispute has brought into active and creative involvement not only many miners who have long been passive members of their union, but also imaginative contributions from thousands who are, formally speaking, 'outside' the NUM — mothers, wives, girl-friends, families, friends, trade unionists and supporters. Whatever errors of tactics and strategy there may have been during the course of the dispute, if these new sources of energy can be mobilized on a long-term basis and across a wider front of activity, they will provide an exciting advance in working–class organization and democracy. Such a development would need to be reflected in extensive changes in union organization, government and policies and the breaching of the divisions between worker and citizen, economics and politics, union and class. No doubt, this is a tall order.

The Conservative Government is probably conscious of this potential and in part this explains its determination to isolate the NUM, to lionize working miners and twist the meaning of the 'right to work' into an individual freedom to scab under the menacing umbrella of intensive policing. But there is too, in the government's attack upon trade unions, a potentially dangerous faith in the unfailing reliability of class power to impose on rank-and-file trade unionists the distorted logic of capitalist rationality. To be sure, there is an enormously persuasive power on the side of employers, politicians, the media — limited understanding and, most importantly, the exigencies of dependence on wage labour. Nor does a supine 'new realism' promise any more hope of resistance. However, the Conservative Government assumes, as the 1984 Act clearly exemplifies, that bypassing or simply dismissing established union leaderships, structures and policies, will of necessity always undermine the collective opposition of union power by fragmenting it into a series of individual decisions at the ballot box. 'Ballotitis', as Mick McGahey has wittily caricatured the government's crude approach to union democracy, provides no guaranteed formula for 'moderation'.

Strangely enough, too many critics of government policy themselves come close to accepting the validity of the government's assumption. They appear to believe that union perspectives are dependent upon the admittedly flawed collectivism of existing union methods and organization. If this simple assumption has any truth at all, it is first because many unions have neglected to encourage internal systems of participation, accountability and debate, irrespective of the precise method and location of decision making adopted. Secondly, the assumption may have some validity so long as trade unionism is separated from other aspects of working-class politics. If trade unionism had been the only arena for the development of working-class culture and working-class consciousness, any neglect and complacency there has been might yet have provided encouragement to the Conservative approach. But new forms of organization have been forged over the past fifteen years or so, often involving trade unionists in novel areas of activity and promising to widen traditional conceptions of the composition and objectives of the 'labour movement'. It is in this respect, especially, that the miners' strike could mark a watershed, not only for mining communities, and the NUM in particular, but for union democracy and working-class politics in general.

Notes

1. Arthur Horner, *Incorrigible Rebel*, London 1960.
2. R. Hyman "The Politics of Workplace Trade Unionism' *Capital and Class*,
3. Leyland Combine Trade Union Committee, *The Edwardes Plan and your Job*.
4. *An excellent summary is provided in J. Hughes, Trade Union Structure and Government* Parts 1 and 2, Royal Commission on Trade Unions and Employers' Associations, Research Paper 5 (London, HMSO, 1967 and 1968).
5. M. Pitt, *The World on our Backs*, London 1979.
6. For an excellent example see ch. 2, 'Countering the Militants', in Robens, *Ten Year Stint*.
7. See for example H. Beynon and T. Austrin, *Global Outpost*, University of Durham, Department of Sociology and M. Bulmer (ed.) *Mining and Social Change*, London, 1978, especially ch. 16.
8. This echoes the views of Alf Robens. Robens' views on picketing have also been taken up by the present Government, see *Ten Year Stint*, pp. 36 and 281.
9. S. and B. Webb, *Industrial Democracy*, London, 1907, p. 26.
10. *Ibid*. p. 35.
11. T. Hall, *King Coal: Miners' Coal and Britain's Industrial Future*, Harmondsworth, 1981, pp. 233–238.
12. *Ibid*. p. 34.

4

Welfare Against the Workers
Benefits as a Political Weapon

Chris Jones and Tony Novak

According to Harry Walker, Secretary of the Miners' Distress Centre, the Durham mining community of Dawdon feels that the Department of Health and Social Security is at war with the families of its striking miners. 'I hate them for what they're doing to the bairns. The system that's laid down is supposed to mirror the country's compassion, but it's put babies on the picket line.' This anger is matched on every coalfield where miners are out on strike. The system of state welfare, once thought to be the symbol of a caring society, has been revealed to have a much nastier side. During the course of this dispute, and more than ever before, the DHSS has taken a place alongside the militarized police forces as part of an increasingly coercive state apparatus facing striking miners and their families.

This is a development of the greatest significance. It is also a reflection of the major changes that have been brought about in important areas of the Welfare State in the past few years. The Welfare State has been fought and struggled for by many millions of workers, not least by the miners themselves, as a way of providing for those in need. This system is now being refashioned and used in an attempt to starve people back to work, to increase the pressure of unemployment, and in general to destroy the capacity of working people to fight for their jobs, their living standards and their communities.

The economic realities of the situation are clear enough. No striker is entitled to claim benefit, and any benefit payable to a dependent wife or child is, regardless of circumstances, automatically reduced by £16 a week. For a couple with no extra resources that means £6.45 a week to live on, with Child Benefit of an extra £2.75 for each child under eleven. Any additional income — from a wife's part-time job, for example —means that benefit is reduced or not paid at all. For the single striker there is no entitlement what-soever. The refusal of the DHSS to meet even urgent needs means that such men are left with nothing, except what is available from friends, families and neighbours. For some, life on strike is simply impossible, and so they are the first to be starved back to work. For the rest, it is a terrible and costly struggle. As a single miner reveals: 'Some days I have nowt at all. I have Sunday dinner at me mam's, but sometimes I don't know where I'll get the next meal. I've six months' mortgage not paid, 20 weeks' telly, six months' council rates and the yearly water rates coming up. There's a £30 telephone bill not paid and they're going to cut it off, and a £15 electric bill.'

To survive in a capitalist society like Britain is impossible without money, without some sort of income, and that is where the bosses have always had the upper hand. Workers have only their labour to bargain with, and their ability to withdraw that labour is a funda-mental form of defence. Yet workers who are out on strike have never been allowed to claim an income from the state. This rule has been followed by both Labour and Conservative Governments on the grounds that government should remain 'neutral' in industrial disputes. It is a curious neutrality that leaves one side with nothing and the other with the comfort and security of wealth. At the same time, governments up till now have agreed — if only to avoid the spectre of starving children displayed all over the television screen — that the dependants of those on strike should at least be provided with minimum subsistence, and that extreme cases of hardship and need should be met. Since the election of the Thatcher Government, even these minimum safeguards have been swept away.

The Turning-Point

The year 1979 marked a turning-point in post-war British history. The election of the first Thatcher Government saw the rise to power of a new, aggressive and class-conscious Conservatism. Its politics were those of confrontation. As Peregrine Worsthorne, one of its adherents, is reported to have said: 'Old fashioned Tories say there isn't any class war. New Tories make no bones about it: we are class warriors and we expect to be victorious.'[1]

This move to the right began long before the actual Tory election victory of 1979. Indeed, in many ways the preceding Labour Government had done much to pave the way for Thatcher. The

Wilson–Callaghan administration, confronted by the most severe economic depression since the 1930s, found its cautious reformism hopelessly inadequate. Its consequent floundering was to involve the Labour Government in exploiting its special relationship with working people, persuading them to make enormous sacrifices for the benefit of the profits and dividends of the wealthy. In this process the Labour Government made breaches in hard-won working-class gains, particularly in areas of state social spending, which were later to be exploited with great effect by Thatcher.

While confusion and division were characteristic of Labour Party politics in the latter half of the 1970s, the Conservatives were undergoing some profound changes under the militant leadership of Margaret Thatcher. Economic depression, the evident bankruptcy of Labour's policies and strategies, and a general loss of confidence within the Establishment about the capacity of the post-war consensus between capital and labour to survive the harsher economic conditions of the 1970s and 1980s, were all eagerly seized upon by a new, aggressive Tory right. In the view of Thatcher and her supporters, the time was now ripe to push for some fundamental changes in British politics.

With considerable skill, the right set about exploiting the situation. Within months of securing the Tory Party leadership, Thatcher had established her own Centre for Policy Studies with Sir Keith Joseph at the helm. This was just one of the initiatives taken in an increasingly energetic mobilization of right-wing intellectuals. During the past fifteen years a flourishing international network of radical conservative thinkers and policy-making institutes has emerged, with particular strongholds in Britain and America. For the Thatcher Government this network has great importance, for the administration has little trust in the ability or even willingness of the Civil Service to come up with the radical schemes and policies required. Consequently, this network stimulates most of the policies and strategies espousing free market dogma and concerning radical change.

With substantial financial support, this Conservative network took advantage of Labour's division and confusion to launch its analysis of economic and social decline in both Britain and the USA. This analysis laid the blame not on capitalism itself but on the power of organized labour and the growth of the Welfare State. Both were accused of encroaching on the operation of the 'free market', of stifling initiative and reducing profitability, of raising popular expectations and increasing discontent. The task set for government was therefore to free capitalism from the restrictive power of trade unions and the demands of the working class on state social provision.

This strategy required an end to the sort of class collaboration that had characterized so much of British politics since the end of the Second World War. It was also a course of action so momentous in terms of its impact on people's lives, jobs and communities, that it carried with it great risks for the right. Such risks of conflict and social unrest are now alarming some Church leaders and 'old fashioned' Tories. Little wonder then that the new right networks have been so industrious in attempting to create an ideological climate favourable to fundamental change with minimal disruption. The 1984 miners' strike is their most crucial test to date. The future of the new right's strategy demands a victory against the miners. For this reason alone this dispute is the most critical confrontation between capital and labour for many decades.

Strikes and Social Security

'There is far too much talk about rights', argued the Tory MP Peggy Fenner in the debate on the 1980 Social Security Acts that were to lead to the present situation, 'whether they be welfare rights or the right to withdraw one's labour.' In the view of the right, the two are inseparably connected: both are symbols of the gains made by working people; both are held to be the cause of Britain's problems; and both have become targets which the right have set out to dismantle.

This was a point many Conservatives tried to make much of during the 1972 and 1974 miners' strikes. As *The Economist* argued in 1972, the existence of social security benefits, which at least provided something for dependants, gave strikers the ability to resist and to prolong a dispute: 'Social security is paid now on the grounds that wives and children should not have to suffer because dad (sic) goes on strike. This is giving the militant dads a freedom to strike for as long and as often as they wish, knowing that although it may put the family holiday in jeopardy, it will not do anything worse, while it may, at the end of the day, bring a memorable wage increase.'

The Economist was, of course, grossly misleading. Going on strike is never easy, and is usually a very costly business. What is more, the vast majority of workers who have gone on strike have, as official figures show, tended to rely upon savings, credit, or families, friends and neighbours rather than on the state. Even the Engineering Employers' Federation admitted that in most disputes no more than one quarter of those eligible took any available benefits. Yet, within months of taking office, the Tory Government elected in 1979 was rushing legislation through Parliament that not only put a squeeze on the social security system as a whole, but also fundamentally changed its role in industrial disputes.

The 1980 Social Security Acts

The two Social Security Acts introduced in 1980 were of great importance. In a general sense they served notice of the Thatcher Government's antagonism towards the welfare system developed since the war by successive Labour and Conservative governments. More specifically, they signalled a strategy of attempting to solve Britain's economic crisis at the expense of the most vulnerable and poor.

The successful and largely unopposed passage of this legislation so early in the administration must have given the radical right great heart. Although social security provision in Britain has never been generous, either in the level of benefits given or in the ways it has treated those dependent on it, this new legislation made matters considerably worse. Taken together, the two Acts achieved an even further tightening up of the social security system; they consolidated the stigmatizing and humiliating role of its means-tested Supplementary Benefits scheme, and at a time of rising unemployment and increasing social needs, made real cuts in benefit levels. No government since the 1930s dared so openly to cut benefits for those dependent on the state (although many, both Labour and Conservative, sought to chip away at whatever gains the poor succeeded in making). Since 1979, however, the cumulative total of the cuts in levels of benefit has amounted to £6,500 million, while at the same time higher-rate taxpayers have received an increase in income of £12,900 million.

That the Tory Government was able to get away with this legislation was the result of a number of factors. One such factor was the attitude of the Parliamentary Labour Party. During the opening debate on the legislation, which now bears so heavily on striking miners and their families, Tory MPs took evident delight in pointing out that at times there were as few as eight Labour members present in the Chamber. The failure of the Parliamentary Labour Party to oppose energetically this open attack on working people's rights and benefits yielded ground to the Tories, who with support from the popular press were able to present the package as a long awaited measure for combating scroungers and the work-shy.

Clause 6

'If it is suggested that in certain circumstances the individual cannot afford it, the answer is simple. There is the choice not to strike, to go back to work and earn the living that is available.'² Of all the changes introduced by the 1980 Social Security Acts, Clause 6, which ordered a compulsory deduction to be made from the benefit payable to strikers' dependants, and which forbade the making of urgent needs payments to them and to single strikers, was the most pernicious and vindictive.

It was, according to Secretary of State Patrick Jenkin, a clause that was 'in a totally different category from the rest of the Bill'. Whereas the other cuts and restrictions introduced were justified on the grounds of saving public expenditure, this particular clause, he went on, 'will save public money to a modest extent, but that is not its main concern. The government was elected, amongst other things, to restore a fairer bargaining balance between employers and trade unions. Clause 6 represents one of the steps taken to that end.'

There should be no doubt that what one Tory MP called this 'excellent clause' in a 'courageous and necessary Bill', while directed at all workers who seek to go on strike (since all those on strike are penalized, whether they belong to a trade union or not), was introduced with the possibility of a confrontation with the miners very much in mind. Clause 6 was one of a number of preparations made by the Thatcher Government to defeat a long and protracted strike, and was shaped largely by what many Tories considered to be the humiliations inflicted on the Heath Government by the miners' strikes of 1972 and 1974.

Frequently acknowledged as the vanguard of the organized working class, the miners were one of the groups identified by the right as potential opponents of their plans to transform British society. According to Alan Walters, Margaret Thatcher's chief economic adviser between 1979 and 1983, the Tory policy of dismantling the large nationalized industries was based on more than a belief in the virtue of so-called free market forces. It was also predicated on the belief that the nationalized industries were a major stronghold of organized labour, and for that reason needed to be taken on. As Walters put it, 'instead of commanding the nationalized industries, governments were largely commanded by them. The graffiti expressed it succinctly: "Miners Rule, OK?" '

Similarly, the final report of a Conservative Party policy group on the nationalized industries, leaked to *The Economist* in May 1978, revealed that 'the most likely battleground will be the coal industry', and added significantly: 'the greatest deterrent to any strike . . . would be to cut off the money supply to the strikers'.

Also, it was more than coincidence that, in terms of benefits paid out during strikes, the years 1972 and 1974 stand head and shoulders above the rest. As a single-industry union, the NUM has never been in a position to afford strike pay, and it was the NUM, probably more than any other union, which was active and successful in persuading and helping its members to claim state benefits. Although very small in terms of the total social security budget, 1972 saw £8 million and 1974 £5 million claimed by strikers' dependants, compared with an annual average of £2 million for the rest of the decade. The situation was even more marked in the case of single strikers. Although not legally entitled to a weekly income they could claim discretionary payments in cases of hardship. As a result of swift action, support and advice, the NUM was again to lead the way in securing payments. In 1972, 52,000 separate urgent needs payments were made to single strikers, as against a total of 5,000 for the whole of the previous ten years.

It is these payments that Clause 6 of the Social Security Acts has severely reduced or, in the case of single strikers, abolished. The consequences are as severe as they were predictable, and intended. Many families have found their income reduced way below the poverty line, and are unable to afford sufficient food, never mind clothing, heating or lighting. This is bad enough for a week or two, but it is now going on month after month. For single strikers, and especially for those living outside mining communities (a development which the Coal Board has sought to encourage with its new super-pits and policies of dispersal), the situation can be even more desperate. Isolated from sources of support, with their only hope the occasional food parcel, it is no exaggeration to talk of starvation.

Turning the Screw

As a result of Tory legislation, a striker's family dependent on the

DHSS is today, in real terms, twenty-five per cent worse off than in 1972. It is not, however, only in financial terms that the so-called 'Welfare' State has exerted pressure on those on strike. Under clear instructions from headquarters, and ultimately from the government itself, the DHSS has imposed further humiliations, hurdles and hardships.

As many other claimants have found to their cost, it is not just the amount of benefit that counts, but the way that claimants are treated. Throughout the strike, welfare rights workers have talked of a deliberate policy of obstruction and bloody-mindedness. Everything, regardless of need or compassion, is played by the book. Forms are found to be unavailable, or out of date. Benefit payments get delayed. Appeals take weeks, and even months to be heard, while in some cases benefit can be suspended pending an outcome. According to one DHSS Regional Controller, when deciding entitlement to Family Income Supplement, payable in certain circumstances where a wife is in low-paid work, 'we are being instructed to include miners' earnings from before the strike, regardless of the fact that miners have had no wages for so long'.

In countless other ways problems have been effected in the path of miners and their dependants. New procedures have been introduced, further reducing any benefits that are payable. For the first time, for example, the value of loans and grants provided to some families by local authorities to prevent children being taken into care have been deducted by the DHSS from weekly benefits. In one Sunderland office, the manager was changed three times during the first six months of the strike, while in other areas special counter staff dealing with the strike have been changed weekly, making it 'almost impossible', according to one welfare rights adviser, to discuss ongoing cases or review previous decisions.

On top of this systematic obstruction there are particular stories of DHSS insensitivity and inhumanity. It is true that the government was forced to relent in the face of public outrage when one couple were denied a funeral benefit — since it did not 'fall within the Regulations' — to bury their son. Other examples abound. Indeed, the DHSS and its lawyers have been meticulous in drafting regulations which exclude those on strike from practically every additional or emergency payment available to other claimants. One such example is that of a miner and his wife (a cleaner at the NCB and also on strike), who are forced to support themselves and their two sons on £13 a week Family Allowance. Both of the boys suffer from cystic fibrosis, and after weeks on a relentless diet of bread complained of severe stomach pains. Their application for an additional allowance from the DHSS was turned down on the grounds that their situation 'did not qualify them for a special diet'. As the father later replied, 'I didn't want a *special* diet. I wanted a diet.'

Yet for all the attempts to starve the miners back to work, for all the planning and legislation, and the systematic obstruction and inhumanity of the DHSS, the Tories' purpose has not been achieved. Ironically, it has probably had the opposite effect. The cuts throughout the Welfare State, that were meant to make workers feel more vulnerable, less militant and more pliable, and in particular first-hand experience of the social security system, have if anything stiffened the resolve of striking miners and their families. As one miner's wife put it: 'In areas like ours that's all there is: pits. Nothing else — only the dole. That's why we're fighting.' When the dole, along with the rest of the social wage, is slashed, and when the welfare state is exposed for what it is, the fight for jobs takes on an even greater urgency.

Help from the Councils

With the DHSS at the forefront of the government's attempt to starve the miners back to work, pressure has mounted on the local authorities to use their powers and resources to meet the consequent hardship. Nevertheless, however generous some may be, the assistance offered by local authorities cannot make up for the loss of benefits imposed by the DHSS, and still less for the loss of a wage.

The amount of help provided by councils has varied across the country. As a rule, the single miners have once again fared the worst because many of the resources available to local authorities are restricted to families with children. In some cases, Barnsley, for example, food and clothing vouchers have been distributed under Child Care legislation in the form of loans, which automatically excludes single miners without children.

A common response by many of the councils in the strike areas has been to increase their welfare advice work, setting up new centres, as in Sunderland, or seconding extra staff to social work offices in the affected coal communities. A smaller number of councils have openly embraced the miners' cause and given grants, such as Lothian's £10,000 to miners' wives' support groups. Others, such as Labour controlled Durham and Lancashire also provided some large cash grants, to be administered by the Salvation Army!

Historically, local councils have had a central role in the provision of social services and benefits. However, throughout this century that role has been gradually limited. From Poplarism in the 1920s to Clay Cross in the 1970s to the GLC and the metropolitan authorities in the 1980s, the British ruling class has experienced local government as a recurring Achilles' heel. For it is at this level that some of the clearest expressions of a truly radical socialist politics have emerged. Margaret Thatcher's government has been acutely aware of this tendency and over the past five years has massively accelerated the process of encroachment on local government powers and spending — the proposed abolition of the GLC and the other metropolitan authorities forms the latest episode in this onslaught.

For the striking miners and their families these attacks on local authorities have effectively limited the amount of assistance available to them. Their room for manoeuvre has been reduced and, as the strike proceeds, new methods are being introduced to curtail what little help remains on offer — the DHSS's decision to deduct from benefits the value of loans and grants made under Child Care laws, for example. Needless to say, while the government is promising reimbursement to meet the extraordinary policing costs that have fallen on councils, there are no matching promises with respect to the costs that have resulted due to the extra provision of free school meals and other forms of help.

Yet even where official council help is available it would seem that it is not always sought out until all other means of survival have been exhausted. As one social services director remarked, 'we are amazed that there is so little demand on us'. That people in such acute poverty should be reluctant to approach local authority welfare services is in part indicative of the reputation that these services have and the ways in which they are administered. At one level they are simply ineffective — 'social workers haven't a clue about welfare rights and benefits', noted one activist working with miners in the north-east of England, 'they're totally unprepared for this sort of situation'. More seriously they can be and are felt to be repressive, and many families worry about their children being taken away should they seek assistance. Social workers are often humiliating, treating the miners and their families as 'second class citizens'. As one striking miner recounts: 'My wife was in this morning to try and get two bags of coal, and was told someone would have to visit before we got it. I have done eight years in the last war. All this bull before getting a bag of coal. Forget it, I don't want someone to visit.'

For many of the dependent poor this is a never ending daily experience.

'The Community Cares for Its Own'

The miners' strike, like many other great working-class struggles of the past, has thrown people and communities onto their own resources. It has created the need to ensure that people are fed, that food and clothing is found and distributed, and that those without family networks to support them are looked after.

The struggle to achieve these things, has brought to light the immense inventive and organizing abilities of working people: skills that are usually ignored in everyday 'working' life, where people are treated as hands without a brain. It has emphasized positive values and emotions: those of togetherness and solidarity, of concern for the welfare of others, and a willingness, even in the most difficult situations, to try and make sure that none go without. In short, values which have no place in the Thatcherite vision of Britain's future, with its stress on individualism and looking after yourself. The strike is also about questions such as these.

Throughout the dispute, and all over the country, mining communities have responded to the failings and withdrawals of the 'official' Welfare State by making their own provisions. This alternative Welfare State is in part the product of necessity, in part a reflection of the closeness of mining communities, and in part a measure of the values and solidarities of working class life. It is hardly surprising that the NCB has sought to disrupt and disperse such communities, as others have been dispersed before them, for they provide a foundation for a culture of opposition and working-class strength.

The scale of these alternative enterprises has varied widely. In some cases it is simply that the wider family helps out, or that a number of families pool their resources. Care is taken to ensure that the elderly or disabled miners are looked after. Where miners are more dispersed or isolated, energy is put into the collection and distribution of food parcels. In many places there are the now-famous kitchens and cafeterias, some providing two or three meals a day, that are important social centres and meeting places.

It is the women who have predominated in this activity: miners' wives, but also other women who have freely given their time and their labour because, as one put it, 'this strike affects everybody'. It is not the first time this has happened — women always bear a heavy burden in any strike — and in 1972 and 1974, miners' wives were actively involved in groups supporting the struggle. There is a danger of overstating the novelty (if only because we need to ask what happened as a consequence of women's earlier involvement and organization), but the scale of involvement and commitment this time is certainly greater.

The activities concerned are usually very practical: 'What we decided was that if everybody could have a hot meal a day, then they could survive. They wouldn't be starved back. In Easington, with there being so many miners, we could put on a kitchen and a cafeteria.' It is also hard and demanding work — in Easington alone five hundred meals a day have to be cooked and served, eight hundred during school holidays — 'It's bedlam. It all starts at 10 o'clock in the morning, and it's pandemonium from then on.' The same sort of thing is repeated up and down the country, day in day out, week after week.

It is virtually impossible to capture the strains that have to be endured and survived as the strike continues in such circumstances of poverty and privation. Yet despite the hard work, the chaos, the hitches, the effort involved in raising money, buying in essentials, and where possible making do with whatever you've got, there is often a sense of excitement, of achievement and of enjoyment.

Celebrations and parties are part of the activities too. In fact, one miners' support group, warned that the meals they were providing might be taken by the DHSS as income in kind and so deducted from benefit, decided they would make each day a birthday celebration. But as the strike has continued these parties have become more than a means of getting around DHSS regulations. They have become a crucial way to maintain morale and lift spirits.

So the struggle goes on, and in the process views and attitudes, as well as activities, are changed. Tasks such as the preparation, cooking and eating of food, previously undertaken in the privacy and isolation of the home, now become collectivized, and are transformed as a result, just as the lives of many of the women, their husbands and their children have been transformed by the strike. Being 'a housewife' no longer has the same meaning for someone active in speaking at meetings, raising money, standing on picket lines, and working collectively to feed and clothe a community.

As the women change so the miners themselves have been forced to consider their attitudes and behaviour towards women. It would seem that, despite some reluctance, many miners *are* changing in this respect. Because of the length of the strike and its accompanying privations, children and youngsters too are being directly involved in the struggle in ways that are unique in recent history. We have yet properly to understand the scale and significance of the changes in relationships, in both families and communities, that a dispute such as this brings about. But it is clear that significant developments have been and are taking place that both sustain the immediate struggle and hold great promise for the future.

In the wider community, an unexpectedly wide range of resources have been discovered and used to help the strike survive. Through a sense of obligation, good business practice, as well as through genuine support, local shops and businesses have responded to calls for help, even though they too have felt the impact of the strike. Extended credit is given, donations made in money and in kind. In some areas, fish and chip shops help by peeling potatoes for the kitchens, while local bakers offer the use of their ovens for baking pies.

Across the country as a whole, support for the miners has been immense despite the cautious and conditional stance taken by the leaders of the official labour movement. There is no record of how much has been donated, in workplace collections, on the streets, or sent in by groups and individuals. It is known, though, that black groups and pensioners have been especially generous despite, in many instances, their own poverty. The *Financial Times* has described it as 'the biggest and most continuous civilian mobilization to confront the government since the Second World War.' And despite the continual misinformation from the NCB, ministers and the media, the support continues. It is — like the provisions made by the mining communities themselves — an indication of a great many people's scale of values. It reflects a generosity and a humanity that, despite the Tory call for people to stand on their own two feet unaided, still runs deep in British society. It is one of the greatest hopes for the future.

In terms of social welfare there is much to be learnt from this strike. Ironically, from the government's standpoint, their policy of changing state welfare into a more abrasive and coercive system to undermine working people has yielded an alternative system of working-class support. While by no means all–embracing it has nevertheless been able to withstand one of the most sustained attempts this century to starve workers into submission. In this resistance, the men, women and children involved talk of strengths and abilities they thought they never had. A stream of confidence has been released; a confidence that so much of the official welfare system, with its array of experts and professionals, had been concerned to contain and control. Is it any wonder that the Thatcher Government cannot contemplate defeat in this strike when the possibilities, the visions, the chances that are being suggested throughout its conduct are so rich in promise and inspiration?

Notes

1. *The Observer*, 5 June, 1983.
2. Reg Prentice, former Labour MP and Conservative Minister for Social Security in the debate on the Social Security Act No. 2, *Hansard*, April 1980.

5
Police and Pickets
The Law Against the Miners

John McIlroy

The Background

The mass picketing of pits in Nottinghamshire, Lancashire and Derbyshire in the first weeks of the miners' dispute presented the National Coal Board and the government with important strategic dilemmas: should the weapons assembled in the legal armoury be used? If so, which, in what combinations and when? These were serious questions as Ministers met in what the *Times* described as 'an atmosphere of mounting confrontation reminiscent of the 1972 and 1974 disputes'. Both these previous disputes with the miners had, of course, seen Tory Governments defeated and specialist legislation intended to deal with extended industrial action revealed as impotent.

Picketing in industrial disputes has generally been dealt with by the police and the criminal law. Between 1906 and 1980 legislation had given pickets and their unions protection against *civil law actions* if they were attending a workplace only to communicate information peacefully or to persuade workers not to work; and if their actions were in furtherance of a trade dispute. A series of important criminal cases from 1960 culminating in the 1974 House of Lords judgement in *Broome v DPP* held that the civil law gave pickets little practical insulation from the commission of *criminal* offences. Pickets, for example, had no right to halt pedestrians or drivers without their consent. To do so could attract a variety of criminal charges. The case law essentially placed picketing in terms of numbers, organization and methods under the regulation of the police. Failure to accept that regulation would court arrest.

The inadequacy of this position from the point of view of the trade unionist and the extent of police powers was widely remarked upon in the 1970s. One authority held that ' . . . the court will always uphold the instructions issued by a policeman, however slight the evidence is, that a breach of the peace might occur.'[1] Another claimed: 'It is fairly obvious that a court will not be over anxious to discuss the assessment of a policeman on the spot.'[2] Britain's fore-most labour lawyer summed up the position prior to 1980: 'The only indisputably lawful pickets are those who attend in small numbers and who keep out of everybody's way. Meanwhile, the workers they have come to persuade to join them, can sweep past in vehicles which the pickets have no right to stop.'[3]

Of course in everyday disputes, the police, utilizing the discretion the courts gave them, often allowed the pickets to communicate their case. But in important, or particularly contentious disputes, this liberty could be withdrawn and the full rigour of the law applied. Police control of picketing came under severe pressure in the 1970s with the intensification of industrial conflict and the re-appearance of mobile mass pickets. The scar the events of the early 1970s left on Tory conceptions of law and order and the proper regulation of trade unions — Saltley Gates mingling with the demise of Heath in 1974 — was a permanent one. Lord Denning was authentically articulating the Tory *grande peur* when, in the Grun-wick case, he stated: 'Our laws are being disregarded right and left. The mobs are out. The police are being subjected to violence. I take no part in the rights and wrongs of these disputes but I do know intimidation and violence are contrary to the law of the land.'

The Conservatives saw their return to power against the back-ground of the militancy of the winter of 1978/9 (and Labour Party and TUC denunciations of picketing) as an affirmation of their his-toric mission to restore order, avenge Heath and exorcise the ghosts of Saltley. Trade unionism needed to be transformed. It needed to be brought within the law. Picketing was the symbol of its excesses and the miners its most important custodian.

'The use of pickets in industrial disputes,' stated the Tory working paper preparing for legislation, 'has been the subject of widespread and increasing public concern'. There had been, it went on to claim, 'an increase in the use of intimidation on picket lines whether directly, through physical violence, or, indirectly, through the threat of loss of union membership and, as a consequence, of jobs'. Law and order concerns were underpinned by economic considera-tions. Secondary picketing could have a disastrous impact on the businesses of those not directly involved in the dispute. Its regulation was essential if union bargaining powers were to be eroded. Secon-dary picketing, moreover, required specific action 'because of its special significance in the context of public order'.

The government decided, despite the law and order rhetoric, to utilize the civil not the criminal law. 'The problem' opined the junior minister, Patrick Mayhew, 'is enforcement. It is not enough to say "if a policeman hears the offence of intimidation being committed he can arrest the offender, end of problem". The policeman must be present at the time. He must hear the words. There must be enough policemen to cope . . . It is not enough to rely on the existence of the criminal law . . .'

Additional civil law, to render forms of industrial action illicit, would buttress public understanding of the problem, illustrate the government's determination to deal with it and, hopefully, galvanize capital to an awareness of its responsibilities in an era where collaborative industrial relations were as outmoded as political consensus. In Thatcher's self-help world, management standing on its own two feet should act together with the police against violence, intimidation and economic loss. The civil law gave them flexibility and discretion to choose when to act and minimize a hostile response from a union movement conditioned by the successes against *In Place of Strife* and the Industrial Relations Act.

The 1980 Employment Act removed from pickets protection against a variety of common law wrongs, from inducement to breach of contract to conspiracy, where liability was attracted through picketing *any workplace other than their own*. The 1982 Employment Act entitled employers to bring such actions not only against the pickets but *against their union* where in specific circumstances it had authorized the industrial action of which the picketing was part or failed to disown it. To give more specific guidance to the legislation the government produced a *Code of Practice on Picketing*. This prescribed for the organization of picketing in restrictive fashion. For example, in paragraph 31: 'Pickets and their organizers should ensure that in general the number of pickets does not exceed six at an entrance.' Mayhew specifically stated that this guidance to the civil law could be taken into account by the criminal courts.

The police themselves were, on the whole, cool on these changes. The Association of Chief Police Officers questioned their efficacy. The Police Federation wanted more criminal law regulations. ACPO were concerned at being drawn into civil law enforcement. Enforcement of specific trade-union control laws could weaken the essential facade of police neutrality. This was a cautious response given the shifts in policing which the 1981 urban riots and the arming of police with riot shields, plastic bullets, tear gas and armoured cars exemplified.

Police support units which could intervene in industrial disputes had been developed since 1970. The National Recording Centre, designed to co-ordinate the activities of Britain's forty-three separate forces, had grown out of discussions between ACPO and the Home Office as a result of the 1972 miners' strike. It had been activated during the 1974 strike when government directions to the police on the tighter control of picketing had not in fact been implemented because of the way the dispute developed. All the ingredients for a militaristic police strategy in a major industrial dispute were available. That the differences expressed by the police on legislation were only tactical could be seen from the police strike-breaking during industrial action by ambulance drivers, social workers and firemen in the late 1970s and their deployment in the 1980 steel strike. If it was needed, a militarized police force was there.

This then was the legal background as Mrs Thatcher and Ian MacGregor faced the confrontation with the miners, planned for at least since the 1978 Ridley Report (see chapter 1.). The decision not to use the civil law to the full in the early phase of the strike occasioned surprise. But the advantage of the civil law, when the direct employer is answerable to the state, is the built-in choice of action and timing. Of course the failure to live up to the rhetoric surrounding the introduction of the Employment Acts, in a situation where their architects were clearly the decision makers, involved a political price which had to be balanced in the accounting. The decision of the NCB to go to the High Court for an injunction against the Yorkshire area on Wednesday 14 March was, in itself, a low-risk opening. Pressing the point in contempt proceedings when the order was ignored was an entirely different matter. There was the fear — justified or not in hindsight — that such an initiative could change the bone of contention, focus the dispute on resistance to industrial relations legislation, and unite a union fragmenting over closures. The situation was developing in an unpredictable and volatile fashion. What evidence there was — such as the announcement of early ballot results — pointed to a 'no strike' vote and another retreat on the lines of the 1983 Tynmawr Lewis Merthyr debacle. Moreover, the scenes of picket-line confrontation, crystallized in Tory minds around the death on the night of 16 March of David Jones, a Yorkshire miner, focused Mrs Thatcher on the law and order issue.

Any dispute such as this would have involved intensive direct policing. But a decision was now taken to use the police and the criminal law to a degree, and in a fashion, unprecedented since 1926. 'The Prime Minister', *The Financial Times* reported on 16 March, 'is understood to be angered by the failure of the police to prevent the disturbances. She is believed to have banged the table while making critical remarks about some chief constables during a meeting with Tory back-benchers. She is thought to have said that chief constables should learn that their job was to uphold the rule of law not turn a blind eye to breaches of it. This line has been transmitted to the chief constables.' Lawrence Byford, HM Inspector of Constabulary was despatched to Nottingham to liaise directly with the Home Secretary. A massive police presence drawn from seventeen different forces was already in the Midlands and the NRC machinery for national co-ordination was in place. Soon the technology and the methods of the militarization of the police that had been developed over recent years would be made available and the police given *carte blanche* in the coalfields. As Police Federation spokesperson Tony Judge was later to say in relation to the decision not to use the Employment Acts, 'It's not simply a case of the employer saying "Well, I won't go to court because it might make things worse". Surely at the back of Mr MacGregor's mind is the knowledge that these policemen are there, that the pits of Nottinghamshire have been kept open and that people have been able to go to work almost solely because of the presence of the police force. And so it looks to us as if there has been a deliberate decision to use the police as the way of keeping the coal industry producing some coal.'

The New Policing

If the strategy of using the criminal law was novel in its scale, intensity and political direction, it must be re-emphasized that the legal justification for such a strategy and the prerequisites for playing the public-order card already existed. Previous court decisions meant that there was, in the end, no right to picket. Attempts by strikers to make a dispute effective and to communicate with fellow workers were rendered illegal not on the Nottingham picket lines in 1984 but on the plush velvet benches of the House of Lords a decade before. Yet because trade unionists perceived approaching fellow workers to be both right and necessary, strikers *would* picket and, if frustrated, would do so in ever greater numbers. As a consequence they would be breaking the criminal law and could legitimately be answered by the growing presence and restraint of the police. The workers' reaction — defence of what they saw as their rights — would then become, in the eyes of the law and of law-abiding citizens, gratuitous and offensive violence.

The root of the problem is the criminal law, not the police. *The legal edifice now works to make effective picketing criminal and therefore acts as a direct agent of the employer in industrial disputes.* In normal circumstances the small change of picketing in a hard–fought dispute would produce a handful of charges of obstruction in keeping the employer's supply lines open. These were not, of course, normal circumstances. Mr Lawson's remark that the then £350 million cost of the strike was a worthwhile investment 'even in narrow financial terms' showed the cabinet's appreciation of what was involved. Whereas at Saltley Gates the view had been that thousands of pickets could not be removed at any price, the reverse was precisely the slogan of government and police in 1984.

Within a few hours of the start of the Nottingham picketing, one thousand police were involved, within days eight thousand, and after the first week over twenty thousand officers from the forty-three different forces were available to police the pickets and patrol the mining communities. The police were determined to match and outnumber the pickets. As early as 21 March, David Hall, president of ACPO reported a ratio of almost 8:1[4]. This degree of commitment continued throughout the dispute. It was graphically highlighted at Cortonwood in the autumn when more than fifteen hundred police stood by to escort one miner to work.

This was the product of central co-ordination by the president of ACPO from the NRC in Room 309 at Scotland Yard. 'Right along one wall are charts and lists of police support unit deployments and of the latest situation in the coalfields. At a glance it is possible to see not only who has sent how many units to whom but also how many injuries and arrests there have been in each area. A separate chart logs the number of pickets. The 'mood' in each area is classified as 'peaceful', 'hostile' or 'violent'. Another table lists special demands on police manpower throughout the country. In the ten weeks of the dispute Hall's team has made a total of 220,000 assignments around the country . . . Every one of the forty-three forces in England and Wales is a giver or receiver'.[5]

If an operational national force was novel, so was its tactical deployment. The road-blocks set up as far away from the scene of the picketing as Dartford in Kent were extremely successful in cutting off the supply of pickets at source. They were the scene of harassment of those travelling to the picket lines, including violent personal attacks and damage to vehicles which were often immobilized. The chief constable of Nottingham estimated that 164,508 individuals, presumed pickets, were stopped from entering the county in the first twenty-seven weeks of the strike.

Those who did reach the picket lines were met by the new riot control tactics and the police support units. There was evidence that right from the start the police were not willing to allow any picketing at what they regarded as key sites. This set in motion a process of escalation, police obstruction stimulating more pickets, mass military-style policing and police violence producing, in turn, a violent reaction. 'Right at the start on March 15 there were just two of us picketing Hucknall. Police tried to move us. When we stood tight they dragged us away. They pulled the sleeve right off my overcoat. Next day there were forty pickets and eighty policemen.'

The experience of pickets in this kind of situation was that assault quickly replaced containment. Pickets were corralled-off, well away from any contact with those they had come to talk to; as the scabs were brought in the pickets would push and shove against the police lines. Those at the front, those who the police came into contact with in the mêlée, those who the police recognized, all would be lifted. If arbitrary and indiscriminate arrests and violence didn't work, snatch squads could intensify the pressure on the pickets. Where large numbers of pickets were involved they were faced with charges by police on foot wielding truncheons and short shields, the use of dogs and specially-armoured police vans ' . . . the atmosphere is light hearted. But all that changes as the coke lorries are spotted. Pushing and fighting begins. Assistant Chief Constable Tony Clement calls out: "Take prisoners!" and the cordon parts "like the Red Sea", said one miner — to let through the more lightly armed PSUs with their round perspex shields and their truncheons. If there is a heavy build up of miners the cordon parts again to let the horses through. Sometimes the mounted police swing down in a pincer movement from the brow of the hill'.

The evidence accumulated of mass military-style policing intended not to regulate picketing, nor to guarantee peaceful picketing, but clearly aimed *at stopping all picketing* is impressive. *Sheffield Police Watch* enumerated case after case of unprovoked violence by the police in six months of systematic observation. 'We have observed that in the majority of cases where violence breaks out this is due to police tactics and when there is what we describe as over-policing. We have repeatedly noted that when the police arrive at a peaceful picket in overwhelming numbers and with dogs, horses, riot equipment and ambulances, then the atmosphere changes. Time and again we have seen this equipment deployed with little or no justification. In our view, it is inevitable that some pickets will retaliate when arrested arbitrarily and for no reason attacked by police dogs . . . '

To break the will of the pickets and undermine the strike, police violence was carried into the mining communities. In Nottingham in May, three specialist police squads were established to patrol pit villages. The *Guardian* reported, 'Cabinet sources confirmed yesterday that the government is hoping that police patrols to stop intimidation in pit villages will lead to more miners breaking the strike and returning to work.' The intimidation in reality came from the police and was aimed against strikers. There were numerous well-documented reports of police in pursuit of pickets breaking into houses, damaging property, and assaulting and intimidating residents. Blidworth, Armthorpe, Fitzwilliam, Hemsworth, Dinnington, Fryston, Grimethorpe, Broosworth, Keresley — the list of police riots is a substantial one. To be known as a strike activist was to court constant routine harassment if not assault and eventual, inevitable arrest.

'A police van arrived close to my house chasing three pickets. Two escaped, the third was cornered by policemen wearing full riot gear. They proceeded to beat and kick the picket until he screamed for mercy. No attempt whatsoever was made to arrest the picket . . . I am not a miner and hold no particular views so that what I heard — saw and heard — is not biased' . . . 'Having surrounded us the police started to tighten the circle. Quite a few women panicked: they were arrested. "Why me?" yelled one young miner's wife as she was being dragged away. "I've fancied you all evening," the arresting officer told her. Another woman charged with using foul and abusive language was told by a police officer, "Call yourself a woman. I wouldn't even piss on you." The women were dragged to the police van with a brutality quite out of proportion to their size or any resistance they were offering' . . . 'They broke down the door, smashed the windows, ripped the phone off the wall and gave everyone a good pasting. They were screaming and shouting "get the bastards" ' . . . 'I was spread-eagled against a wall and interrogated about my union membership beliefs and reasons for being in Notts. I was told that miners' families could starve to death before I would be allowed to deliver the food. I was pushed, jostled, my arms beaten with something hard, my instep stamped on. A police officer removed my glasses and pushed my face into the wall. I was told that if I returned to Notts, both my arms would be broken' . . . 'The police kept the pressure up until the Yorkshire pickets decided to withdraw later that day fearing for the safety of their Notts hosts and their families. This was clearly the objective of Sergeant Wright and his Special Police Squad.'[7]

It would be possible to document in a similar way other aspects of the police strategy. Detailed evidence of political surveillance and intelligence gathering, telephone tapping and interception of correspondence was accumulated by Jim Coulter, Susan Miller and Martin Walker in their book, *State of Siege*. The experience of arrest was used to break the will of activists. Pickets were held in custody for long periods without being charged and were subjected to abuse and assault. Those held attested to widespread disregard of statutory rights to notify relatives and the Judges Rules which gives suspects the right to make telephone calls and see a solicitor. Forcible photographing and fingerprinting were common.

That *agent provocateurs* and plain clothes men mingled with the pickets was openly admitted by the police who used video equipment to identify and keep tabs on activists. There were reports of an army presence on the picket lines. NUM members described the use of informers, confrontational identification, police posing as solicitors, and beatings in police stations. ' "Smile", he said, "I'm taking your picture". "No you're fucking not" said I. The officer no. 7337 of the Greater Manchester Police replied by applying his fist hard into my mouth. "Shut your fucking mouth". He hit me twice in the face. The same officer then put his fingers in my eyes and pulled my head back. The chap with the camera stuck the boot in three times.'[8]

The police tentacles stretched well beyond the mining areas. By the end of 1984 several hundred members of miners' support groups had been arrested collecting for the strike. The *Guardian*'s comment in April — 'with every day that passes in this dispute evidence is accumulating of police activity that may or may not be legal but in any event should be considered quite outrageous in a democratic society' — seemed to many by the turn of the year an understatement and the European Parliament voted to set up an inquiry into the police violence.

Few miners have used the procedures that exist to complain about the police. As Lord Scarman pointed out in 1981, there is a lack of confidence in these procedures because it is the police who investigate the police. When I discussed this with two arrested miners they felt that the complaints procedure was not only toothless, to use it was to court further surveillance, intimidation and possible assault. 'Those animals are completely out of control. They are a complete law unto themselves.'

Important Criminal Law Cases

March Mr Justice Watkins refuses to grant Kent miners an interim injunction against police using road-blocks on the technical grounds that, if they win the issue at a full trial, the damages that they receive from the police will be an adequate remedy.

July 6th Lord Justice Watkins, in the High Court, orders the South Yorkshire Police Committee not to proceed with two resolutions attempting to control the Chief Constable's spending on the miners' dispute in a case brought by Attorney General, Sir Michael Havers.

October 12th The High Court rules that bail conditions imposed by Nottinghamshire magistrates preventing nine pickets from demonstrating outside any collieries other than their own are legal.

November 9th A Clerkenwell Stipendiary Magistrate rules that the 1979 regulations giving responsibility to the Metropolitan Police Commission to grant or refuse permits for street collections are unlawful. The charge of collecting for the miners without a permit brought against James Wood is dismissed. The police announce their intention to appeal.

November 22nd The High Court rules that striking miners were lawfully arrested for obstructing the police in the course of their duty when they refused to turn back at a road-block.

The Criminal Courts

'When the miner demanded to know what law gave the officer the right to stop him going home the officer pointed at his blue uniform and said, "This law".'⁹

    The available evidence shows that during the dispute, far from acting as a curb on the police, the criminal courts acted to ratify, legitimize and amplify their actions. A deputy chief constable told *Labour Weekly*, 'We can do all sorts of things and the legality of them can be determined later.' The determination was inevitably a positive one for the police.

    The use of arrest as a means of intimidating pickets and removing them, at least temporarily, from the combat zone is illustrated by the statistics. By December 1984, 8,731 arrests had been made. But about one thousand of those arrested, about a seventh of the total, were not charged. NUM solicitors also argue that the majority of those charged should not have been; and if the cases *were* brought then they should have resulted in acquittal. Yorkshire NUM lawyer, Steve Gallagher, referred in June to the twelve hundred cases then produced by that area: 'I believe that in the law, as I undersand it, no offence was committed in eighty per cent of the cases. They are the victims of aggressive policing. The majority have never been in trouble before. Many of them are totally bewildered.'

The majority of arrests, initially about eighty per cent, involved relatively minor charges such as obstruction and breach of the peace. But by the end of the year such charges were declining as a proportion and there was an increase in the more serious charges such as unlawful assembly, conspiracy and riot — offences which are imprecisely determined, carry a maximum sentence of life imprisonment, and are ideal for the vigorous prosecutor. More than five hundred people, for example, had been charged with unlawful assembly. More than two hundred charges had been made under section 7 of the Conspiracy and Protection of Property Act 1875 — the old offence of 'watching and besetting'. As the NCCL commented: 'The use of a charge that has been almost unknown in recent industrial relations' history can also appear as an attempt to "throw the book" at those arrested'. The use of this offence seems to have been suggested in a March issue of *Justice of the Peace* magazine in an article written by J.B. Hill, one of the prosecuting solicitors for the Nottingham Police.

Charges directly connected with violence such as assault still constituted less than ten per cent of the figures. But as Christmas approached, there were three cases of threats to kill, three explosives charges and the South Wales murder case. By now the acquittal rate was about twenty per cent. For the majority convicted there was a tendency to more serious sentences. By December more than fifty people had been jailed and six sent to detention centres. Sixty-six per cent of those sentenced received fines and a third of these were for sums over £100. Additional expense is involved in the payment of costs. A miner fined £100 may be ordered to pay, say, £40 towards prosecution costs at a time of financial hardship. Some magistrates allowed payment by instalments. Others did not. In one case an order of costs of £250 was made by a North East Bench. In such cases the magistrates are well aware that the miners have no resources to pay themselves and are clearly seeking to fine the union as well as the member.

Many criticisms have been made about the conduct of these cases. The granting of legal aid has attracted attention. In Scotland, the NUM and lawyers complained that miners appearing before the sheriffs in Dunfermline and Kilmarnock were refused legal aid in circumstances where it was granted in Edinburgh, Kirkcaldy, Hamilton and Linlithgow. In the North East, solicitors reported that practice varied between different benches for miners arrested on breach of the peace charges. Sunderland was cited as an example of an area where legal aid has been refused in the majority of cases.

Miners have often discovered that the police offer no evidence against them but instead ask the magistrates to bind them over to keep the peace on pain of paying a considerable sum. This again, is a means of rendering pickets *hors de combat*. But faced with the alternative of being bound over or answering to a substantive offence — with the possibility of conviction and a further period on remand — many miners wer ewilling to accept the courts' terms. Others have refused on the grounds that while being bound over is not a criminal conviction, it is regarded as such.

Police have regularly offered to drop charges in return for binding over, sometimes coupling the offer with a threat of harsher charges if the offer is refused. For example, on 5 May four Yorkshire miners were charged in Nottingham, one with breach of the peace, one with obstruction, and two with using threatening words and behaviour. They pleaded not guilty. Three months later, with them still not having been brought to trial, the police offered to drop charges if they agreed to be bound over. If they refused, their solicitor was told, the charge of obstruction would be accompanied by one of obstructing the highway, the breach of the peace charge would be accompanied by one of using threatening words and behaviour, and the other two pickets would additionally be charged under section 7 of the Conspiracy and Protection of Property Act.

In the Sunderland Magistrates Court a trend developed of simply refusing bail to miners arrested previously in the dispute and remanding them in custody pending trial. The upshot was that several pickets found themselves locked up in Durham Gaol awaiting trial on charges for which, even if found guilty, they would be most unlikely to be given prison sentences. In every such case applications to judges succeeded in securing the release of those remanded on bail — but with very stringent conditions. In one case the judge commented that he considered such remand to be wrong, particularly where the union's resources were expended on obtaining release.

Conditions attached to bail have also been a major problem. Whilst a majority of those charged have been released on bail, there have been more than four thousand cases where the bail has been subject to stringent conditions. Pressure from the Nottingham deputy chief constable led to Mansfield Magistrates Court adopting as standard conditions of bail that miners should not visit 'any premises or place for the purpose of picketing or demonstrating in connection with the current trade dispute between the National Union of Mineworkers and the National Coal Board other than peacefully to picket or demonstrate at your usual place of employment.'

This condition was attached to bail forms even before applications for unconditional bail had been heard by the magistrates, apparently in breach of the 1976 Bail Act. No conviction or scrutiny of the defendant's previous record, or examination of the likelihood of the commission of a further offence, had taken place. This practice was used by other benches. In some cases bail conditions have been even more restrictive. In May the National Association of Probation Officers described bail conditions on three Doncaster miners charged with offences under the 1875 Conspiracy Act — intimidation and actual bodily harm — as, 'extremely harsh and almost unparalleled'. The three miners were ordered to have no contact with each other, maintain an 8 a.m. to 8 p.m. curfew, report to the police daily, and keep out of Nottinghamshire — conditions described by the assistant general secretary of NAPO, which had dealt with two thousand pickets arrested, as 'moving towards house arrest'.

Miners who refused to accept bail conditions as a matter of principle were remanded in custody. Miners who ignored the conditions, most notably Kent NUM President Malcolm Pitt, then received jail sentences for breaking their bail. Mr Pitt claimed that the Lord Chancellor's office had gone as far as to advise magistrates to grant bail only with conditions. His case illustrates just how draconian this procedure is. He was sentenced to nineteen days in prison for breaking his bail. But when he was convicted for the original charge he was only fined.

Bail with conditions provided an excellent means for the authorities to stigmatize even those charged with minor offences. It provided a justification for intensive police surveillance during the bail period. It 'took out' pickets. It meant, once more, that those who kept to the court-imposed conditions could often play little active part in the front line of the dispute. It worked, in other words, to weaken the NUM and to strengthen the NCB and the government.

But when this procedure was taken to the higher courts which supervise the practice of police and magistrates it was upheld. The Lord Chief Justice, Lord Lane, sitting in the Divisional Court of Queen's Bench, heard arguments on behalf of nine Yorkshire miners that magistrates had imposed bail conditions without scrutiny and assessment of individual circumstances and, therefore, had breached the Bail Act. Police evidence on the violent nature of the picketing does not appear to have been challenged. On the basis of this, Lord Lane felt that: 'By the time these defendants appeared in court it must have been clear to everyone and to the magistrates in particular that any suggestion of peaceful picketing was a colourful pretence and that it was a question of picketing by intimidation and threat'. To *attend* a picket was, he felt, automatically and knowingly to involve oneself in violence and criminality. 'It must have been obvious to all those participating in the picketing that their presence, in large numbers, was part of the intimidation and threats. It must have been clear to them that *their presence* would, at the least, encourage others to threats and/or violence even if they themselves said nothing' (our emphasis). Presence at a mass picket, according to this logic, makes one guilty of a criminal offence. Magistrates who were aware that mass picketing was occurring locally were entitled to take account of this in relation to the individuals charged. 'Against that background the magistrates were right to conclude that, if no conditions were imposed, offences would be committed by these defendants whilst on bail. The nine men's good character did not affect the likelihood that they would involve themselves in mass picketing and thus commit public order offences'. Lord Lane's judgement did criticize the magistrates for their use of the standard bail conditions form. But its substance acted to legitimize the new law of the coalfields: all picketing was violent, all picketing was criminal, all picketing must be banned.

Similar judicial support for the mass military-style policing and criminalization of picketing came in the other major case heard during the dispute, the challenge to the use of police road-blocks. In response to representations from counsel that Lord Lane had made clear in the previous case — on the basis of police affidavits — his view that a mass picket inevitably leads to intimidation and violence, which was not challenged in this case, his Lordship stepped down from the hearing. Nonetheless, Mr Justice Skinner and Mr Justice Otten, hearing the case in his absence, found in favour of the police.

Michael Mansfield, representing four Yorkshire miners, argued that they should not have been stopped on the grounds of police apprehension of a breach of the peace unless that breach was imminent in time and place. Nothing in the miners' conduct at the road-block could lead to that conclusion and, indeed, the police had no knowledge of which out of four or five possible collieries they intended to picket. The court dismissed the appeal against the magistrate's decision. Mr Justice Skinner stated: ' . . . the law on this subject is clear. If a constable apprehends, on reasonable grounds, that a breach of the peace may be committed he is not only entitled but is under a duty to take reasonable steps to prevent it'. The situation had to be assessed by police officers on the spot. 'Provided they honestly and reasonably form the opinion that there is a real risk of a breach of the peace, in the sense that it is in close proximity, both in place and in time, then the conditions exist for reasonable preventative action, including, if necessary, the measures taken in this case.'

Whilst this test did not substantially differ from the defence submission, the court found that the magistrate's findings of fact made it clear that the police had acted reasonably in the specific circumstances of this case. With twenty-five cars containing sixty pickets converging on four or five collieries, an apprehension of a proximate breach of the peace *was* reasonable.

These decisions were in the long tradition of cases dealing with picketing. Broad principles have been enunciated which, when applied to specific facts, function to legitimize police action and strengthen the employer's day to day conduct of the dispute. They provided a useful focus for state propaganda: the police, the refrain went, are not acting outside the law: the respected custodians of that law, after a fair and detailed inquiry, have said so themselves.

The Use of the Civil Law

The direct policing strategy combined with the state propaganda machine to create a material basis for the incessant talk of 'thugs', 'anarchy', 'violence', and 'the rule of law'. It created violence and it created criminals. It bore an important burden in the government's attempts to isolate the strikers from other workers. Employment Minister, Tom King, for example, argued, 'Some scenes in recent months have nothing to do with the traditions of trade unionism as people understand it in this country'. His sentiments were amplified and given greater point within the movement by the leader of the Labour Party and the general secretary of the TUC.

The policing approach enabled the government to maintain some vestige of its spurious stance of non-involvement whilst other state agencies operated directly on its behalf. It bought time for the splits in the NUM to reach maturity and, by playing a small role in further dividing miner from miner, it reinforced those splits. The division within the union allowed the state to sound the themes of civil war and democracy, and of internecine strife where one side stood for law and order, freedom, liberty and basic decency and the other side constituted 'the enemy within'. The state constantly strove to remove the dispute from the terrain of confrontation between trade union and state-capitalist employer to the more favourable ground of a struggle between society and the prince of darkness. The framework was clearly articulated by Warwickshire Police Chief, Peter Jospin: 'What we are seeing in this dispute is a deliberate challenge to law and order in this country. The mass picketing and the intimidation of working miners are an attempt by bully boys in society to impose their will on those wishing to exercise that most democratic right — the right to work.'

The use of the civil law enabled the scab to take the stage not only as hero but as crusader. In the '*On the Waterfront*' drama served up to Britain's workers the blackleg was the Brando hero, Terry Molloy, while Arthur Scargill was cast in the role of gang boss, Johnny Friendly.

The NCB hesitated over the use of the Employment Acts. In the end they didn't use the available legal apparatus to discipline the union. They didn't need to. The working miners did the job for them. And they did it in a way that was qualitatively superior. The right of union members to take their union to court, arguing breach of rules, had long been accepted by the labour movement. It was not perceived as partisan industrial relations legislation. The resort to the courts by the working miners provided tangible living evidence, in the maelstrom of a life and death struggle, for the Tory view that out of touch, militant union leaders oppress and manipulate a reluctant rank and file. What better proof of the democracy argument than the spectacle of miners, with their well known traditional solidarity, suing their own organization? And, of course, in the end, given the NUM policy of non-co-operation, the outcome would be the same as if Ian MacGregor himself had instructed counsel — the state would act to punish the NUM's contempt. But in this case, coercion wore the clothes of popular rebellion. The state would sequestrate the NUM's assets and drive it down to defeat, not in the interest of government or employer, but to *protect the union's own members*.

The actions brought by working miners in May, June and July were limited and defensive, intended to protect those working against disciplinary action and give them legitimacy, identity and self-respect. Nonetheless, the spate of judgements stating that the strike was unofficial in key areas helped to strengthen the outlaw stereotype of the union and stimulate waverers in going over to the employer's side. A picket in Ollerton commented that the police, 'have stopped official pickets altogether because they say the High Court in London has declared the strike in Notts unofficial'. The early civil cases illustrated the vast powers that the right to interpret a union's rules gave the judiciary in substituting their own prejudices for union democracy. Like the criminal cases, they provided a pulpit for condemnation of the strike which could be powerfully used in propaganda.

What had been a relatively modest probing by working miners began to escalate with the initiation of the case against the Yorkshire NUM by two Manton miners, Robert Taylor and Ken Foulstone, advised by the solicitors Hodgkinson and Tallents, a firm with a wealth of Tory Party connections. The legal avalanche gathered momentum in August. With the failure of the back to work movement the cabinet intensified its propaganda campaign and searched for some institutional Trojan horse capable of stimulating a substantial return. On the second weekend in August as Peter Walker, Tom King and Leon Brittan all made speeches calling on miners to cross picket lines and return to work, the National Working Miners' Committee held its first meeting. Like the group around 'Silver Birch', this was largely a paper organization. Its significance lay in its advisers: moral rearmament figures such as journalist Graham Turner, Thatcher adviser David Hart, Saatchi and Saatchi director Tim Bell but, crucially, David Negus of Derbyshire solicitors, Ellis Fermor.

Although not active politically since involvement in the Tory Party as a student, Negus was firmly opposed to the strike and supportive of Thatcherite values: 'Individual rights are being trampled on. It is the role of the courts to stop powerful interests stepping on those rights and in the twentieth century those powerful interests tend to be trade unions. They appear to be the only group in society who believe that they are above the law'. At the 1984 Tory Party conference, Negus was to be found addressing the Society of Conservative Lawyers in this fashion.

The legal advisers, knowledgeable and determined, were aware of the full potential of action against the NUM and of the fact that, thus far, it had hardly been exploited. They could not but have been impressed by the success of the sequestration proceedings taken by Reads Haulage against the South Wales NUM. This had made clear that other trade unions were not prepared or not able to come to the aid of the miners, that the card which had demobilized the Industrial Relations Act in 1972 was no longer in the pack. If the state took over the NUM the union would simply be unable to up the ante. The era of using the law as self–protection was over. Now, working miners, urged on by right-wing politicians and lawyers, could use the law *offensively* to protect their democratic rights or alternatively to destroy the NUM and break the strike.

Events moved with rapidity. On 10 October the NUM and Arthur Scargill, personally, were fined for contempt of interim injunctions declaring the strike unlawful. The NUM continued its defiance. A fortnight later the union's assets were sequestrated. The legal tempo quickened as the back to work movement became significant for the first time. Pre-emptive action of the union executive meant that the funds were dispersed outside of Britain. By 11 November, the sequestrators Price and Waterhouse had only managed to lay hands on a derisory £8,000. The charade of government non-intervention was again spotlighted when the High Court refused to indemnify the sequestrators against further expenses incurred in pursuing NUM accounts. The government, unsolicited by Price and Waterhouse, took the position that as upholding the law was in the public interest the Treasury should give them a financial guarantee. This unprecedented move was only revealed on close scrutiny of the small print of supplementary estimates almost a month later.

The success of the union in foiling the sequestrators prompted a further and potentially decisive move by David Negus. Acting on behalf of the National Working Miners' Committee member, Colin Clarke, he began an action to remove control of all NUM assets from the union's trustees and place them in the hands of the receiver. The decision to press the case quickly resulted from a desire to influence the judgement of a Luxembourg court about unfreezing £4.38 million of the miners' money. The announcement that the NUM was to be placed in the hands of the Derbyshire solicitor and former Tory Councillor, Herbert Brewer, provoked a crisis in the union's stance of total defiance of the law. The majority of the NUM's cash had by now been located in Dublin and Luxembourg. The financial collapse of the union with the consequent disastrous impact on the organiza-tion of the strike appeared imminent. For the first time the leading officials of the national union offered to co-operate with the courts by agreeing to freeze the funds held in Luxembourg. However, Mr Justice Meryn Davies refused to accept this gesture unless the union agreed to submit fully to the court and accept all past orders against it.

The position had now changed dramatically. The civil law was no longer sniping dangerously at the union's flank. It was at its throat and threatening to paralyse its operations. Writs were flying thick and fast. For the first time in the dispute the NUM leaders were in constant consultation with lawyers. In a break with past practice an unsuccessful appeal was initiated. Whilst a recommendation from the national executive for some measure of co-operation with the receiver was rejected by a Special Delegate Conference which reiterated its total defiance of the judiciary, the isolation of the miners was reinforced when a formal approach to the TUC for help proved fruitless. The representatives of the General Council responsible for liaising with the miners, including left-wingers Ray Buckton and Bill Keys, refused to pursue even limited measures such as providing accommodation, office facilities and services for the NUM which might place them, in their turn, in contempt of court.

The striking miners remained isolated and battered, but still defiant and unbowed. However, it seemed only a matter of time before an organization built with sweat and blood over centuries would be completely appropriated by the state so that the strike would either be broken or enter a new phase of guerilla warfare.

Some Lessons

It is neither rhetoric nor exaggeration to state that, in 1984, every possible component of the system of law and order was utilized to defeat the miners' strike. In such a situation, one union standing alone cannot triumph. The strike paved the way for greater state regulation of industrial relations. It finally set the seal on the militancy of the late 1960s and 1970s and illuminated its crucial weaknesses. We cannot rehearse here the arguments for the building of a new socialist trade unionism. But such a movement will certainly require a deeper, more complete analysis of the state and legal system.

It is a tragedy that the stock of socialist ideas that does exist has not in recent years been drawn upon and developed. There is, for example, a long–running socialist critique of the judiciary as a cohesive, homogeneous elite, recruited largely from the ruling class and representing a relatively autonomous component of the state, protecting the owners of property against the producers of wealth. There is relatively detailed documentation of the magistracy, its anti-working class constitution and functions. And the left has increasingly come to realize that the changes within the police force and their growing lack of accountability simply reinforce their role like that of the judiciary, as a class force. When a police inspector states, "If Scargill wins like this, then there's no future in this country for any of us. We might as well clear out and let the rabble take over" [10], he represents not deviancy from the norm but the norm itself, the authentic voice of a force dedicated to the maintenance of the capitalist system.

But if socialist explanations of the rule of law in class society are long standing it would be wrong to overestimate their impact on even labour movement activists. The view of the legal apparatus as independent and impartial, if given to misuse at times, is enduring. Most working-class criticism has tended to operate within the framework of 'bad law', 'abuse' and 'bent coppers'. The untenable nature of this kind of distinction is underlined by the use of the long–standing and accepted judicial power to regulate union rules via the law of contract, which lead to the state take-over of the NUM far more effectively than the 'class' law of the Employment Acts. Though recent events have opened many eyes to this fact, there is a vast educational task before us.

Moreover, relevant socialist critiques have not been reflected in the politics of labour-movement decision makers, still less in their policies. The limited discussion there *has* been, for example on what kind of law should replace the Tory Employment Acts, has stopped short of looking at how to change the judiciary which has foiled so many past attempts at changing substantive legislation. It is only recently that we have seen plans for greater control of the police force carried at the Labour Party Conference — against the opposition of the leadership. It is this leadership who mis-educate workers by repeating what the state, and often their own experience, tells them — in Gerald Kaufman's words for example, 'the police force is not an arm of the state but the servant of the community'.

The miners' strike has been important in raising some of these issues but unfortunately has done so against the background of labour movement leaders' pieties about 'the need to condemn all violence'. Such statements are not only intellectually and politically bankrupt but legitimize the role of the state and squander the opportunity to deepen an understanding of its oppressive nature. There are, however, exceptions: Tony Benn has put the case for the election of magistrates and parliamentary confirmation of judicial appointments. The argument that all police forces should be placed under the control of elected local councils with power to hire, fire and instruct police chiefs has gained wider resonance.

We need to look more closely at these arguments and develop policies which can be implemented by a socialist government. This will require the mobilization of popular support. The last Labour Government, for example, far from grappling with the legal apparatus, refused even to change the law on picketing which has caused so many problems in this strike. That takes us back to the trade unions and other groupings of women, blacks, and gays, who have been inspired by the miners. There has been much talk, in the light of the developments discussed here and others, such as the new Police Act, of Britain becoming a 'police state'. This is quite understandable in the circumstances. But the police and judiciary remain very much as they have always been. Whenever class conflict has intensified there have been tactical adjustments according to the balance of forces. This was as true in 1926 as it is today. We have seen some shift within the mechanisms of social control from consent to coercion. But Thatcher, perhaps more so than Stanley Baldwin, still governs through *consent*.

The importance of this point is that it directs us towards *the centrality of the battle of ideas within the labour movement and amongst its allies*. It has been the continuing weakness of socialist ideas, despite Saltley Gates and the Pentonville Five, which turned the victories of the 1970s into the defeats of the 1980s. The judiciary, the police and the law have not been the main barrier to winning the miners' strike. All the police and legal judgements in the world could not have kept the Nottingham pits working, the steel industry operating, and the power stations functioning if the workers had laid down their tools and supported the miners. We saw in the early 1970s how the police and the judiciary could be beaten. If they are to be beaten today, if we are to change the law and change society, we will have to change minds and change methods. That is the real challenge of the miners' strike.

122

Notes

1. P. O'Higgins, 'Picketing and the Law', in E. E. Coker and C. Stuttard (eds.), *Industrial Studies*.

2. R. W. Rideout, *Principles of Labour Law*.

3. K. W. Wedderburn, *The Worker and the Law*.

4. *The Guardian*, 22 March 1984.

5. *Sunday Times*, 20 May 1984.

6. *The Observer*, 24 June 1984.

7. *Yorkshire Miner*, December 1984; *The Guardian*, 15 August 1984; *The Miner*, July 1984; *London Labour Briefing*, August 1984; *New Statesman*, 17 August 1984.

8. *Briefing National Supplement*, July 1984.

9. *The Observer*, 24 June 1984.

10. *Police*, July 1984.

6

The Role of the Media

Bill Schwarz and Alan Fountain

Redefining the National Interest

The declining fortunes of the labour movement in recent years have given rise to increasingly fierce denunciations of the media by labour activists. These denunciations have frequently been accompanied by implicit suggestions that the crisis of the labour movement can somehow be attributed to the false ideas peddled by the media. With good reason the protracted and often desperate conflict of the miners' strike has encouraged such a perspective. Representatives of the NUM have expressed horror at the blatant manipulation of news reports. Arthur Scargill has been particularly vehement in his condemnation of the lies produced in the media; during the course of the strike these criticisms have come to form a substantial part of the union's case, with Scargill insisting that the media, and Fleet Street in particular, has been recruited as an active agent against the strike.

The force with which these arguments are expressed reflects a deep appreciation of the political significance of the mass media. After all, it is through newsprint and television, rather than rallies and mass meetings, that public representations of the strike are daily given form. It is a matter of some irony that Scargill himself is an accomplished media figure, and more than any other trade union leader has risen to prominence via his skilfull use of television and the press. Throughout the dispute he has been determined whenever possible to turn the public attention he receives to the advantage of the union. During his television debate with MacGregor there was little doubt about who was going to be the winner. The irony here is a telling one and has never been lost upon Scargill's detractors: Why, they ask, if he criticizes the media so much does he also seek it out? The irony masks a real problem.

Without doubt the NUM has been absolutely correct in seeing the media as central, on occasions decisively so, in determining the balance of forces between the strikers and those ranged against them.

In this light the union has also been right in its attempts to use and influence the media. At the same time, for people who have persistently been subjected to attacks by the press, the idea of the media as intrinsically and totally malevolent makes a lot of sense. Certainly there is more than a kernel of truth in this view. However to over-emphasize it is to risk losing a wider battle. Whilst people in the heat of struggle can see the media as grotesque and interfering, this is far from so for those who have never directly experienced the vindictiveness of its attacks. For them the argument that the media is simply a lie machine, producing one distortion after another, often appears unconvincing and biased in its own turn. In addition, such a line does little to assist in the battle for determining *how* the strike is represented day–by–day — it obstructs attempts to utilise whatever openings for sympathetic coverage are available.

Lest this be understood as an apology for the media, it is as well to insist from the start that lies and blatant manipulation do indeed have their place in the reporting of the strike. There was for example the notorious occasion of the Scargill 'confession' — 'The Truth that Scargill Dare not Tell' — a complete invention published in The *Daily Express* on 9 May. Another example was the attempt by The *Sun* on 20 November, in the short span between its first and second editions, to inflate by fifteen thousand the number of miners supposedly at work by adding into the figures all the auxiliary workers. These cases are notorious for their unabashed cynicism. So, too, are the desperate attempts to seek out working miners in an insatiable bid to create yet more tabloid 'martyrs' ready to castigate the evil of Scargillism. Such moves by the press have frequently been handled with minimal skill, and have more than once backfired. They form only the most dramatic moments in the long and difficult struggle for the management of public opinion.

Paul Foot, for one, has done great service in beginning coolly and carefully to monitor the fabrication and debasement of journaltistic standards which at moments seem to have corroded, not just this paper or that, but the very institution of the press. The treatment of the strike by the Tory tabloids and *The Times* has been disgraceful, inflicting permanent damage on any idea of the press as a free institution on which democratic and pluralist culture depends. It is now more than ever clear that there firmly exists an undisguised, conservative–dominated news oligarchy — notwithstanding the idiosyncratic, baronial socialism of which Robert Maxwell boasts. Maxwell, Murdoch and Matthews between them control seventy-five per cent of the national dailies sold, and eighty-four per cent of the Sunday press. Editorial support from Fleet Street for the striking miners is non-existent. There is no doubt that this is a deep source of resentment in their ranks; equally it raises important questions about the very idea of a democratic society and freedom of speech.

However it certainly cannot be assumed that the existence of a Tory-dominated press has been the primary cause in preventing the emergence of a mass, unified working-class movement in support of the strike. This would be to attribute to the press an enormous power it does not possess and to discredit entirely the capacity of its readers to think for themselves. It is important not to underestimate the profound scepticism which permeates working-class culture; for all the changes that have taken place, the continued strength of that corporate opposition which separates 'us' from 'them', and which feeds the popular suspicion that 'it's all a pack of lies anyway' is still clearly in evidence. The press may be a significant organizer of popular beliefs in selecting, categorizing and contextualising information so as to make sense of the world for its readers, but it does not create these ideas from the abstract. On the contrary, to be effective in breaking down scepticism these ideas must, at least partially, connect with and conform to the lived experiences of the readers themselves.

It is too easy to argue that television and the media in general are inseparable from government, simply providing it with its most effective channel to the public. Of course, the connections can be close. Collusion does take place. It seems most likely that it was governmental pressure which persuaded the editor of *The Sunday Telegraph* to drop a story of proposed involvement of the troops from the second edition of his paper on 25 March. Similarly, if the government is sufficiently astute, the nervousness of BBC directors can be strung out into perpetuity by way of the occasional well-chosen short, sharp reprimand from Downing Street. And, again, there can be no denying the close political relations between the government and sycophantic admirers, suitably rewarded, of the stripe of Sir Larry Lamb or Sir Alastair Burnett. But such a mono-lithic view of the media as a government conspiracy cannot take account of those moments when real conflicts do flare up between the managers of public opinion and cabinet ministers, and result in deep political difference. A most spectacular example of this in recent years was the open struggle between the government and some sections of the media during the war with Argentina. Equally, it is necessary to explain the limited diversity of perspective which *is* given space in both news reports and current affairs. During the dispute the characteristic animosity to the NUM which lay barely beneath the surface of BBC television news contrasted with the attempts by the Channel 4 news reports to at least explore the issues with a modicum of journalistic seriousness and integrity.

Unlike the newspapers, television and radio are institutions which (under the regulation of the BBC and the IBA) are required to forgo the privileges of partisan editorial loyalty in favour of 'impartiality'. Whenever challenged, the mandarins of the BBC and the IBA insist that they are neutral, dedicated to their famous commitment to 'balance'. This concept needs to be investigated. It is evident that in the reporting of the strike in 1984/5 representatives of the NUM have been given their say alongside the NCB. It is too early yet, without the benefit of the findings of detailed research, to tell whether the overall time allocated to the miners' representatives has equalled that of the NCB. On past evidence this is unlikely. But if we put this on one side for a moment it has to be admitted that an attempt at some kind of formal balance has been made and that the BBC and IBA managers are not being entirely untruthful when they reiterate their commitment to a formal balance between the two sides. It is still necessary to see how this works in practice.

Critiques of the notion of balance, in its practical manifestations, have been developed by the Glasow University Media Group and by the Campaign for Press and Broadcasting Freedom. The general points do not need to be rehearsed in detail here — the identification of trade unions with disruption, the concentration on scenes of conflict, the loaded language, the distortions resulting from inadequate contextualization and the editing of stories, and so on. During the strike, even at the most elementary level, there is reason to be dissatisfied with the 'impartiality' achieved. Some random examples can be cited: For the duration of the strike it has never been clear with whom the striking miners should be 'balanced'. Has the principle of impartiality been fulfilled if the government, the coal board, and the police as well as on occasions working miners are all given their say as separate interests? At moments it was seen appropriate for elected representatives of the NUM to be balanced by whoever appeared as the self-appointed leader of working miners in Nottingham.

Another example relates to the disparity in financial resources between the NUM and the NCB. For much of the strike the NUM has been without funds. The coal board on the other hand has massive spending power and has used this to invest heavily in advertising in the press. This advertising, in turn, has been used to create news stories and publicity for the NCB free of charge. This was clearly seen on 2 January when the NCB, through advertisements it had taken, virtually bought the lead news on national and local television and radio. The flow of media material, undoubtedly favourable in sum to the NCB, has swamped occasional stories which strongly support the striking miners. For example, *The Observer*'s detailed analysis of the coal board's July figures of working miners showed them to be shot through with errors, and the paper carried the strong suggestion that the NCB were primarily engaged in a propaganda exercise. But *The Observer*'s report did not result in a general re-assessment of the reporting of the figures. No scepticism was expressed on the next occasion that the NCB stepped up its propaganda war by announcing numbers returning to work. The report's analysis was simply ignored.

Yet another example shows that 'balance' does not always work in a way that opens up issues: The *ad hoc* inquiry at Grimethorpe resulted from local anger at what, in effect, was a police riot in the village. The Chief Constable of West Yorkshire attended the 'inquiry' — a meeting on 17 October in a local hall to which television crews were admitted. At the meeting hostility towards the police was repeated in statement after statement from residents. The Chairman of the Police Committee made the charge that the police had acted like 'stormtroopers'. The Chief Constable declared himself 'shocked' at what had happened and expressed his sincere concern to do something about it. But the news bulletins which reported this event managed to create the impression of anything but unanimity. The voices of the villagers themselves were not heard. Instead 'balance' was achieved by opposing the statement about 'stormtroopers' with the Chief Constable's expression of shock. The impression given was that it was the chairman of the police committee's description of the police, rather than the action of the police themselves, which had upset the Chief Constable. Here was a case of an attempt at 'balance' creating a deeply misleading picture of antagonism and conflict.

Other examples could be given. In the public debate at the Edinburgh Film and Television Festival even the most astute of the media executives and programme directors were thrown on the defensive. The NUM's case had to be accepted. Even if a formal commitment to

impartiality and equality had framed the conception of their programmes, the practices and mechanisms of broadcasting had clearly
shifted the ground in favour of the anti-strike forces, leaving the
strikers peculiarly exposed. It is important to ask why this was so.

Paradoxically, part of the reason must lie in the very objective of
balance, as it is understood by most media practitioners. As they see
it, the institutions of the media exist in order to represent the general
or national interest. No particular interest, not even that of the
government, can override this goal. They attempt to achieve it by
securing a range of competing accounts from the different interests
involved in any story. Television reporters doggedly search out an
'NUM spokesman' for each item on the strike — the NUM is not to be
excluded; on the contrary, it is seen as desirable and even essential
that it be given a voice. This is necessary in order to give substance to
the idea of the general interest. It also explains why, within certain
limits, 'hard-hitting' and 'concerned' journalists can challenge and
sometimes directly attack the Prime Minister and her senior cabinet
ministers. This is not simply tokenism; it is an integral part of the
role the media assumes in the broader culture, as the guardian of the
collective interest and as tribune for us, the public.

However, this idea of a general or national interest, which the
media functions to preserve, is closely linked to the concept of two
party constitutionalism. Differences can be countenanced, even encouraged, so long as the broad principles and framework of the
existing system are adhered to. It is this schema which results in the
invitation of both a government and an opposition MP, or a trade
unionist and a manager, to speak on any issue being covered. As a
previous Director-General of the BBC admitted, the BBC is biased
towards the system of parliamentary democracy.

But what happens when a representative of a particular interest
appears not to abide by the unwritten rules of English constitutionalism? The answer provided by the strike seems to be that it then
becomes quite *legitimate*, within the underlying rules and codes of the
profession, to single them out for special treatment, to provoke,
challenge, and badger them. This is justified not by personal vindictiveness but as a duty to the public. In such a case the norms of
everyday journalistic practice no longer hold and yesterday's profes-
sional transgression becomes today's code of practice.

Having said this, it is crucial to remind ourselves that there is no
evidence whatever to suggest that the NUM organized 'its' strike
with the intention of destroying parliamentary democracy. Yet the

mass media have gone a long way to construct an idea of 'Scargillism' which is devoted to just that. Consequently Scargill, and the case he puts, can be denied the status of a recognized partial interest which, like any other, has a rightful claim in the polity.

This accounts for the most profound transformation in the media during its strike. The media consensus has narrowed considerably and the underlying rules are shifting. The terrain on which balance is founded has moved although this has not been a homogeneous process. So it is that, today, the political exclusion of 'the enemy within' coexists in the media's coverage of the dispute with a pronounced philanthropic attitude to the privation of the striking miners. The current coverage of the mainstream media attempts to reconcile a newly-defined plurality of viewpoints and construct a new unity on this ground. This transmutation of media ideologies is unnerving and dangerous. It disrupts and transforms even the most settled conventions of established programmes, completely collapsing traditional distinctions between news and current affairs. This by no means signifies the capture of the mass media by the formal apparatus of government. But it is a worrying sign of an intensifying authoritarianism.

The full and detailed story of the media and the strike, scrupulously documented and researched, needs to be told. It is one of the many tasks to be undertaken at the end of the dispute.

Bill Schwarz.

The Miners and Television

One of the most remarkable aspects of the strike has been the awareness on the part of the miners and the NUM leadership of television's crucial role in representing the cause and course of the struggle. The power of television to interpret instantly events going on in isolated communities to the rest of the country and crucially, to other mining areas, has made it a particularly powerful element in this strike.

While television certainly plays an important role in determining people's views of the world, there is ample evidence that it also generates resistance to its seemingly endless and repetitious distortions. The widespread support for the strike, both in the trade unions and support groups, belies the pessimistic view that television can completley obliterate people's understanding of their class position. Nevertheless television *is* the dominant means of receiving sounds and images purporting to describe the world to us at home and, therefore, has to be taken seriously by socialists.

The miners have been acutely aware of television's role in reporting the strike to millions of people. They are justifiably condemnatory of the vast majority of broadcast material about the strike, and rightly mistrustful of wandering television crews who are persistently unwilling or unable to cede any of their power to the people at the wrong end of the camera.

The widely publicized aggression towards television crews on the picket lines has resulted in sharp contradictions within the ACTT which, though supportive of the strike, has had to deal with censure motions on the miners from its members. Indeed the inability of the union to make any effective practical efforts to remedy the biased television output is one of the harsh lessons of the dispute.

The miners' forceful criticisms of television are part of an increasing awareness of its potential role within the labour movement. Until recently the movement has tended to focus on the printed word as a means of communication. Its analysis and use of television, tape and films, has not been sufficiently developed. What follows here does not represent in any sense a full analysis of television coverage of the strike, but rather a preliminary contribution towards the development of a fuller debate within the left.

At the outset, it is worth noting the wide range of programmes on the strike. There are several loose categories: the main news programmes on BBC, ITV and Channel 4; a range of current affairs programmes — e.g. *Panorama, Newsnight, World in Action, TV Eye, Weekend World*, and *Diverse Reports*; a broad band of apparently 'lighter' coverage – on *Afternoon Plus, TV AM, Breakfast Time*; regional coverage by ITV companies supplementing the national network; various one-off documentaries made from a clearly sup-portive class perspective, such as Chris Curling's *The Last Pit in the Rhondda* and Ken Loach's *Which Side Are You On?*; and finally programmes which, to some extent, have been made with the collaboration of their participants, *Taking Liberties, Coal not Dole, Notts Women Strike Back*, and *Get It Shown*.

All these programmes were made and shown, without exception, by broadcasting institutions that have ultimate editorial, financial and scheduling control over them. It is worth reminding ourselves that not only are the individual companies completely undemocratic in their organization, structure and decision making, but also that their controlling bodies – the BBC Governors and the IBA board –are constituted entirely by appointment. Because of their composition, the dice are loaded heavily in these institutions against the interests of the working class and its allies. Even the right wing of the Labour Party and the Trades Union Congress is barely represented in the upper echelons of the television companies. It is noteworthy that the IBA did not appoint a single person with a labour movement back-ground to the board of Channel 4, yet well-known SDP and Conservative figures were much in evidence.

The great majority of television executives and producers are firmly middle-class by background and education, are paid ex-tremely high salaries and operate within rigidly hierarchical struc-tures. The introversion of those employed in television has led to the development of a complacent media culture that in general reflects the interests of the ruling class, but does not always coincide exactly with the views of government at any particular time: television has its own interests, its own notions of 'professionalism', 'good tele-vision', 'service' and, of course, a need for audiences and – in the case of ITV – for profits.

These factors indicate an area that needs more detailed analysis. British television can be characterized as a body that represents a world hostile to progressive politics, yet is still subject to sufficient contradictions and ambiguities to enable some programme-making of a socialist character to take place. From these rather general features of television as a whole we can now return to the miners' specific problems.

Without doubt the vast majority of news and current affairs output has worked against the interests of the miners and their supporters. It is not true to say, however, that this is the result of a conscious media conspiracy – the variety of approaches in different programmes cannot be reduced to one reactionary type. There is a clear category of news reports and programmes blatantly biased in favour of the coal board and the government. The miners themselves have cited many instances of serious ommisions, total distortions and even lies. But perhaps an even deeper problem than this obvious bias is the combination of television practice and a dominant ideology which produces a system intrinsically incapable of fairness. If we look at concepts like 'news agenda' or 'balance', or the natural practices of television news reporters and presenters, we discover a network of beliefs, habits and interests so deep that the participants are incapable of seeing the politics implicit in their everyday work.

What is 'the news'? Five men crossing a picket line, or five thousand trying to stop them? From whose perspective is the event reported? Inevitably, the news is not a neutral 'window on the world'. Every act in constituting a news item, in deciding in which order the items should be placed and in what accent the items are read, involves the adoption of a position. The fact that the vast majority of television makers do not accept this is a critical aspect of maintaining the system's conservatism.

The obligations placed on television to 'balance' output is apparently taken very seriously. Indeed the incomprehension that greeted Arthur Scargill's criticism of TV coverage of the strike at the 1984 Ediburgh Television Festival centred on this crucial question. The television makers and executives at Edinburgh were surprised at the hostile response to what they regarded as their fair and even-handed approach to reporting the strike. But their arguments, resting on numerical evidence of the number of times NCB and NUM spokespersons had appeared, were simply not credible. They ignored the context of those appearances. The media's role in creating a persona for Scargill that bears little relation to reality, and still less to the perceptions of the majority of NUM members made, it impossible for him to appear in a favourable light. The negative connotations attached by the media to his image, even before the strike commenced, meant that his every utterance would be presented as ideologically unacceptable.

The very notion of balanced reporting implies a position 'outside' class interest and ideology. With the sharp political, regional differences produced by this strike it is inevitable that even where a reporter has tried to be 'balanced' his or her report will inevitably favour one side or another.

There is a further argument in the debate over the issue of balance: should it operate within individual programmes, within each company's output, or across all four channels? At Channel 4 the company has persistently been required to balance programmes made from a left viewpoint. The station's *Comment* programme featuring Jimmy Reid criticizing Scargill's handling of the strike was the result of an IBA suggestion that Ken Loach's *Which Side Are You On?* should be balanced. This flew in the face of those who have argued at Channel 4 that its coverage should be balanced not internally but across the entire network. Such a view is not accepted by the IBA nor by the company's board. The board's current position in negotiations with the IBA is that they will aim for balance across their own scheduling. This contrasts with the ITV companies which, with much greater audience figures, are generally expected to balance within particular programmes or news reports.

During the miners' strike a handful of programmes have been transmitted that in various ways have made a clear break with the predominant tone in coverage of the dispute. On one occasion Channel 4 news offered a camera and crew to both Scargill and MacGregor to make their own short pieces outlining their respective views of the strike. This was such a distinct break because it ceded some degree of control to the participants. Scargill, for once, could say what he chose rather than having to fight off a battery of hostile questions. It was an experiment apparently applauded within television but not yet repeated by Channel 4 or, for that matter, by any other news programme.

Other examples of programmes outside the normal range of treatment of the strike were Ken Loach's *Which Side are You On?* and Chris Curling's *Last Pit in the Rhondda*. Loach's film was initially considered unsuitable for showing on ITV because of its highly partisan approach and was eventually broadcast to a much smaller audience on Channel 4. ITV's view that this film was too biased for them to show suggests a quite extraordinary assessment by the staion of their overall coverage of the strike. Certainly from the miners' point of view it would only have been a beginning in balancing their previous eight months' output.

The *People to People* programmes shown on Channel 4 — *Coal*

Not Dole, Get It Shown and *Notts Women Strike Back* — were made collaboratively between programme makers and members of the mining communities. They could not have been shown in their final form without the editorial approval of those represented. It is nevertheless important to remember that, contractually, final control remained with Channel 4. The problem of contractual control also affected the programme makers responsible for *Taking Liberties*. This remarkable programme about policing and civil liberties during the strike was restricted to the *Open Space* slot on BBC2 and shown only after considerable internal hesitations and delays.

At Channel 4, there has been a positive, if cautious response to the programmes dealing with the strike. The Channel's particular remit, endorsed by an act of Parliament, to seek 'new voices', and its policy of trying to represent the regions, created a space for programmes supportive of the miners. In addition, the Channel's commitment to innovation has facilitated the institution of an hour-long news programme that has been perceived by many miners as more sensitive and honest than those of the BBC or ITV.

There are certain specific demands that can and must be made of the television companies in the future. During the Edinburgh Festival debate, Scargill suggested that fifteen minutes a week of television time be placed at the NUM's disposal. This demand has hitherto fallen on deaf ears, although it is hard to see how one could ask much less of a TV system seriously engaged in offering its audience a balanced view of the strike. Television in a democratic society should surely be made available in this way to a genuine diversity of interests and viewpoints.

The notion of a right of reply represents another crucial demand and has formed the basis of much of the Campaign for Press and Broadcasting Freedom's work. It is obviously an important demand, though one that the television companies might well be able to assimilate, marginalize or cynically manipulate. The right of reply is essentially a responsive and defensive demand. A positive input into the regular schedules is what is really needed. The wider democratizing of television to transform it into something that can truly be called a 'service' to the people will be a long-term task. But socialists could achieve far more than they have done until now.

Having sketched out some of the familiar problems of the politics of television it is appropriate to look briefly at the prospects for the future.

First, it has to be emphasized that progressive movements must spend much more time and energy in developing media analysis and policy for action. Successive Labour governments have done nothing in this area and, at the least, have held extremely conventional views about film and television.

One of the most impressive examples of oppositional media activity during the strike has been the production of a series of independently produced and distributed video tapes — *The Miners' Tapes*. Produced by a group of people working outside the television establishment, these films have been used widely at miners' meetings and benefits. Close links with independent programme makers have certainly benefited the union during the strike, and the construction of such relationships is an important task for the labour movement in future. So too is the opening up of the possibility of establishing a significant video tape production and distribution network working on behalf of the labour movement.

Alan Fountain

PART TWO
Digging in for Coal:
The Miners and their Supporters

7
Stopping Out
The Birth of a New Kind of Politics

Kim Howells

In mid–December 1984 reporters began trekking into the valleys of South Wales like prospectors into a new goldfield. They wanted to know why the coalfield was virtually scab-free when every other area, apart from sections of Yorkshire, had become badly tainted by the NCB's back-to-work campaign during the previous six weeks.

They flocked to the area headquarters in Pontypridd and, without a flicker of a smile on their earnest faces, they asked 'What's the magic ingredient? There aren't any mass pickets down here. Is it the nature of the communities? Perhaps it's genetic? Is it to do with hating the English coal board bosses in London?'

Maybe it was some or all of those things, mixed up in a stew of radical political consciousness, an area leadership which genuinely reflected rank-and-file thinking, a humorous, and free-and-easy strike administration, a superb string of fund-raising centres and back-up organizations. Maybe it was the way that, within weeks of the strike starting, South Wales women threw off all that garbage about being 'behind' their men and began occupying coal board offices, blockading steel-works' gates and touring Europe putting the case for the defence of their communities.

Certainly, the doggedness and sheer guts and imagination of the strikers in South Wales was best expressed not more than a few miles from the 'English' headquarters of the coal board in London.

In a huge, packed town hall in Brixton a young striker from the Betws pit near Ammanford in the west of the coalfield sat chain-smoking on the stage, alongside Peter Heathfield. He listened and smoked and bit his nails to the quick as Heathfield wound the enthusiastic audience up into knots of revolutionary tension with superb oratory.

The Ammanford boy had to follow him to the microphone. He had never before spoken in public; still less had he found himself trapped before several thousand people who wanted to hear some magic truth from the mountains. After Heathfield's inevitable standing ovation, he wobbled forward, grabbed the mike with shaking hands and started thanking the Lambeth council for allowing the Ammanford Support Group the use of the town hall's nuclear bunker as a working office and headquarters in London.

The audience began to laugh and, being a sharp lad, he realized that out there, beyond his veil of terror, he had struck a rich vein. 'Yeah', he said in his nasal Ammanford drawl, 'they've given us their nuclear bunker under this building. And Thatcher there, up the road, better remember this . . . If she ever goes crazy enough to press the nuclear button; and if the missiles start flying about . . . if she manages to survive the holocaust in *her* nuclear bunker . . . Well, at the end of it — when she thinks it's safe — she's going to stick her head out of her bunker and she'll look down the road, and do you know what she'll see? She'll see six South Wales miners crawling out of *their* bunker shouting, "The strike's still on." '

Mike Reynolds, the Ammanford boy, had tapped a little more of his potential. Like the rest of us, he'd begun tapping it right at the start of the strike when we found ourselves battling for the hearts and souls of our own brothers in South Wales pits during the first hours of the stoppage.

There was a big problem in Wales during those early moments. A large section of our twenty-one thousand miners and cokemen were in no mood to take the lead once again in confronting a national government. South Wales had led every major coal stoppage since the balmy days of the mid-1970s: the fight to keep Deep Duffryn open in 1978/79; the temporary defeat in support of the steel workers in 1980; the successful opposition to Thatcher's first pit hit-list in February 1981; the bitter campaign in 1983 to prevent the board closing the Tymawr/Lewis Merthyr mine.

On each of these occasions many Welshmen had detected varying degrees of reluctance amongst miners in even the most militant sister coalfields to come forward with generous physical support. They remembered all too vividly how, just twelve months earlier, they had travelled to every pit in Britain in a vain attempt to drum-up support for our strike against the closure of Tymawr/Lewis Merthyr. They recalled that far too many pits had given them ' . . . everything bar their votes.'

They sensed that, once again, they would find themselves isolated in splendid heroism — ready to be picked off one by one after returning to work with their tails between their legs.

But it didn't turn out like that. Most pits struck spontaneously on the first morning or within the next twenty-four hours. A couple had stragglers who were picketed out. But once stopped, there was no strike more solid anywhere in Europe. Once that was a confirmed fact then the potential of our men and women began showing itself everywhere.

South Wales and Kent are probably physically more remote from the big English coalfields than any others in these islands. Yet both share the distinction of consistently and methodically picketing targets across an enormous geographic area. It was a logistical task of major proportions simply to transport and sustain forty pickets in, say, Leicestershire for a week. It involved hundreds of miles of travel, sleeping night after night on coaches or in vans or, later, in community halls and separate digs.

It involved evaluating targets, deciding if they were sensible and how best to tackle them. It involved learning from experience how to avoid mistakes and time-wasting, how to approach working miners without alienating them and driving them into defensive packs which could never be persuaded to change their minds and join the strike.

It involved gathering intelligence: which power stations, in *practice* not in theory, were the important ones to isolate; which midlands pits were more open to debate; which communities might be cajoled into allowing us to put our case calmly and sensibly; which town councils might allow us to use their buildings to sleep, eat and wash in; which ports were likely to welcome coal imports and which ones would boycott them.

By May 1984 South Wales pickets were operating as far north as the Heysham nuclear power station near Lancaster. They were in the coalfields of Lancashire, Derbyshire, Staffordshire, Warwickshire, Nottinghamshire and Leicestershire. They were covering the Wash ports, helping out in the Essex ports, picketing cement works and power stations in Cambridgeshire, Birmingham, Oxfordshire, Hampshire, Devon, Cornwall and in all of the counties bordering on Wales as well as in the whole of Wales itself. At one time, our pickets were camped twenty-four hours a day, seven days a week outside twenty-two power stations: coal-fired, oil-fired and nuclear, from Sizewell to Pembroke and from Wylfa to Fawley.

The cost was astronomic and the effort enormous. For month after month, the coalfield despatched an average of four to five thousand pickets to these various targets. South Wales coach hire companies had never experienced anything like it. Men whose previous expertise had revolved around supporting roofs or ripping roadways forward suddenly found themselves becoming experts at interpreting ordnance survey maps or organizing transport or dishing out legal advice or sniffing out likely sources of accommodation or food and funds. Others, like Mike Reynolds, rapidly became accomplished speakers, organizers and fund-raisers.

Networks of telephone numbers were woven across the coalfield; lists of permanently available pickets were pinned up for future reference; information was exchanged about which territory was friendly and which was hostile. Conversation abounded everywhere about locations no one in South Wales had previously heard of: places like Coalville, Ironbridge, Barrington and Hythe.

From the very beginning the main picketing emphasis was placed firmly on the power stations and ports. The national NUM headquarters appeared a good deal less interested than us in these targets. Cokeworks, like Orgreave, and the continuing saga of trying to winkle out the pits of Nottingham were closer to their hearts. Experience in that county had taught us very early on that a siege mentality was developing in the Dukeries — a mentality which, when combined with the ruthless use of thousands of police, would inevitably result in a stalemate and thousands of our men being arrested.

If we could stop the power stations on the other hand . . . The first team to reach the Heysham nuclear station had previously spent a hard fortnight picketing the pits of the Stoke area. They'd been directed to Heysham as a means of taking the pressure off them and we were looking to them to provide us with some explanation as to why it was that so many other NUM areas seemed very reluctant to stick at the daily grind of picketing power stations. We knew that it was less spectacular work than the daily round of battling with the police outside pits, but in our eyes it was much more vital in any long-term quest for victory.

The team arrived there around mid-morning. After two hours of stopping all traffic moving in and out of the plant, their co-ordinator rang the Pontypridd headquarters: 'Listen,' he bawled down the line, 'we've been here a couple of hours and we haven't seen a single tonne of coal pass this spot.' 'Jesus Christ,' screamed the picket organizer in Pontypridd, 'it's a bloody *nuclear* station, you idiot. They use uranium in the place. Find out how we can stop it.'

Within three days a report, hand-written in block capitals, was on the organizer's desk in Pontypridd, pointing out that even though it was almost impossible to stop the uranium, the nukes were nevertheless theoretically vulnerable to picketing because they needed large supplies of CO_2 and other gases to control the various production processes. The same team co-ordinator who had searched for coal outside Heysham had researched it and written it. Our headquarters found it invaluable. We immediately contacted the TGWU tanker drivers' representatives with a view to restricting supplies to all of the nuclear stations. We succeeded only partially, but that can come later.

We were learning our lessons and learning them fast. Men and women who in normal times rarely left their villages and valleys were rapidly becoming lay-experts in matters which had never before impinged on their lives. They were travelling vast distances day after day, discovering allies and enemies in the most unlikely places: friendly Hindu communities in Birmingham, hostile steelworkers in Newport; magnificently supportive farmers in the wilds of Dyfed and hostile city councillors in the chambers of Cardiff.

They also began penetrating the outer walls of the 'Great Citadel' of the left and they were finding all too often that the brickwork crumbled at the first kick, stairways to higher levels collapsed spontaneously, and that the telephone wires had frequently been eaten right through by rats.

As far as South Wales was concerned, the main keep of this citadel was the so-called Triple Alliance. It was an imposing structure but as rickety as the rest of the building. Theoretically, we had the support of the steelworkers on the giant strip-mills on the coast, the railwaymen, and the seamen and dockers. All of this was underpinned by the mighty TGWU in Cardiff and co-ordinated by the Wales TUC.

Surprisingly enough, it worked for the first couple of months of the strike. We ran down the stockpiles of coking coal inside the steelworks and attempted (unsuccessfully) to prevent the mighty coal-carriers docking at Europe's largest man-made harbour at Port Talbot. Then, on hearing that the Scottish miners were allowing regular deliveries of coal from Hunterston to Ravenscraig, we negotiated with our Triple Alliance partners an arrangement whereby Llanwern received about ten thousand tonnes of coal and coke a week by rail under the strict supervision of the NUR, ASLEF and ourselves.

This succeeded in limiting steel production and in raising a howl of protest from the Welsh Office that we were threatening the future of the great steel plants. For a while, something approaching peace and harmony reigned on the coastal strip. It lasted only until the moment of the NUM declaration, at an ASLEF delegate conference, that a complete block was to be placed on deliveries of all fuels to the country's steelworks.

The steelworkers reacted angrily and the Triple Alliance disintegrated. The following week brought an awesome and depressing sight: massive convoys of scab haulage firms roaring between Port Talbot and Llanwern on the M4. The steelworkers opened their arms to the coal and coke supplied, often, by the same haulage firms which had worked four years earlier at the behest of the British Steel Corporation to break their own strike. Miners, their wives and supporters flocked in their hundreds to the gates of both strip-mills and attempted to enforce the blockade.

Despite mass arrests, the use of an extraordinary range of tactics and twenty four-hour picketing costing many thousands of pounds for month after month, we never succeeded in halting the convoy for more than a few days. It ploughed on remorselessly — even after we imposed a blockade on iron-ore deliveries. As many as two hundred lorries would frequently be lined up under heavy police escort to make the hazardous run. The M4 became ochred with the dust of iron ore and its bridges filmed with small-coal.

Supplies to the steelworks were supplemented with shiploads of coal and coke landed at private wharves on the river Usk at Newport. Here, too, dozens of arrests were made and all to no avail, save teaching ordinary men and women a short, sharp lesson in understanding the power of the state.

By October, the steelmen were receiving over twenty thousand tonnes of coal and coke a week — over twice the amount we'd allowed them before the total 'blockade' had been declared. The Triple Alliance lay in ruins and our morale needed lifting.

We did it by co-ordinating, within an hour of each other, two imaginative and daring occupations. Using split-second timing, a party of over a hundred men from the central wedge of the coalfield managed to penetrate the centre of the huge Port Talbot steel complex and occupy the massive cranes on the unloading wharf of the docks. Meanwhile, a group of Gwent miners took over the enormous transporter bridge spanning the river Usk at Newport. Realizing that if they could suspend the bridge's gondola in mid-stream they would effectively block access to wharves upstream, they forced the authorities to review completely their whole attitude to the security of these vital public facilities.

Both occupations highlighted the differences of approach to picketing by rival police forces on and around the coalfield. The

South Wales police, acting in unison with the British Transport Police played it relatively softly, softly at Port Talbot while their comrades in Gwent took the opportunity to show off their riot gear and their lack of basic human decency. Both occupations were peaceful and a conscious alternative to challenging lines of single-minded and well-equipped policemen, a tactic which had already been tried in most spectacular fashion at the Orgreave coking plant near Sheffield.

Unfortunately, it was the latter type of tactic which came to dominate the headlines and capture most people's imagination. It never succeeded in stopping a single lorry nor a scab and taught us in South Wales a good deal about what to do to win friends and influence people during industrial disputes.

These heady events needed effective and complex support structures. South Wales was relatively late in following areas like Kent and (striking) Nottinghamshire in setting up networks of fund-raising centres across the country. Complaints, some of them justified, began filtering back to the Pontypridd headquarters that we should ease up on the picketing and pay more attention to raising money.

This need immediately became more intense after the sequestration of the South Wales area funds at the end of July 1984. The area became the first mining victim of the new Tebbit laws and it was felt, with great justification, that South Wales had been singled out because of the enormous breadth of its picketing involvement. Suddenly, the organization had virtually no funds of its own. The sequestrators had even seized independent food funds right across the coalfield. Families were in danger of going hungry and the pickets were in danger of being unable to purchase petrol for their vans, cars and buses.

Within weeks, Welsh men and women were everywhere, from Preston to Peterborough and from Stoke Newington to St Ives. They addressed hundreds of meetings each week, twinned pit villages with factories and constituency Labour Parties, organized large and efficient co-ordinating centres in Liverpool, Birmingham, Oxford, Bristol, Southampton, Swindon, Reading and London as well as scores of smaller centres elsewhere.

But still it wasn't enough. To feed up to twenty thousand families each week, as well as paying the huge and myriad costs of picketing, was a problem which was resolved only by creating what amounted to an alternative Welfare State inside Wales. Everyone was mobilized: MPs who had supported us from the beginning as well as those who had been less forthcoming; borough and county councillors; other trade unions; all were told, 'Even if you will not support us physically, we need your money' and often they gave it; the chapels, churches and political parties both inside and outside of the UK. We stepped up our delegations to Europe; Belgium, France, Italy and Denmark gave magnificently, others followed. Meetings of over ten thousand were addressed by Welsh miners in Bologna and Milan. A constant stream of visitors tramped up the Rhondda and across east and west Wales from all parts of the world.

At one moment, during a street battle outside a cokeworks in the Aberdare valley, there were visitors from six different countries watching or participating in the event. A film crew from Japan worked alongside crews from Paris, London and Cardiff. A week later, a benefit concert at Onllwyn was partly paid for by several gay and lesbian groups from London and the food provided by a London Turkish Society.

The coalfield had developed a new collective spirit which revived community life and re-awoke in ordinary people the understanding that it was possible to take the first, concrete steps towards creating a more humanitarian and socialist society now, in the dreary midst of Thatcherism, and that it was idiotic to assume that such steps were only possible after some special kind of electoral victory or a triumph on the barricades.

With no prompting from *Marxism Today*, the *New Left Review* or *Labour Weekly*, the people of the coalfields created the basis for a new politics which grew out of experience and necessity. Old politos — especially many of the crocodile-skinned varieties from Westminster — found themselves straggling badly behind, lost in a mist of worries about parliamentary whips and TUC guidelines. Others became near-sighted, so hard did they search the small print of their constitutions and manifestos for guidance on how to relate Trotsky and Tawney to food-parcel distribution in Cwm Llantwit.

Even within the NUM there were individuals who failed to understand that this strike was going to be won or sustained (it became difficult to differentiate between those two activities after a while), not simply through the deployment of mass pickets but by mobilizing and tapping the enormous potential of *whole communities*. 1984 and Thatcher could have been a century away from 1972 and Edward Heath. We faced an opponent in 1984 who took her task seriously. And that task was nothing less than the destruction of the organized British labour movement. Pit closures were merely the pretext for dismantling the sharp end of the only independent working-class movement which had survived anywhere in Europe intact through the 1930s and 1940s.

Our defences were found badly wanting. The citadel was falling apart. The people of the coalfields had no choice but to create new defences and in building them they rediscovered old socialist and collectivist truths. They realised that by uniting and sharing all that they had, they could survive and overcome the worst that the present state apparatus could throw at them.

In South Wales we also rediscovered something else: that we are a part of a real nation which extends northwards beyond the coalfield, into the mountains of Powys, Dyfed and Gwynnedd. For the first time since the industrial revolution in Wales, the two halves of the nation came together in mutual support. Pickets from the south travelled to the nuclear and hydro-stations in the north. Support groups in the north brought food, money and clothes to the south. Friendships and alliances flourished; old differences of attitude and accent withered and out of it all grew the most important 'formal' political organization to emerge during the course of the strike —the Wales Congress in Support of Mining Communities.

Backed by MPs and elected officers of the Labour Party, Plaid Cymru and the Communist Party, it embraced organizations as diverse as the Welsh Language Society and the Wales TUC. It forced people out of their political trenches and provided a forum for debate and action of the kind sadly missing, not merely in Wales but throughout these islands. It has opened up the possibility of mutual action to defend and strengthen communities, whether their life-blood is coal or farming or engineering or oil refining. Its existence has given certain established politicians nightmares; it has perplexed others and given a new lease of life to still more. Its potential has hardly been realized. It is a fledgling, still growing in the shadow of the citadel and it will continue to draw sustenance from the communities which gave birth to it, whatever happens to its midwife, the strike.

Its existence is proof that we have already achieved victories, however they are measured in the jaundiced public eye of the media. Our communities have survived hell and high water and come back fighting. They have begun to realize their potential for creating change and have moved with astonishing speed and imagination towards a new and practical politics which builds upon existing structures.

It is clearly the duty of all other socialists and of everyone who cares for the future to ensure that these momentous beginnings are not crushed, forgotten or smothered after the strike.

8
Beyond the Coalfields
The Work of the Miners' Support Groups

Doreen Massey and Hilary Wainwright

The miners' strike seems to epitomize those aspects of the labour movement and class politics that certain interpreters have found 'old fashioned', sectional and, by implication, bankrupt. Male manual workers, the old working class with a vengeance, fighting to save jobs in what is officially described as a declining industry, state-owned and located in isolated declining regions. And yet around this struggle a massive support movement has grown up — almost un-reported — with as broad a social and geographical base as any post-war radical political movement.

The Coalfields

The social structure of the mining communities reflects the industry which is their livelihood: lack of white-collar jobs, their proletarian nature, the overwhelming dominance of male, manual labour. The regions are distinctive in other ways too. They are predominantly white; they are socially conservative; traditional sexual divisions of labour — woman as home-maker, man as bread-winner — have been deeply ingrained and only recently begun to break down.

Their politics have been workplace-based. They are the fiefdoms of one of the most important unions in labour movement history, symbolizing — at least for men — the old strengths of a solidarity born of mutual dependence at work, and the reliance of a whole community on a single industry. The themes of discipline and collectivism run deep and strong in the political atmosphere. These are regions owned, regulated, fed and watered by the central state. The industry is nationalized, high proportions of the inhabitants live on state subsidies, and for an alternative to work in the pit they appeal to state regional policy. They have voted Labour for years, through thick and (mainly) thin. And the local state, for ages too, has been in the hands of the Labour Party right wing. They are the heartlands of labourism. What this means is that the strike is taking place in some of the most self-enclosed and socially homogeneous regions of the country. And indeed that geography is part of the rationale and the character of the strike. The one-to-one relationship between community and coal, at least for male employment, has been one of the bases of its solidarity. Levels of militancy have been in part related to dependence on the industry (this, it should be noted in passing, is a nice boomerang of that 1950s 'anti-regional policy' of keeping alternative employment for men out of the coalfields). And that dependence on a single industry has also been one of the bases for the struggle going beyond the workplace, to become an issue of community survival. Again there is some kind of relationship: it is the coalfields most affected by the reconstruction of the 1950s and 1960s, for instance by new workers moving in from other areas, and therefore the more recently constituted communities, which have been least solid in the strike. Geographical coherence therefore has been an element of strength but its corollary — geographical separation — has, potentially been an isolating factor.

Put these social and geographical characteristics together and the strike could easily be seen as an old politics, slogging away in its own redoubts, far away from where 'the rest of us' live. And indeed, several commentators on the left (as well as the right) have seen it in those terms. The last gasp of the old labour movement, in its decaying heartlands, isolated, sectional, macho, and with little resonance beyond its regions, its unions, and — of course — what they call the 'hard left'.

Support from Elsewhere

What has actually happened has been quite different. One of the most stunning aspects of the strike has been that in many ways it has not remained locked within those characterizations. With trade-union leadership at sixes and sevens, their creaking structures, and their lack of credibility, unable to lead any response, and with party political leadership embarrassed by the whole affair — in spite of, maybe because of, all this heavy-footed inertia — there has sprung up a completely different way of organizing support, indeed an expansion of what the concept of support means. 'The grass roots', people of all sorts, previously politically active and not, have just got on with it. Often in the most unexpected ways and places, support networks have been organized, fundraising events launched, and distribution systems established.

The Cities

Some of the strongest support has come from Labour's other base — and Thatcher's other opposition — the big cities. What the cities share with the coalfields — apart from Labour MPs — is industrial decline and the feeling that they have been singled out for attack. The Prime Minister knows the geographical bases of her enemies. In the cities, in addition to economic devastation, the assault comes in the form of rate-capping and the proposed abolition of the GLC and the Metropolitan Counties.

In other ways, however, the cities and the coalfield regions are very different from each other. In the cities there is generally a great mix of industries, including services, and a variety of jobs. Many of those in work are on low pay, in casual occupations, working in small firms, and in many areas levels of unionization are low. There is a different kind of physical dereliction. In the middle of all this lives an enormously diverse population; in many cities ethnic minorities, gay and lesbian communities, women's groups and 'alternative' networks of many kinds form an important element. The trade-union movement is also different from that in the coalfields. Here its very industrial variety has been the basis for a tradition of local links and networks. Public sector and white-collar unions are especially important.

All this in recent years has begun to spawn a politics quite distinct from coalfield labourism. It is often anarchistic, socially adventurous, with a commitment to politics outside the work-place as well as within. It is the radical, as opposed to the labourist, end of the labour movement — if you like; a different kind of trade unionism in uneasy combination with an alliance of the dispossessed.

And yet, in spite of these contrasts, the support from the cities has been massive. On Merseyside there are fourteen support groups, which between them have sent off £1 million so far (a *million* pounds — from a city itself in desperate poverty), and that's not including work-place collections, and new groups are still being formed. There are normally fifty to sixty miners out in the city centre. From Birmingham support goes to South Wales, and also to other more local coalfields. From London it has gone to Kent, South

Wales, Staffordshire and the North East; individual boroughs and support groups of various sorts have twinning arrangements with pits in many different coalfields. There are people with buckets, collections of food, on high streets everywhere, an anarchy of support groups and what appear to be a number of different attempts to form umbrella organizations.

The Garston Miners' Support Group in Liverpool typifies the close links which are beginning to be formed between city and coalfield. 'Each week', notes John Bohanna, one of the group, 'at least some of the group go knocking on people's doors asking for food for the striking miners. Equally, each week some of the group go asking for money in the local pubs. Raffles and two huge jumble sales have taken place during the summer. The raffles concentrated in work places and any sympathetic individual the group could encourage support from. The group had transported car-loads of food to North Wales striking miners' families and has provided van-loads for the striking miners' families in the Lancashire Pits. It has also developed links with Bolsover families.' The latest high point in the groups' work was organizing a party for 150 kids in Bolsover. It was a bit like transporting a prefabricated house and a prefabricated party (almost) complete with balloons, presents, sandwiches, ice cream, jelly and Father Christmas, 120 miles. John Bohanna takes over the story: 'Never in the history of partying have preparations been so disorganized. But never in history can the efficiency of that group be equalled in its work-rate and determination to provide all that a children's party should have. We found pleasure in seeing many fathers of the children along with mothers at the party. A miner taking photographs was heard to remark — "Orgreave was safer than this". It gave an opportunity to embrace our (small) physical display of solidarity with our verbal concern and wishes to the adults. Leaving the little town of Bolsover we saw parents and children lining the pavement and waving their thanks. But we had thanks to give them for allowing us into their lives.' The 'two ends of the labour movement' are linking up.

The nature of the support from the cities reflects the characteristics of the conurbations, and grows out of a constellation of very varied connections people have made. Movingly, impressive support has come from those who are themselves experiencing industrial dereliction. Liverpool 8 (Toxteth) was one of the first places on Merseyside to spawn a support group: 'it grew up literally overnight at the end of April'. The support group in Kirkby, a 1950s outer-city council area shattered by economic collapse, has achieved a fifty per

cent response to its door-to-door collections. In London, people in
the areas round the Royal Docks have set up the Durham-Docklands
Miners' Support Group. On an early visit they took £750 with them
to the North East. As they handed over the cheque to the Durham
Women's group 'there were tears in their eyes — and ours'. The
secretary of the Docklands Group recalls: 'It was the derelict villages
that shook me. You could see how much they depended on the pit.
The villages without a pit were dead. New factories had once been
built but they've been closed long since. We know from the experience of what happened to us what will happen to them.' The
Docklands, like the coalfields, was a community dependent on a
single dominant economic focus. The slogan of the Durham–Docklands Miners' Support Group is 'Don't let the mines go the same way
as the docks'.

Support comes, too, from the trade unions in the cities. In Liverpool although some of the work-place collections seem to have been
slower to build up momentum there are now contributions from
most factories. The body plant at Ford, Halewood gets about £1,000
every fornight and the PTA plant between £900 and £1,300 every
week. The collections are for different, specific needs each time, so
people know how they are helping. In London a vast variety of
branches, chapels and work-place communities have regular collections, have adopted pits, and organize special appeals and events.
Support has been especially strong in Fleet Street, Inner London
local authorities, the Civil Service, hospitals and schools.

Perhaps the most notable of all has been the support from marginalized and oppressed groups. The Labour Party women's section
is central to the organization of support in Merseyside. Afro-
Caribbean groups, Cypriot groups, the Asian community and
Turkish people have contributed and organized support. As early as
May two coach-loads of miners and their families came from Kent to
the Multi–racial Carnival in Brent. And unemployed people have
been prominent in the work of many groups. On Merseyside it's
unemployed people who keep the co-ordinating centre going for the
support groups. And centres for the unemployed are often the
physical base for the support organizations. In Southampton,
Cardiff, Manchester, York, Glasgow and Edinburgh there are
'Lesbians and Gays Support the Miners' groups. In London by
December over £3,000 had been raised through regular collections at
lesbian and gay clubs. All these social groups have been important
sources of support for the strike in all parts of the country, but in the
cities they also form a crucial element in the recent emergence of a

new radical urban politics.

Fringe culture has been drawn in as well. There are gigs, collections at fringe theatres (such as the Half Moon) and at clubs (such as Islington's Wrong Horse), benefit discos and day-long benefit variety shows (e.g. at the Tricycle) with films, food, comedy and music. In Liverpool at a concert — for two to three thousand people — local bands played free and several friendly sound companies lent equipment cheap.

And finally the left-wing local authorities themselves play a part, though necessarily circumscribed by red (i.e. blue) tape. Both City and County Councils are part of Merseyside's Trade Union Labour Party Campaign Committee, a central part of the support activity. In London Ken Livingstone chairs the 'Mineworkers' Defence Committee' set up to co-ordinate support from the different political groups, and in Camden and Islington women from Kent were given mayoral receptions. The GLC's evidence to the Sizewell enquiry is part of the wider case for coal and more recently the Council has produced *London In the Dark*, a pamphlet on the possibilities and impact of coal shortages and power cuts in London. And developing plans for combined heat and power systems (for instance in Newcastle, Sheffield, London, Edinburgh and Glasgow) will make more efficient use of energy. Local state politics and policies can be part of constructing a long term national energy plan. The cities may not produce much coal (though there is a joke going around about Islington Main Colliery, due to all the strike-related activity in that borough), but they are major consumers of it.

Thatcherland

Most unexpected of all has been the support which has come from the outer-metropolitan and more rural stretches of south and east England. Electorally this has been Thatcher's strongest base, with the Alliance coming second. It is not an area without its problems. Here too older manufacturing industry is in decline (the railways at Swindon for example), and unskilled school leavers have little to look forward to other than unemployment or a job at a routine, repetitive end of a service industry (insurance perhaps), or one of the much vaunted high-tech growth industries. But the dominant image at least is affluence, confidence, prosperity. Unemployment is below the national average, both jobs and people are moving into the area, and there are high proportions of the new middle class and their social accoutrements — the gin-and-Jaguar belt.

Much has been made in recent political speeches about the increasing gap between North and South. It is a political and ideological divide as well as an economic one. And yet, during this strike, thousands of people from such unlikely sounding places as Borehamwood (Cecil Parkinson's seat) and Rottingdean not only contributed to the Christmas Appeal for the miners and their families, but also wrote letters saying why, expressing their support, and urging the miners to go on. St Albans and Wivenhoe have become reknowned, through media coverage, for their organization, activity and generosity. It would be wrong to pretend that this stretch of the country had suddenly turned radical. The very high proportion of Christmas letters which came from Thatcher country may well have been precisely a result of the relative lack of more organized campaigning in such areas. Contributors to the Appeal expressed a strong desire to dissociate themselves from the popular image of satisfied southerners: 'Even in rural Somerset there is support and admiration for *our* miners' stated one.

In some letters there is a real sense of embarrassment at geographical privilege: 'Many of us in the prosperous south are appalled at the treatment miners are receiving, my small contribution is perhaps the only positive action my family can take' wrote a contributor from New Milton, Hampshire.

At times the letters create an impression of people outside the mining communities almost *willing* the miners to win, and not only for the sake of the mining communities. The appeal seemed to have opened up an opportunity for people to express themselves, to become involved. For instance, one contributor wrote: 'Please tell the miners and their families we are with them and not to give in'.

But support has not been confined to donating money and writing letters. There has also been, even in these parts of the country, the development of active support groups with direct involvement in the strike. Two examples may help to illustrate what is happening.

Cambridge is one of the hearts of high-tech land. It is set in a basically Tory area, but the town has a hung council and Labour local control (which has had its advantages — such as getting a licence for collecting). The university has always resisted the development of manufacturing industry, so there is no major manual trade-union base. Its Labour Party is large — the result, perhaps of the social nature of the town — for the bulk of the membership comes from the white-collar and intellectual sections, those who live in the terraced houses of the centre, rather than from the small outer-council estates, though the latter do vote solidly Labour.

The social group involved in what is now a major and sophisticated support network reflect that 'sunbelt' Cambridge image. The most important elements are intellectuals and white-collar strata in general, together with people active in issue-politics, particularly feminism and the nuclear question. But the organizational contribution of unemployed people has also been very important. The initiative for the support group came from the trades council but its political composition includes members from just about every left party or group and many non-aligned — it is a 'very important political development locally in itself'. The weekly meetings have between fifteen and fifty people attending.

Cambridge has twinned with Blidworth and Rainworth, two pit villages in Nottinghamshire where only a minority came out on strike. The choice was based on a mixture of personal contact (through a left political group) and the belief that life for strikers might be harder here than in more 'solid' areas. And in support of those strikers, Cambridge has had gigs, ceilidhs, house meetings, college collections, jumble sales, an art sale, and numerous other things. The main sources of money are private donations, the Labour Party levy from members and awards, and — above all — the big Saturday street collections in town. All told, Cambridge Miners' Support Group sends off £600 a week to Blidworth and Rainworth (and they also give some support to Gwent, but there isn't the space to tell everything here). Each village gets about £150 in cash and £150 in food, regularly, every week.

Milton Keynes is a very different bit of the British sunbelt. Not ancient academic spires, but Britain's biggest new town. Like most new towns Milton Keynes shares one thing with Cambridge — the lack of a major tradition of manual-labour trade unionism. When they began the support group the organizers reflected on this and were cautious about how much support they would raise — 'It's a strange place Milton Keynes, it's not like an old labour movement area. It's not like Liverpool and places . . . it's bred into them in Liverpool'. In the event, a major organization has been established, drawing together all kinds of local groups and individuals including 'lots of people completely new to politics'. Milton Keynes Miners' Support Group began through the trades council and is based in the Unemployed Workers' Centre. Between 150 and 200 people are associated with it, not all coming to meetings, but available to provide meals, accommodation and help. People are there as individuals, but very important links have been established with the Afro-Caribbean Club, the Sikh Society, the large local Peace Group and the Ecology Party. In contrast to Cambridge, the political parties have not been significant here. The constituency Labour Party seems to have been very reticent 'but individual branches have been great' (another case yet further down the structure, of the 'lowest orders' not waiting for the higher echelons to move but just getting on with it).

Milton Keynes today supports South Derbyshire and contributes to Cannock, Staffs. From the initial work-place collections, activities have now branched out to become wide-ranging. As elsewhere there have been numerous visits to the coalfield, 'bus-loads of people . . . to see what's going on', and a special fund, started with amazing foresight on September 1, for Christmas. Each pit got £800 and all 380-odd children got a present. A number of local shops came up with quite spectacular donations of food, clothes and toys. More regularly, there are weekly or twice-weekly collections in Milton Keynes, Bletchley, Newport Pagnall and the Open University. All houses in Milton Keynes are being leafleted with requests and then visited each day for collections — 'we get food, clothes, and some abuse'. In total this activity brings in between £800 and £1,000 per week in support of the strike.' 'Milton Keynes must have sent getting in for £30,000 already'.

All this activity, in the cities, in Thatcherland and throughout the country has been far more than simply giving aid to some distant struggle. It has had an integral relation to the strike. A typical comment, this one in fact from Liverpool, runs 'there is a constant flow of information about the strike . . . people feel really involved in the strike . . . it doesn't feel like charity. When miners arrive they are immediately put to work. They feel involved in the organization, part of the same movement, rather than the recipients of charity'. And in Milton Keynes there is a keen awareness that although one of the areas it supports has only a small minority out on strike, aid there is vital for the strike as a whole — 'those few strikers are vital. Keeping them able to stay out stops the NCB being able to say any area is back completely'. So all this organization and support is essential, and the people involved see that; they have a strategic sense of what they are involved in.

Explanations

What has led such diverse groups of people to feel that this strike, however geographically and socially distant, concerns and involves them? There is no single explanation but there are several common themes. They crop up in letters sending donations, in conversations duing street collections, in discussions about why a particular group is giving an unexpected amount of support.

Resonance

A recurring theme is the resonance — sometimes based on sympathy, sometimes on respect, on fond memories or past friendships and family connections — which the miners have with people of every region and nearly every social group. The letters to the national Christmas Appeal express this resonance most vividly.

Many letters recall experiences of the generosity of the miners and their families. A retired social worker writes: 'I worked in the coalfields for seventeen years. I know how quickly miners responded to the appeals for help from those who were less fortunate than themselves. They most certainly do not deserve the abuse that flows from those who know so little about them'. Two pensioners from Herne Bay remember: 'the wonderful friendship shown to us in Derbyshire. For me it was as a lonely soldier during the war, training amongst strange people and far from home. For my wife it meant being offered a refuge for two very young children. We never forgot how our buckets of coal came to us after that'. The strike brought back other memories of the war: 'I am old enough to remember how much the miners responded to all that was asked of them during the war and feel indignant that this be forgotten in hard times now'. Shades of the Earl of Stockton. There were contributions 'with thanks for comradeship of those miners I knew as a Bevin Boy forty years ago', from people who worked on the 'Save the Miners' Fund in London in 1926' and 'on behalf of my late husband, born and bred in Tonypandy — whose family experienced the troops in 1911'.

A Common Cause Against Thatcher

The pent-up hostility expressed towards Thatcher is overwhelming, whatever people's views on the strike itself. 'Anti-Scargill, anti-all violence but above all *anti-Thatcher*. Good luck' says, one Home Counties' contributor to the Christmas Appeal. 'Thank God for the NUM, at least one union has the guts to stand up to her' writes a contributor from Hastings, expressing a view of many who feel that the NUM is taking on a common enemy. 'As a civil servant', another man wrote starkly, 'I feel that your cause is ours, if you fail we all fail'.

Street collectors found a similar sense of common cause. During a first collection in Milton Keynes an unemployed man with a family gave £10 after cashing his giro. 'You can't afford to give that much surely?' said the collector. 'I can't afford not to', was the response.

Support groups from all over report that the people most deprived and battered by Thatcher's policies give with greatest generosity. We've just seen that in Liverpool support is strongest in Toxteth and Kirkby and that in London's Docklands the experience has been similar. One of the organizers describes the response to their weekly collection: 'Pensioners nearly always give, so do the Asian and Afro-Carribean Community and young people. The well-dressed people give less. We didn't do as well as I expected from them'.

In Toxteth, Brixton, Chapeltown in Leeds and other inner-city areas where blacks are in a majority, an understanding of what it is like to live under police occupation lies behind the strong feelings of support. Memories of police aggression are also a factor behind the support of one of the most well paid and traditionally sectional trade-union groups in the country: the Fleet Street Chapels of the NGA. Most of these chapels raise £1–2 per member per week and there are regular exchange visits. Coach loads of NGA members travel up to Bold in St Helens and Birch Coppice in Staffordshire and pit villages in Durham and Northumberland. 'It's Warrington that's produced this response', says Mike Power, Father of an NGA chapel at the Daily Mail, 'the Warrington picket line on the night of November 31st 1983 has changed the NGA. There's a real feeling of solidarity with the miners especially because of the police.' On 31 November NGA members including five hundred from Fleet Street were on the picket line and experienced police violence for themselves.

The reasons for NGA support are typical of the wider pattern of labour movement support, especially in the cities. Where workers have already had their own clashes with the government, whether they've won or lost, whether they have traditionally been left or moderate, there is a groundswell of sympathy and considerable contact between pit villages and work-place support groups. Civil servants for instance were among the most numerous of those who identified themselves in contributing to the national Christmas Appeal. They included a trade unionist from the GCHQ who had refused to resign from the union. He sent £250. In London campaigning groups in schools that came into being to defend the Inner London Education Authority have in many cases become the basis of miners' support groups.

The sense of a common threat is one factor behind the support of women's groups for the strike. A Midlands Women's Aid Centre for instance, wrote with a cheque for the Christmas Appeal: 'We too are suffering at the hands of the Tory Government. Next year our Urban Aid grant will be halved, the following year none at all. We fully support your struggle'.

Finding Allies

But the wholehearted and enthusiastic involvement of all kinds of women's groups, Labour Party women's sections, women's peace groups, and childcare campaigns, in the industrial action of a notoriously male-chauvanist union is not based just on anti-Thatcherism. Their involvement has been inspired by the power and confidence of the women in the mining communities.

The response of the Enfield women's peace group in London sums it up: 'We were inspired by the women. We wanted to show them that they weren't alone, that we need each other. Our links with the women in Cannock have helped to overcome our isolation and sense of powerlessness'. The involvement of the women had helped people outside the coalfields to understand the community issues at stake.

The people who set up the Durham-Docklands support group illustrate this. Eddie Corbett explains: 'Before I met the women (from Durham) I'd felt sympathetic to the miners but I didn't really want to be involved. I saw them collecting outside tube stations and thought of them just as trade unionists. After hearing the women and their stories of hardship and the police I understood it was families and communities at stake.' It was then that he and the other made the connection between their fight for democratic control over their community against a non-elected government quango, the London Docklands Development Corporation and the miners' defence of their communities against the government-appointed

NCB. 'They are fighting the same regime, the same undemocratic process as we are.'

Other groups which have made positive links include the environmental movement, the peace movement and the anti-nuclear movement. In Milton Keynes for instance the Ecology Party is very active. They quickly saw the links between the strike, the nuclear issue, the open-cast mining which they are against for environmental reasons. In the same town the large peace group, which itself involves a broad coalition, has put over the miners' case in several meetings. 'Mines not Missiles' is now a common theme at rallies organized by CND and miners' support groups. Miners' support meetings increasingly reflect these and other links and the speakers most in demand are those who make the connections. Tony Benn has done nearly three hundred miners' support meetings, most of them packed to overflowing, since the Chesterfield by-election. From the figures we have, he must have addressed over two hundred thousand people. Platforms often include speakers from other campaigns and these multi-purpose platforms are not only speaking to the converted. People new to political activity, though often involved in local community issues, have been turning up and getting involved. At a rally of nine hundred in Liverpool, three hundred new people signed up to become involved and twenty-five per cent of these are now active in their local support group.

Political Catalysts

These are some elements, then, of an explanation for the extra-ordinarily widespread support which exists for the miners, behind the media picture of an isolated and sectorial strike. But an adequate explanation must include the driving forces behind the initial formation of the larger support groups. In most cases, town or city-wide support groups have been initiated by trades councils or local Labour Parties, with socialists outside the Labour Party providing important support. The impetus to create support groups was more than trade-union solidarity. Memories of the 1972 and 1974 miners' strikes provide a powerful image, a source of great expectations. When the miners take action, governments fall. At the beginning there was a strong sense of the miners' power to break Thatcher's grip. It was not that people wanted to leave it to the miners; it was rather a feeling that Thatcher would find it difficult if another front was opened up, especially in the coalfields. In the cities, campaigning alliances were already forming to fight abolition and rate-capping. There was a feeling that at last a trade-union battalion, the most militant, had gone into action. As the strike developed and the other big battalions held back, not so big now, as the women became an organized force and the strike increasingly became a strike about communities, the significance of the support groups became clearer. It seemed increasingly that their work was crucial to the miners' power and their chances of success. Personal links and the adoption of pits created a momentum of their own. A new, or at least more confident, do it yourself politics flourished out of necessity.

Forms of Organization

That phrase 'out of necessity' comes up again and again as people explain the work of their support groups. It helps to explain the form that the support movement takes. Out of necessity, the support movement has started from existing organizations and resources. Picking up whatever in the old structures suited their urgent purpose. They grew from whatever organizations could be most rapidly geared into action, from networks of friends, to tightly organized NGA chapels. They used whatever resources were available from church halls to county halls, from the Labour Party's duplicator to the WRP's newsletter. Out of necessity the initial organizations have moved outwards to extend support.

In doing so they have often changed themselves. The NGA for instance, normally a rather exclusive organization, has helped to co-ordinate and extend a miners' support group in small offices and work-places throughout the City. Women who come together for a women's canvass in the Chesterfield by-election became the Chesterfield Women's Action Group to support the miners. In January it organized a women's march through all the nearby pit villages.

Co-ordination

In most towns and cities there are miners' support groups that play a co-ordinating role, organizing big functions, rallies, concerts, etc. In the larger cities the co-ordinating meetings also play an important role in sorting out some of the problems which arise within groups, between groups and in relations with strike centres. As we have already said these groups have usually been initiated through the local Labour Party or trades councils. All left parties are normally involved, though the Socialist Workers Party was a latecomer to the support groups, and initially chose its own forms of direct support for the strikers. Everyone comments on the unique degree of co-operation between political groups. On at least one occasion it has gone so far as discussing with each other whether or not to sell their papers during street collections and deciding against! In addition to city-wide support groups there is an immense variety of smaller community and work-place groups which spring from groups of friends, from collections by individuals and from visits from miners themselves. The Garston Miners' Support Group is a good example of a community group, though most of its members also organize regular collections at work. It started with a group of friends who had worked together on other issues.

One of its members describes its organization: 'There are no regulations in the group. GMSG doesn't have standing orders. No bureaucracy, just straightforward action to help the section of the class that had the guts to challenge the rich. No command structure, no leaders, just a grouping of socialists that did what it could. However, there was a need for a co-ordinator that kept the energy of the group ticking over. That fell to Eileen and Mark.'

Twinning and the Distribution of Food

Connections of personal friendship, political commitment, and material sustenance between the support groups and the pits are the energy supply of the support movement as much as the life-blood of the strike.

Take Cambridge for instance. They've organized holidays for miners' families; there was a massive exercise at Christmas with, amongst much else, an individually chosen present and collection of stocking-fillers for each child (over two hundred of them); there's at least one trip a week from Cambridge to Notts, and there have been long and short visits, both ways. 'We've had speakers down from them and spoken ourselves up there. We've picketed, had women pickets, worked in the kitchens, gone to the Cash and Carry, looked after the children, joined in parties, pub sessions and gigs'.

Sometimes the connections are called 'twinning' but the associations are more flexible and varied than such a one-to-one relationship implies. At the beginning of the strike there were problems when groups adopted the pit with which they first had contact — often through visiting miners. Some pits received more money than others. Such problems remain, but there is a growing bush telegraph and an acute awareness of the need to achieve an equitable distribution. The Milton Keynes Support Group for instance now supports South Derbyshire and contributes to Cannock in Staffs. But this has not always been so. The story behind it tells a lot about the sensitivity and flexibility of the 'alternative distribution systems' which have developed during the strike. Milton Keynes is in the South East Region of the TUC and its money was originally sent off along the 'normal channels' of organization to the centre, and to Kent (also SERTUC). It soon became apparent, however, that Kent was getting a lot of support, especially from London, so it was decided to adopt pits in Leicestershire. This lasted for about six months until Leicestershire, too, began getting more from its local towns. So Leicestershire suggested Staffordshire and South Derbyshire with whom they had had close relations, and who were having a rough time. This carefully thought out allocation of aid is vital for the strike.

Many support groups, like Garston, share funds between pits. Or, like the Durham–Docklands support group, they contribute to a regional co-ordinating centre. *Socialist Worker* carries a list of strike kitchens in need. *Labour Briefing* lists pits which are not yet twinned. In the mining communities themselves the womens' support groups have become well organized. They have had to — managing hundreds of pounds each week, feeding over three hundred people every day. They co-ordinate regionally and do their best to ensure that funds and provisions reach areas of need. In South Wales, there is a particularly co-ordinated multi-level system, providing channels of support (from urban and rural areas of Wales, from England and from international sources to the coalfields).

Preaching to the Unconverted

Just as groups have improvised to find the best way of distributing the support, so they have tried all kinds of ingenious ways of collecting funds and putting across their arguments. Individuals have been buying and selling British Telecom shares and sending the proceeds to the Christmas Appeal. Greenham Women have marched from pit heads to nuclear power stations, giving out leaflets and holding meetings on the way to make the connection between the case against nuclear power and the miners' demands. The most impressive thing about this aspect of the work of the support groups is the emphasis on reaching out to the uncommitted. It is as if all the heart-searching about the left being stuck in a ghetto, shop-floor leaders being out of touch with their members and so on, has produced an almost evangelical commitment to win support on the street, in the pubs, on the shop floor and in door to door collections. In Kirkby for instance the support group has leafletted each house at least three times and visited at least once. Few election campaigns could better that! Its political importance is that arguments are reaching people, independently of the media.

The forms of organization in the support movement, and in the mining communities are an extraordinary combination of traditional labour-movement structures with the open, campaigning styles of CND and the women's movement. The women in the mining communities have played perhaps a leading role in inspiring the support movement. And their relationship with the NUM nationally as well as locally sets the example for this combination. In a sense their organization and its importance is sustaining the strike and extending support has given a new legitimacy to the demands of women outside the coalfields for real power within labour-movement organizations. A recent national meeting of Women Against Pit Closures was symbolic. There they were sitting around the board table in the reserved seats of the NUM executive. Ann Lilburn, a grandmother from Whittle, Northumberland, sat in the seat reserved for A. Scargill and Katherine Slater, a miners' wife from Barnsley in the seat for P. Heathfield. They were discussing the distribution of £1–2 million. Their treasurer, Jean McCrindle, has handled nearly £1 million this year, in her spare time. At one point Arthur Scargill in person put his head round the door smiling benignly, but no-one really noticed.

Conclusions

Whatever the outcome of the strike, labour movement politics will never be the same again. There will no doubt be attempts to block, if not stamp out, the new initiatives that cut across so many traditional procedures and hierarchies. It will be a struggle to consolidate and develop the improvised democracy produced inside the coalfields and beyond, by the strike.

But the pressures to continue the process of change will be strong.

Through the strike and the support movement many people new to political involvement have become experienced, effective speakers, expert organizers and confident socialists. A lot has been learned. Amongst these new activities a gut anti-Thatcherism has begun to be more precisely articulated to win a positive belief in another way of organizing society.

This is partly the result of learning about the problems of other groups. Miners, for instance, learned through their visits to the cities of the problems of racism. As one Nottingham miner put it 'I'd never been racist, I don't think, but I'd never really understood it before.' Support groups in the rural south learnt from the solidarity and collectivism of the mining areas, from 'the steadfastness and sheer courage up there,' as one of the Cambridge group told us. Travelling and exchange visits across the country are an important source of power. Usually it is only the leadership that has an over-view of what is going on. Moreover these visits help create unity at the base, across the old structures. They have also created connections between different, previously quite separate, sections of the working class; cleaners fighting privatization in London speaking on one platform at miners' meetings, miners from Nottingham joining the picket line at Addenbrooks Hospital in Cambridge; miners promising to join the people of Docklands in action to stop a business-men's airport. Finally, there has been a learning of an immensely practical sort; learning to manage thousands of pounds on behalf of hundreds of pepople; facing up to the real problems of building an alternative welfare system, a system of distribution according to need. Such experience leaves more than memory.

The support groups we have talked to in most detail already have plans for the future. In Cambridge, they want to find a way of consolidating the network into a more permanent organization after the strike is over. In Liverpool they feel they have established a strong organization which they will need again and won't let col-lapse. In Milton Keynes they are already planning a 'trade-union month' as part of an attempt to strengthen the unions there.

One of the most politically decisive experiences of many who have been part of the support movement is that they have tried the traditional hierarchies and leadership of the labour movement and found them severely wanting. The lack of political leadership has been most important. It has been the failure of some of the Labour Party's Parliamentary leaders to get across the economic and social arguments for the mining communities which has created the vacuum that the support groups are trying to fill. Even now the parliamentary leadership seems to be making little attempt to give effective national backing to the support movement or even draw media attention to its size and scope.

But instead of wasting time passing resolutions calling on the leadership to do the things that will never materialize, people in the localities have, on the whole, just got on with it. This has not only been on a local basis but also nationally. A conference attended by over 1,500 support groups was held in December at Camden Town Hall. This confidence amongst the support groups to take the initiative in their own hands, rather than simply making calls on the leadership, sets an important precedent for the future.

In much of their work many support groups illustrate in practice the kind of movement we need to build in order to achieve socialism: A commitment to change through building up democratic power at the base, in the factories and in the communities; a breaking down of the traditional, inhibiting boundary between politics and trade unionism; a sense of local strength and identity which at the same time is not parochial; a commitment to a non-sectarian but principled form of unity, in which different political tendencies are respected and work together; an emphasis on reaching out, a confidence that radical demands can be popular if they are argued for.

It would be wrong to pretend that all this has happened without problems. In all this activity there have of course been tensions; tensions between different political perspectives and groups, conflicts between the new-found strength of women and the power-bases previously established as male, suspicions of the white left on the part of some black groups. But constructing links between groups, between areas, between issues can never be achieved without tensions. There are real contradictions between the multiple issues which have become linked to the support network during the strike and no genuine democratic 'alliance' could ever be built without recognizing and facing up to them. In this context the strength of the support networks is precisely that 'alliances' have been built in the course of real, day-to-day, political action. These are not 'links' established simply by writing out lists of policies, nor are they a 'common programme' negotiated between party leaders.

We are not claiming the world. But nonetheless something radically different has emerged out of a movement in support of what was seen as an 'old' struggle. Many thought this impossible. They have argued that the left must move with the times — that 'old-fashioned' class struggles are doomed to isolation, without resonance or relevance to present-day socialist policies. Behind this argument is an equation of class politics, on the one hand, and the existing institutions of the labour movement on the other. To make such an equation leads to an incorrect assessment of the political choice before us, as one between industrial muscle and the new social movements. The existing institutions of labour *are* old fashioned and sectional. But what the miners' strike has shown is that these institutions can be superseded and challenged without abandoning class politics. It has shown that it is not a question of *either* industrial action *or* the new social movements, nor is it one of just adding the two together. What is important is a recognition of a mutual dependence and a new openness to influence, of the one upon the other. What this strike has demonstrated is a different direction for class politics. New institutions can be built through which 'class politics' can be seen as more than simply industrial militancy plus parliamentary representation.

In this article we have written mainly as reporters of an aspect of the strike which has been almost completely ignored outside the left press. We have interviewed people throughout the country about their support activity but have focused on four groups in particular. We would like to thank the following for their assistance although none of them are responsible for our political interpretations: Tony Benn, Kate Bennett, John and Joan Bohanna, Eddie Corbett, Bill Dewsbury, Vic Graves, Doreen Humber, Dave Hailwood, Liz Knight, Alison New, Kevin Machin, Bernard Regan, Mike Power, Liane Philips.

9

We'll Be Here Right to the End . . . and After

Women in the Miners' Strike

Loretta Loach

'There is no "beginning" of feminism in the sense that there is no beginning to defiance in women. But there is a beginning of feminist possibility — even before it is conceived as such. Female resistance has taken several historical shapes.''

It would be quite wrong to say that the movement of women in the miners' strike was a feminist one. Why ever would it have been? Pit villages embrace a tightly knit community in which the focus on men and masculinity is more pronounced than most. Apart from the fact that male strength is held in high esteem, the cultural activity of the community revolves predominantly around men. The actions of the women in the dispute were motivated by very direct and immediate needs; overwhelmingly the need to defend their livelihoods and their communities. Nevertheless, the work they undertook and often the way in which they organized came from their specific situation as women. From it they drew a strength and courage which made them unshrinking in their determination, fearless in the face of the police and bolder in relation to their men folk.

The movement of Women Against Pit Closures did not owe its existence to the womens' liberation movement. Yet some of the challenges it has made and some of the new consciousness that has been created could not have occurred without the influence of feminism. In turn, the movement has tested some of the problems that have preoccupied feminists since the mid-1970s. Through the links that have been established a learning process has taken place. It is an uneven and contradictory process, one that has been mutually beneficial to working-class women and middle-class feminists.

When the miners' strike began the movement that had made the single most imaginative and audacious challenge to the policies of the government was already entering its third year. The Greenham Common peace women had appeared on television screens throughout Europe and America and had become a thorn in the side of the Defence Ministry. The moral of their message — which the sympathetic media identified with all things motherly — popularized the issue of peace and won the hearts and minds of millions. The theories and experiences of a decade of feminism were brought to bear on the women's peace movement influencing its form and direction. What the movement lacked in material strength and effectiveness was compensated for by its powerful emotional appeal to public opinion and the left. This picture of women's self-activity became a regular reference point for the more progressive sections of the labour movement and perhaps, even before direct links were established, an inspiration to the women in the mining communities.

The most important industrial dispute of the 1980s also developed against a background of intense self-scrutiny on the left. The apparent shifts and changes in the social and economic structure of the country and the second term of Thatcherism starkly posed the question: Where did we go wrong? Different strands within the socialist movement competed to define our ills and to develop a strategy to overcome them. Feminism featured as a small component in this important debate. It demanded a change of policies and more open, democratic forms of organization better able to present a popular political alternative both to Thatcherism and Labourism. The feminist demands made good economic and political sense yet, for the most part, 'the left has consistently ignored, marginalized or rendered irrelevant feminist arguments'.[2]

The response of the left to the women's involvement in the miners' strike both proved many of these criticisms of the socialist movement and at the same time provided the force and momentum through which the potential for change would emerge. If the argument against feminism is that class oppression is paramount what better challenge could there be but from working–class women who not only identified with the needs and requirements of their class and community, but who through personal struggle had glimpsed some of the oppression they feel in relation to men.

Lorraine Bowler from Barnsley Women's Action Group expressed some of these problems in her speech to a mass rally in Barnsley Civic Hall. The hundreds of women who had gathered could identify with most if not all that she was saying: 'At the beginning of the strike women from the Barnsley group wanted to go picketing and we were told that it was a bad enough job organizing the men. All I can say to that is women do not need anyone to organize them. They can organize themselves. The proof of that is shown in this hall today.

'I'm sure that for some or most of the women here today it is the same in their homes as it has been in mine over the weeks. There are arguments now as to whose turn it is to go on a demonstration or picket, and whose turn it is to babysit. Talk about job sharing! We've seen it at its best over the past eight or nine weeks.

'In this country we aren't just separated as a class. We are separated as men and women. We, as women, have not often been encouraged to be involved actively in trade unions and organizing. Organization has always been seen as an area belonging to men. We are seen to be the domesticated element of a family. This for too many years has been the role expected of us. I have seen change coming for years and the last few weeks has seen it at its best.'³

The trade-union and Labour leaders of the left have cultivated the heroines of the miners' strike with a sentimental passion that is both endearing and frustrating. Their soulful proclamations on the women's strength and energy are consistently undermined by the reality of a socialist movement based on sexist assumptions and informed by sexist practices. It is these features of left-wing organizations which render the qualities and contributions of women inessential, irrelevant and unimportant to the dominant political process.

It will not be because women were equal with men that their struggle in the 1984 miners' strike will never be obscured or forgotten. It will be because as women they were visible and active in their own right, separately and apart from men and not simply tagging along behind them. The following interview demonstrates this point. It is a celebration of just two women who surfaced in the strike and showed a capacity for organizing that offended the pride of many a miner.

Bobby and Sue come from a small pit village called Bentley in South Yorkshire. They are sisters and their family has been part of the mining community for over a hundred years. The decisions that affect their lives and those of other working-class communities are remote from them. 'It happens down in London,' said Sue, the younger of the two. 'It were nothing to do with us. We imagined that people in London thought we were still in clogs and flat caps. We're northerners, you're southerners. When you had snow down in London we'd say "well they've got everything else, they may as well have that as well." Before, we didn't used to care two sods what

Margaret Thatcher were doin' with oil or price of oil, now we do because it affects us.' 'Put it this way' says Bobby carefully 'you read more and you're more wary of what you read. At one time I didn't care about coal, I were a wife, those things didn't concern me, but now we're taking some of those things on.'

Until the moves to safeguard their livelihoods, Bobby and Sue have never been involved in anything even distantly political. Their action, like those of other women in the coalfields, grew out of the practical needs of the community, but through their energy and initiative they and the other women who make up Bentley Women's Action Group have created a profound and unprecedented change in the essentially male culture of the mining community. 'Now when we're in pub we sit with the men and join in instead of chatting about kids and the home and things. We can sit with 'em and talk about pit. We want to know about things, about what's happening in the union.' 'Some mornings I've been picketing before him and I've come home and he's done the housework.' 'I've always thought well, men do thinking. But I speak my mind now more than I've ever done. I've always been outspoken but I've never pushed myself.'

The women are now central in the community, they have extended their influence to every area of village life, even the sacred male institution of Sunday cricket has been brought within their remit. 'By weekend we've no money left out of Social and we don't do meals in kitchen, that's the time when you can get depressed. So we've organized games on Sunday. Women play men at cricket and rounders.' How have the men responded to that? 'You know, you'd think we were playing test cricket at Lords. They take it so seriously, you know, "we'll show them women". ' 'One day,' Sue said imitating them, 'they said "if there's any cheating we're not playing anymore." They even make us mark it officially on sheet — Bentley Women's Action Group versus Bentley pickets. They made us wear bloody pads and they couldn't stand it if a women hit a good one.'

How did it all Start?

'We went on a rally for Women Against Pit Closures and said if anyone is interested in setting up a kitchen let's get in contact with one another. Our first meeting were about five weeks into strike. We thought kitchens were a good idea because we women could then play a part and keep everybody together. We'd be able to feed everybody so we could keep fighting against pit closures, but we didn't expect it to last as long as this. At first you only got men in for food, women never came, they thought it were only for men, now they come, and kids. Everybody sits in with everybody, women don't just sit together. We talk about everything: picketing, what's been happening — they should have strike headquarters down at kitchen because everybody's there.'

When I arrived at Bentley pavilion just before lunch-time the kitchen was just preparing to dish up. There were about five women and two men in there, one being a retired chef who offers his services freely in support of the strike. Do men help? 'They do come in and wash up for us', said Bobby. 'If we're busy they'll muck in. They'll do shoppin' and sweep floor. Before if they'd been asked to do those things they'd have said "who she bloody talking to", now they do it — don't get me wrong, you can't change 'em in twenty-two weeks but they do it.'

But getting men to help seems to them undignified and compromising. When the group was first set up, the union offered them fifty pounds. The women chose to regard it as a loan saying 'we want to be self-supporting we don't want nowt to do with NUM. We wanted our own control. Can you imagine having men, they'd say "I think you can do it like this or you can just have this", we didn't want none of that. We wanted to have money, we wanted to have control of the place. At first we said let them go picketing, we'll feed 'em all, we don't need them, we'll do it ourselves. We've made every decision as far as running the thing is concerned.'

Whilst wishing to be independent of men they did not rest content with the arduous labour of 'women's work' in the kitchen. They wanted more involvement in the dispute, they wanted to go picketing and initially they were met with stubborn resistance. 'When they wouldn't let us go picketing we all got together and played hell with the union. The treasurer of the union locally wasn't keen at first and he said we weren't on books anymore' (that means you are not covered by the NUM if you are arrested) 'but that were just a threat.' Bobby laughs. 'They hate to think that women's getting top dog of 'em.'

Bobby is the sort of woman who believes things can only be achieved if you contribute every bit of yourself to the fight. It's not a position, that's just the way she is, pushed strongly and powerfully by the emotional waves of the strike. The first time she went picketing was a mass picket at Harworth colliery. 'I was petrified. I'd never seen so many police, you just don't in a little village like this. It were a weird feelin'. Then, you only have to see one scab and police talking into their machines and down the line goes the whisper, "They're coming" and you just erupt. There was no stoppin' me, I broke through and got over the other side of the road because it was near scabs. At first they wouldn't let me through, it was too dangerous, but I said I'd catch a bus round there if they didn't. First time on a picket line and I turned two blokes back. I've told 'im', she said, nodding in the direction of her husband, 'If you'd have let women go picketing in the beginning you'd have got through to them long ago.'

'Have you ever seen a woman on a picket line when you watch TV?' asked Sue, who now takes it in turns with her husband to go picketing, so one of them can look after their two young children. 'It never shows women on a picket line, the camera seems to stop dead at women. If the Notts women saw Yorkshire women on a picket line they'd think differently about the strike. When Anne Scargill got arrested the cameras went mad. Don't get me wrong, I think she does a wonderful job, but there's plenty of ordinary women doing the same but the telly ignores them.'

Standing Up to the Men

Through their activity, the women have experienced the more general oppression they feel in relation to men, though they would not refer to it as such. 'We've stood up for ourselves. We've stood up to them. Like, we say we're going to London. At first it were "can we go to London," we used to think that we should give a few days notice; break it to them gently and get housework and washing done. Now sometimes you get a phone call two hours before you've got to go and we just drop everything and it's "I'm off to London." ' The action group is a place where, apart from business, the women exchange stories about the men's reaction to what they are doing. The example they give to each other provides the momentum and opportunity to overcome some of the traditional passivity and timidity in the home. One woman bargained with her husband to be allowed to go to London for a rally. She exchanged sex for his permission. When she mentioned this to some of the women in the group she said 'I thought, what the hell am I giving in to him for', recognizing what she was doing in order to keep him quiet. In the beginning they were asking. Now they are just doing. 'If it's an issue we're fighting on' said Sue 'If the husbands say no the women come back and tell us and we'll get on to them and say "what do you bloody mean no". There'll be no comeback because he knows it would come straight back to the group. When we first met in a pub it were "Oh he'll not let me go to pub" and we'd say, ask him, and if he said no we'd be on to him.'

The Bentley Women's Action Group, and no doubt others like it, has rivalled the union as the key organizing vehicle in the community. The implications of this for women hardly need emphasizing. Out of the material need to provide food their energy has been released and they have drawn strength from the powerful role they now play. Through their impulse, challenges are being made to myths and assumptions cherished for centuries in the mining community. Mr Scargill may walk on water but he does so because unknown to him, the imagination and initiative of women is providing the scope and thrust of this rebellion. 'Margaret Thatcher didn't bargain for us. Can you imagine what would happen to strike if Kitchen fell through — they're depending on us.'

'I think women wanted a say before about coal issue, about strike. But nobody has ever let them, nobody has ever, ever wanted to listen. The NUM being all men; they wouldn't listen, no one is ever allowed near when there's a meeting, even kids aren't allowed near. Keith took Neil, he's only ten, when I were in London. They turned him out. They wouldn't speak in front of a non-NUM member and everyone looked round wondering who they were referring to.' 'You see' said Bobby 'we're trying to change all this not just in Bentley.' The women believe they should be allowed in union meetings when they are discussing business which concerns them. 'This strike has been on for twenty-four weeks and we've done everything the men have, we've done more, we've done kitchens, speaking, rallying, picketing, the only thing we haven't done is go down pit and we intend to do that when the strike is over.'

Men's Jealousy

Are some of the men jealous of the trips to London, the meetings, the sheer excitement of being active? Bobby's husband has been in the NUM for twenty-two years and he said to her 'you've done more mouthing in twenty-two weeks than I've done ever, the whole time I've been in the union.' Sue said, 'they'd never in their wildest dreams have imagined that we would be where we are today. They thought we'd be saying "we've got to have help." They make remarks, like when we got union mini-bus to go to Nottingham they said "bloody marvellous they can get mini-bus when they want." And if we had committee meeting in pub we'd stay for a drink after, that niggled them at first. When we got to kitchens the day after we'd have conflab, "owt said last night when you got home? were it alright?" "Aye, nowt mentioned." A lot of the men have gone for women's action groups but we're not scared, we've got gobs, we'll use 'em.'

Unsurprisingly, hesitation and lack of confidence characterized the early days of women's involvement in the strike and this was felt as much in relation to 'educated' women in London as it was to men. 'When I first went to London' said Bobby 'I expected to be laughed at, the way I spoke, the way I am, but I made some friends and that gives you more guts to do what you're doing. It's not really me, speaking in public, I get nervous but I think, well we are somebody and we've got to do it. If more women could see and hear women such as me who's not had a right good education they'd see they could do it and we'd get on much better.' Sue, the more businesslike one of the two, normally speaks at union meetings. 'I make notes beforehand. I don't go into great detail. I say what I've got to say and that's it.' She mentions proudly her sister's capacity to rouse an audience. 'She makes 'em cry. I mean, she jumps around from one thing to another but it's all her, from her heart, it's truth.'

When they visited women's groups in London the Greek Cypriot women met them with a table of food, fifty pounds donation and the warmth and understanding of another community who had faced strife. Maria, one of the workers, said 'Our community is very sensitive to issues like these, they have a long history of struggle, and they relate to it straight away.' Bobby thanked them, shook all their hands and embraced them, their kindness had moved her to tears.

Through the experience of the Bentley women the language of politics has woven its way, giving shape and meaning to the wealth of things they are encountering. Do terms like sexism have any meaning for you? They paused. 'Oh you mean men slaggin' off women? Yes, they'd shout things at women on picket lines and we'd go up and say "we're not here for stuff like that." It makes 'em think.' Sue believes that one of the reasons women have had the confidence to speak out is because of Greenham Common. 'It was only women that made peace camps, it was the women that made a stand for peace. I know men agree with it but it took women to get up off their arses and do something before things moved.' Bobby mentioned a rally where 'even the men' gave a standing ovation to a woman from Greenham. 'They're brilliant those women!'

'The line up here was that they were scruffy lesbians and there were lesbians in one camp and junkies in another. I know they do that, I know they do have lesbians there, but they're fighting for a cause. I could see that the people shouldn't slag 'em off for what they do.'

I'm Not a Feminist but . . .

'I'm not a feminist,' said Sue 'I don't know though, I've got feminist views on some things, I read *Spare Rib*, I agree with some of it but I'm not what yous are, you're too feminist you are, but when they appeal to you' she gives an example 'like when police called you (Bobby) a fucking lesbian on the picket lines you were saying "I was scared, did he think I was?" ' Bobby joins in, 'when we talked about it with these feminists they said, "why be scared, there's nowt to be ashamed of" and they put their point to us and it were logical, so I said to young Anne, "your place or mine!" ' Sue interrupted, 'But that's makin' a mockery of lesbians!' 'We weren't though' replied Bobby.

'When Maggie Thatcher came to power a lot of it were to do with women. I think we thought, great, woman rulin' country, it'll be money in pockets and for women high-up in the country with good jobs, educated women, it was. She said we could buy our council houses but she conned us, she wanted us to have a mortgage so we would be frightened. You know, "give 'em everything they want and they'll not come out on strike". Before we'd have never talked politics or religion now I'd have my say on both.'

The women have sustained their organizing effort for over six months. When they speak of the group they refer to the friendship and bond that has grown between them. 'We really want to stick together and we've said that after the strike we can't let it go, and when we meet we always say don't forget it's our fight and we'll be here right to the end and after it. We no longer stand behind men, we stand with them.' It has given them all confidence. 'Linda who lives up the road, we took her to London and she hardly opened her mouth. She does now. If she hears anyone pullin' us down she'll stand up to 'em. Her mam has said, "God, this has really brought you out of your shell." We'd have all cracked up if we'd not had the group.' Such a long dispute like this places an immense strain on the women and their relationships. Managing on social security, worrying about feeding and clothing a family, arrears on HP payments can all prove too much. 'One woman in the group split up from her husband, she'd got three little kids and it got her down, she's gone home to her mam.' For the most part, the existence of the group lessens the feelings of anxiety and isolation that all of the women feel. By sharing day to day problems some of the pressure is relieved. Have things changed in the home at all? 'Yes, Kit' (Bobby's husband) 'has to do more. This morning I thought, I can't shop I'm too tired, and before I knew it he'd looked to see what was needed and gone. Any other time it would have been me saying, "go for a loaf duck." It's the same if we go to one of our houses for meetings, none of us make tea we say to 'em "put kettle on love".' Do you think that after the strike the changes that have taken place will go back? 'I don't think any of us will alow that, it will be job share. The women have had a good thing, they'll not go back to it, especially the young lasses.'

But this is not a normal time for the people of Bentley. It is an exceptional period of industrial and social militancy. Even if the women have the confidence and energy to continue organizing after the strike, their bargaining power in relation to men will no doubt diminish. Being politically involved in matters relating to the men is one thing but when it comes to issues independent of them will they be so tolerant?

Nevertheless, things in the coalfields of Britain will never be as they were prior to the strike. The working-class women in these communities have, through intense personal struggle, realized some of their strength and potential. 'We can't lose this close bond. Instead of asking a bloke we have asked each other. It's brilliant. W've fought for this. After, we might join the Labour Party and form a women's section. I've told yer we'll be here right to the end and after.'

Whilst the women I met in Bentley would not formally identify with the language of feminism the more they spoke about their lives the clearer it became that their experiences were not in contradiction with much that 'educated' London women had discussed with them. Perhaps if their activity survives the strike, whatever the outcome, and feminist influence prevails these women may develop an explanation for their own specific world, relevant to their needs and aspirations, that will expand the scope and broaden the appeal of feminism and socialism alike, and provide the challenge to this government that is urgently required.

Notes

1. S. Rowbotham, *Women, Resistance and Revolution*, Harmondsworth, 1972.
2. K. Myers quoting Tricia Davies, 'Viewpoint', *Marxism Today*, March 1984.
3. Printed in full in Barnsley Women, *Women Against Pit Closures*, Barnsley, 1984.

Donations and Messages of support to: Bentley Women's Action Group, 53 Briar Road, Armthorpe, Doncaster. National Women Against Pit Closures Group, c/o NUM St James House, Vicar Lane, Sheffield.

This is an expanded version of an article which first appeared in *Spare Rib*, no 147, October 1984.

10

'Where's Ramsay MacKinnock?'
Labour Leadership and the Miners

David Howell

The question "Where's Ramsay MacKinnock?" was posed on a banner at a rally of South Wales Miners in Aberavon on 13 November 1984. The underlying assumption makes perhaps the harshest charge that can be levelled at a Labour Party leader — an accusation which was expanded in the Aberavon Rally post-mortem by Kim Howells, Research Officer to the South Wales NUM: 'It ill-becomes Neil Kinnock to forget what the dispute is about. South Wales miners note that he is very ready to condemn retaliation by pickets to police provocation, but is far less willing to involve himself in arguing the case for the continuation of mining in places like South Wales.'[1] Ironically, Ramsay MacDonald was MP for Aberavon at the time of the 1926 dispute. As a venue for a demonstration of strikers' anger in 1984, it provokes fundamental questions about the relationship between Labour leaders and industrial action.

There are two simple responses to such questions. One simply asserts that in 1984, as in 1926, there is abundant evidence of the bankruptcy of Labourism squeezed between workers engaged in a fundamental, albeit defensive, struggle, and a class-conscious government. Such an automatic verdict is breathtaking in its insensitivity towards the industrial and political changes of the last sixty years, a denunciation that utilizes timeless categories. The argument moves easily towards its inexorable conclusion.

Alternatively, there is the curt response that the parallel is absurd. Kinnock is emphatically not another MacDonald. The defence has been made for every Labour leader since 1931. It points to a significant sentiment insofar as all subsequent leaders have fought shy of another fundamental split. But the core of MacDonald's political strategy should not be identified too closely with the events of 1931. The actions of Wilson and Callaghan have forcibly demonstrated that subsequent Labour leaders have shared some of MacDonald's basic assumptions without such common ground leading to their quitting the party. They too have had their defenders against any charge of 'MacDonaldism' — but the validity of such defence must rest, in part, on the precise nature of the charge. The question on the banner raises complex issues; easy verdicts should be avoided. An adequate analysis requires a comparison of 1926 and 1984.

The miners

In one obvious sense, a coal dispute in 1926 was a more significant event. There were over a million miners then compared with approximately 180,000 in 1984. South Wales, the radical vanguard of the Miners' Federation, had about 200,000 miners in 1926; still demonstrating its traditional solidarity today, the number is little over ten per cent of the old figure. Besides this diminishing industrial significance, the old stereotypes of the mining community, industrial homogeneity and solidarity are of diminishing relevance. Massive closure programmes have often ruptured the umbilical cord between the pit and the community. The solidarity of miners — 1984 style — is not a timeless quality inherited readily from past battles. It has had to be constructed, often in the face of forbidding difficulties.

But a significant parallel does stand out against this kaleidescope of changes. The issues at stake in both disputes involved much more than the future of the coal industry. The complex Glaswegian politician John Wheatley expressed this judgement forcibly in 1926, as he condemned the weakness of many of Labour's most prominent figures: 'The miners are fighting alone but they are fighting the battle of the whole nation. If they lose, we all lose.'[2] Then, the miners stood out against the doctrine that the export trade demand required wage reductions. Moreover '1926' marked the last battle in a series of confrontations that had dominated industrial relations since 1910. In 1984, the battle raised issues fundamental to Thatcher's Britain — employment, the 'rights' of management, and above all responses to that harsh process that is turning large tracts of Britain into a separate country where the age of retirement is often sixteen. And again, there is the longer perspective: for the Government, 1984 could count as a second leg to 1972 and 1974. This time, as in 1926, the Government played on its own ground.

One reason for the unfavourable terrain in 1984 has been the issue. The solidarity achieved in 1972 and 1974 over a national wage demand has been eroded, firstly through the introduction of area productivity schemes, and then by the nature of the closure issue. Among the many propagated in recent months, there exist few more misleading stereotypes than the claim that miners' disputes have always been notable for their solidarity, and that the recent actions of some NUM officials have damaged this resource. But '1972' and '1974' were, arguably, exceptional. In 1926, the issue was again potentially divisive. The threatened shift to District Agreements indicated draconian reductions in exporting coalfields such as Durham and South Wales, but in Derbyshire, Nottinghamshire and other Midlands Districts, the likely wage cuts often seemed small. In both disputes, it was in the latter coalfields that the union's strategy had its weakest point. It was there in 1926 that the return to work began in the late summer. The problem of solidarity was reflected in the loose structure of the Miners' Federation; it still leaves its mark on the organization and actions of the NUM. Solidarity within a mining community has been achieved frequently; solidarity between coalfields has often been far more problematic. 1926 and 1984 stand as sombre monuments to this.

The problem of mobilizing the NUM membership over the issue of pit closures was highlighted in the argument over the absence of a national ballot. It was an issue in which Labour parliamentarians largely accepted the orthodoxy that such an individual ballot counted as the ultimate in democratic procedures. Accordingly they not only marginalized other participatory forms of decision-making but also failed to focus on a fundamental problem of democratic theory. Whilst it may be argued that a national ballot would be appropriate on an issue that affected all participants equally — a national wage demand, for example — it is less obviously appropriate for dealing with so divisive an issue as pit closures. In such cases, the impact may be seen not simply as uneven, but as bleak for some while advantageous for others. The basic argument has been heard before. In June 1926, a Derbyshire coalowner wrote to *The Times*: 'If the ballot were secret, taken in a constitutional manner, the men would go back to work immediately . . . Neither Mr Smith nor Mr Cook dares face a secret ballot.'[3] On both occasions, a union forced to fight on an issue that worked against the maximization of solidarity had to develop methods of achieving and maintaining unity. In 1926, the initial stoppage was more complete, but significantly less than unanimous; divisive tendencies were present then as in 1984.

The party

If the comparison of '1926' and '1984' on the industrial side shows a complex variety of parallels and divergences, initially there seem to be far fewer common features politically. The problems of the Labour Party as it faced the challenge of the 1984 coal dispute are well known. The electoral disaster nine months earlier had left much debris — of reputations, of hopes, of assumptions. There could be no easy road back to office. Most immediately Labour faced the challenge of the SDP-Liberal Alliance. Already the party's leadership had committed itself to the gamble that the Euro-elections of June 1984 could serve as a significant indicator of Labour's recovery. Among the leadership some were too ready to see traditional industrial confrontation as a handicap to electoral revival. They had looked with alarm at the political implications of the National Graphical Association's dispute with the Messenger Group of newspapers; they were apprehensive about forthcoming union ballots on political funds. Given their perspective, the issues raised by a lengthy coal dispute were hardly welcome.

At first sight, this pessimism seems far removed from Labour's position in 1926. The Party had already held office for a brief period; three years later it was again elected. In broad terms, the contrast is valid. Labour strategists in the twenties were optimistic about future electoral success in a way that was simply impossible after June 1983. Although Labour had been defeated in October 1924, and faced a huge Conservative majority in the House of Commons, its aggregate vote had actually increased. Much of this reflected an increase in the number of candidates, but this in itself was a symptom of fundamental optimism. Nevertheless, Labour leaders in 1926, perhaps MacDonald especially, were concerned about electoral strategy. The previous election had suggested that the Liberal vote was collapsing; in the context of the 'Red Scares' of 1924, this had benefitted the Conservatives. But Labour could achieve a parliamentary majority only if it acquired a substantial share of this vote. Otherwise it seemed doomed to a permanent second place. In 1926, as in 1984, Labour leaders faced the question of how a prolonged industrial struggle would affect its attempts to construct a broad anti-Tory majority.

Faced with this problem, MacDonald had one resource denied to his counterpart in 1984. He was able to dominate his party in a way that Kinnock could not. Since his election as leader of the Parliamentary Party in November 1922, he had emerged as a Labour Party leader in an unprecedented fashion. Aided by the party's electoral growth and by his short term as Prime Minister, he was normally able to dominate not just the PLP but also the National Executive Committee, and the party conference. It was a hegemony that Labour supporters after 1931 preferred to forget, but its strength highlighted much about the nature of Labour politics in the 1920s.

Certainly, MacDonald had faced considerable criticism after the defeat of October 1924, but at the Liverpool conference a year later, this came to nothing. Partly this was because behind the rhetoric of MacDonald, there lay the organizational skills of Arthur Henderson. The brittle leader and the sometimes avuncular, sometimes authoritarian 'machine-politician' complemented one another. From 1926 onwards Labour conferences were typically stages for MacDonald's empty but soothing rhetoric.

The contrast comes over sharply in the responses of the 1926 and 1984 conferences to the coal dispute. Robert Williams, once an eminent supporter of 'Direct Action', chaired the 1926 gathering; his treatment of the miners' struggle showed how far this one-time sympathizer with syndicalism had embraced a cautious parliamentary gradualism: 'The miners' decision to continue the dispute is heroic. They may be likened to the sightless Samson feeling for a grip on the pillars of the Temple, the crushing of which may engulf this thing we call British civilization . . . This despairing policy may be magnificent, but it is not war'.[4] But in 1984, the speech from the chair came from Eric Heffer. He unreservedly supported the NUM's position and attacked recent legal decisions on the dispute as demonstrating the class prejudices of the judiciary. This was followed by a conference opening day dominated by the dispute, a speech by Arthur Scargill that was enthusiastically received, and a series of contributions critical of police tactics. The 1926 conference spent little time debating the substantive issue. Nothing was offered to the miners except sympathy and the long-term hope of mines' nationalization. Although there were protests from the MFGB delegation and others, alternative proposals were side-tracked or voted out.

One reason for MacDonald's domination of significant party bodies was that he could normally count on support from the major unions. The NUR, for example, was influenced heavily by his close associate, Jimmy Thomas. More broadly, union leaders backed MacDonald as they sought compensation for industrial weakness in the hope of a Labour Government. This investment in an electoral route to trade union influence was a powerful factor uniting trade unionists and the parliamentary leadership; it was buttressed by the increasing tendency of union officials to identify all left-wing criticism with the Communist factionalism that they often experienced inside their organizations. A crucial feature in the containment of the Labour-left was the skill with which party managers identified all left positions with the priorities of the Communist Party. The tactic was facilitated by the fact that Communists still attended Labour Party conferences as members of trade union delegations. A critical left alternative was only beginning to emerge in 1926 through an ILP shift from a concern with socialist theory towards a critique of Labour policies. Some of its most prominent members such as James Maxton and John Wheatley were already keen critics of MacDonald, but others remained political allies. As yet, the ILP stood at a moment of transition, unable to offer a clear focus for the left. The terms of any controversy could be manipulated so long as it was possible to indicate the involvement of Communists at Labour Party meetings.

This fragmentation of the left had its counterpart in 1984. The apparent Bennite consensus of 1981 had disintegrated, in part as a result of divergent responses to the defeat of 1983, and Kinnock's successful bid for the leadership may be seen as both a cause and a consequence of this disarray. Ultimately however, the contrast is most significant. Both MacDonald and Kinnock faced a left that was relatively weak, but in 1926, the party's structure was controllable from the top in a way that was not the case in 1984. Kinnock and MacDonald led the same party but they had to operate within very different political environments. For MacDonald, party affairs had a predictability that Kinnock could only envy.

The Leaders

None of MacDonald's formative experiences were likely to generate real understanding of the miners' predicament. Significant episodes in the moulding of his political style were provided by rural Morayshire, the Radical politics of late nineteenth century London and the early ILP. The last, especially, went along with a dismissal of class conflict as the basis for any movement towards socialism, and a scepticism about trade unions as the vehicle for achieving a worthwhile community: 'each of the wings of an army for carrying on the class war is bound in the nature of things to fight its battles mainly for its own hand. Trade solidarity rather than proletarian solidarity is the real outcome of a class war in practice, and trade interest is ultimately individual interest.'[5] This outlook produced a sharp anti-

pathy towards the 'Direct Action' strategies advocated by some
trade unionists from 1910 onwards. Prior to the 1912 coal strike, he
attacked some within the MFGB as: 'syndicalist Anarchists of the
ordinary type, who find in Socialism the greatest obstacle to their
absurd economic and political ideas.'[6] The dichotomy between
'Direct Action' and his conception of evolutionary socialism was
apparent again in 1925. He reacted with dismay to 'Red Friday' when
the Baldwin Government responded to the prospect of sympathetic
industrial action by granting a nine month subsidy to the coal
industry: 'It has handed over the appearance of victory to the very
forces that sane, well-considered, thoroughly well-examined
Socialism feels to be probably its greatest enemy.'[7] When the subsidy
expired, conflict was predictable. MacDonald's political record suggested that he was unlikely to offer unambiguous support to the
miners.

Kinnock's formative experiences provide the sharpest of contrasts. A miner's son from Tredegar, he was born at a time when the
socialist culture of South Wales remained a vital force, but born also
into a fortunate generation free from the worst deprivations of that
industrial community. His early years as an MP coincided with the
trade-union-based confrontations of the early 1970s. Industrial
action seemed to carry a radical potential that had not been seen since
the aftermath of World War One. In the coalfields, the 1972 strike
was often viewed as a reversal of 1926. Kinnock's response was very
different from MacDonald's hostility to aggressive industrial tactics.
Faced in 1972 with Conservative accusations of picket-line violence,
he responded in terms that revealed his origins in a self-consciously
working-class, traditional community: — 'What would be the in-
stinct of any red-blooded man in this House, having put his family to
all that inconvenience and near-misery, if he saw someone riding
roughshod over his picket line? I know what my attitude would be.
In fact, I should be worried if it were not the case.'[8]

Over the next seven years Kinnock continued to appear as a
left critic of Labour's established leadership — refusing office in the
Callaghan Government, criticizing what he saw as a retreat from the
radical promises of 1974, elected to the NEC as an opponent of
government policies and condemning the economic strategy that
precipitated the public-sector disputes of early 1979. But after that
year's electoral defeat, a distance developed between him and several
prominent figures on the parliamentary left. One symbol was his
early appointment to the front-bench; more substantively he was
unhappy about some aspects of the left's campaign for party demo-

cratization. Perhaps most fundamentally, he came to believe that the 1979 defeat necessitated a thorough reappraisal of the party's strategic assumptions. Any such examination would include a sceptical survey of the role that traditional class-based institutions and actions could play in a Labour revival. It was a reappraisal that many on the left remained reluctant to contemplate. The separation became embittered when Kinnock refused to back Benn in his 1981 campaign for the deputy leadership. The resulting hostility was to have its implications for March 1984: Kinnock's rejection of Benn's campaign brought him into angry confrontation with Arthur Scargill, soon to be elected president of the NUM.

Any understanding of the reactions of MacDonald and Kinnock to '1926' and '1984' requires a special consideration of their relationship with the miners' union. In each case this was influenced by the emergence of a new national official of the union who advocated the miners' case in a distinctive — and to many — disturbing style. The relationship between MacDonald and Arthur Cook seems to have involved little personal animosity. Yet Cook's strategy, declared openly on his election as MFGB Secretary early in 1924, was guaranteed to provoke MacDonald's hostility. It was not simply Cook's admiration for the Soviet Union, although this provided opponents with abundant opportunities for scurrilous comments. More fundamentally, he advocated the development of industrial strength as a first priority. He favoured aggressive action including sympathy strikes and the expansion of rank-and-file control. In appropriate circumstances this could be a strategy for social transformation; at a less propitious moment it was presented as the most effective tactic for defending working-class rights. Originating in the rich pre-war debates that produced *The Miners' Next Step* and maturing in the radical environment of the Rhondda, Cook's emphases were bound to antagonize MacDonald. Yet many within the MFGB leadership differed fundamentally from the Federation's secretary. Many were elderly conventional trade unionists, sometimes doubling as Labour MPs. Normally they backed the party leader's proposals, although once the gauntlet had been thrown down in April 1926, they mostly stuck firmly by the MFGB's policy. Indeed, it seems clear that Cook, despite his 'Not a penny off the pay, not a minute on the day' slogan was more likely to be flexible in private negotiations than some of his more orthodox colleagues. Yet it was against him that MacDonald eventually directed his criticism. In a private letter after the dispute had collapsed the party leader articulated the hostility that he had largely suppressed for so long: 'In all my experience of Trade Union leadership . . . I have never known one so incompetent as your-self.'[9] The judgement is echoed by one made privately by Kinnock of Scargill: 'He's destroying the coal-industry single-handed. He's the labour movement's nearest equivalent to a First World War general.'[10] Certainly Scargill's industrial strategy closely resembles that of Cook; in part it was a reaction to the pit closures of the 1960s, carried out by a Labour Government, often without any effective response from a cautious NUM leadership. It led on from early strike actions in Yorkshire to the Battle of Saltley Gate, and was viewed widely as a major factor in the successes of 1972 and 1974. As with Cook, Scargill came to symbolize a strategy and a sentiment that had diverse tributaries and a wide body of support within the union.

The relationship between Kinnock and the new NUM President was exacerbated by two factors. One was the personal antagonism that remained after their angry conflict in 1981, a legacy that perhaps fed into wider tensions between the NUM and the Labour Party. But the distancing was increased by the composition of the NUM Executive. Whereas MacDonald could rely on a sympathetic hearing from some miners' officials, Kinnock could relate politically to few of the NUM leadership. The union's left showed more in common with those MPs from whom Kinnock had become remote; the NUM right were no more congenial and rarely took political initiatives.

Beyond the strategic arguments and the personal antipathies, the most fundamental challenge offered by the two Arthurs was perhaps one of style. It is a challenge captured in images: of Cook speaking to a miners' rally — no jacket, no collar, sleeves rolled up, or of Scargill in his baseball cap on the Orgreave picket line. Such presentations of the miners' case express the emotions that fuel a dispute; they stand remote from the political conventional etiquette of parliamentary debate.

The Responses

Even in the autumn of 1925, MacDonald had anticipated with gloom the conflict that seemed likely to follow the end of the coal subsidy and the publication of the Samuel Report. He viewed any widespread dependence on sympathetic action as disastrous; by March 1926, he was quarrelling with Cook over the latter's assertion that the Labour Party had pledged itself to support the miners in the impending dispute. As hope of settlement collapsed, MacDonald privately noted what he saw as an unreasonable stance by the MFGB. They had an 'impossible formula' on wages and hours. Ultimately he personalized the issue in terms that would be echoed in some quarters in 1984. 'It really looks tonight as though there was to be a General Strike to save Mr Cook's face. Important man! . . . The election of this fool as miners' secretary looks as though it would be the most calamitous thing that ever happened to the TU movement. The chief criminal however is the Government.'[11] Similarly, MacDonald backed the General Council's decision to terminate the General Strike and resented the MFGB's bleak response. He defended the Federation's commitment on wages, however, but despite his recognition of the harsh necessity of its position, he offered little as a strategy.

The initial responses of Labour's leadership in the spring of 1984 were muted. The dramatic countdown in 1926 forced politicians into making declarations. Yet although developments in 1984 lacked this sharp focus, there were abundant signs that a conflict was likely. The Government's 1981 retreat on pit closures would not be the last word; the NUM failed to prevent the closure of the Lewis Merthyr Pit; four months of an overtime ban and the NCB's response in certain coalfields generated further hostility. All of this, plus the appointment of MacGregor, should have suggested that the proper question was not 'whether' but 'when'. The answer was dictated by the NCB; Cortonwood provided a flash point that the NUM could ignore only at grave risk to its future credibility.

Given this sequence, the quiescent response of Labour's front bench requires explanation. It is clear that several were sceptical about the dispute's durability. Moreover, political priorities could generate the hope that the strike would be transitory. A wish not to be associated too closely with an embattled trade union could produce a belief that perhaps the association would not be necessary, and that a potential threat to electoral recovery could be avoided. Within this confused initial response, the issue of a national ballot acquired a special prominence. Labour leaders hoped for its use, a pro-strike verdict would remove a political difficulty; the opposite would kill the whole issue. On this issue Neil Kinnock acquitted himself badly. During a parliamentary exchange with Margaret Thatcher on 12 April, he welcomed the 'clearer and closer prospect' of a ballot within the NUM.[12] It was a preference that proved politically damaging as the prospect receded. This early exchange highlighted a consistent weakness in the responses of Labour's front-bench. All too often there was an acceptance of the terms of the argument as laid down by the government along with an inadequate sensitivity towards the problems facing the NUM. In this case, they accepted too easily that such a ballot was the last word in democratic procedure, an acquiescence with implications for trade union procedures that went far beyond the coal dispute.

Once the early activity had died down, MacDonald and Kinnock faced similar prospects. By mid-May 1926, sympathetic action had ended, but the coalfields remained virtually solid; by mid-May 1984 it was clear that Nottinghamshire and some smaller coalfields would continue to produce, but elsewhere the strike held firm. Throughout the long months of the 1926 lock-out Labour leaders made speeches in the Commons, but the National Executive Committee never discussed the issue. Both party and miners accepted a division of labour based on the premise that the question was purely industrial. MacDonald's responses demonstrated an increasing concern with the role of the government. He reacted angrily to the government's introduction of an Eight Hours' Bill: 'This is not peace; this is a sword.'[13] By the end of August, his accusation had become more fundamental: 'The Cabinet . . . has been a very efficient, a very faithful and a very loyal sub-committee of the Owners' Association.'[14] His basic case was that 'the government cannot afford to stand outside'.[15] In 1984, Kinnock repeatedly proclaimed the same argument: 'I believe it is the duty of government not to inflame, the duty of government not to exacerbate, the duty of government not to alienate, but to conciliate, to produce negotiation, to secure peace.'[16] This commitment was highlighted in 1984 in the repeated attempts by Stan Orme to initiate negotiations; in 1926, it led MacDonald into ultimately abortive discussions with Winston Churchill.

Such statements and activities rested on a shared belief that the state could and should represent a communal interest above that of contending classes. Labour front-bench criticisms of the Baldwin and Thatcher Governments rested on their failures to act as more than the representatives of a section. On both occasions Labour's front-bench presented an economic defence of the miners' position that could be maintained independently of any commitment to the union's strategy. MacDonald's diagnosis pointed towards the redundancy of strike action on issues that had significant social consequences: 'Every day presses upon us the question of how far the community as a whole can allow these major disputes to be fought out as though only the two chief parties alone were involved.'[17] In 1926, the intellectual self-confidence of Labour could point to the nationalization of the mines as a panacea; the 1984 leadership could not offer so simple an answer. But at least, they could agree in their reservations about the miners' strategy. Kinnock could claim dismissively that he had no interest 'in achieving a Gallipoli';[18] MacDonald could confide in readers of the *Socialist Review*: 'I find that now a few of our old Socialist friends reflect gravely in private on the way that the miners' case has been handled.'[19] The reservations in 1926 tended to focus on the bargaining position of the MFGB. Similarly Peter Shore in 1984 could accuse both sides of intransigence, but recent Labour doubts have focused much more around the issue of picket-line violence.

Kinnock's position on this has been clear throughout, although not wholly consistent with his 1972 position. On the second day of the 1984 dispute, he thoroughly condemned violence: 'in pursuit of industrial disputes even when it occurs among people who feel impotent in the face of the destruction of their jobs, their industry and their communities . . . '[20] Similarly, he reacted to police claims about picket violence at Harworth, early in August: 'violence is no part of British trade unionism.'[21] MacDonald in 1926 did not confront directly the question of violence but there is abundant evidence to suggest that his abhorrence was, if anything, even deeper than Kinnock's.

Such positions indicate much about these leaders' perceptions of British political developments and in particular, their view of the state's role in industrial disputes. Kinnock's attempt to write violent confrontation out of British industrial relations is simply wrong on historical grounds. Many episodes have been marked by violence — the 'New Unionist' battles of 1889–1893; the confrontations of the pre-1914 years including the Tonypandy riots and the shooting of two people by troops at Llanelly; and within the coalfields, the disputes of 1921 and 1926 were not gentle affairs. Blanket claims about the British labour movement's pacific qualities are not only Pharisaical; they misrepresent the past; they misleadingly isolate certain responses as abnormal and they present an idealized portrait of the liberality of the British State.

Violence in the coalfields in 1926 and in 1984 flowed directly from police actions to protect scabs. In 1926, violence escalated from August as some miners returned to work; in 1984 the basis for confrontation was always present in the Nottinghamshire coalfield. Sir William Joynson-Hicks, home secretary in 1926, wrote to chief constables in the late summer in terms that would be echoed by Leon Brittan: 'It is the distinct wish and intention of his Majesty's Government that the utmost protection should be afforded to every man who desires to work in the coal mines of this country.'[22] Police responses in both disputes involved the abrogation of the right of pickets to approach those going to work. The normally cautious South Wales miners' leader Vernon Hartshorn claimed in 1926: 'the police are refusing to allow the lodge officials even when they go in ones or twos to see workmen, and telling them that it is illegal to do so.'[23] Violent conflict was inevitable. In the earlier dispute the most moderate miners' leaders condemned some police actions. George Spencer, a few days before his expulsion from the Federation, quoted a police threat to some Nottinghamshire strikers: 'You have had two days' quiet now, but we are going to get into you b–s tonight.'[24] When coalfield MPs provided evidence of police violence, the government response in 1926 paralleled that in 1984: 'You cannot make a baton charge without people being hurt . . . if men are there when a baton charge takes place, they must accept the consequences . . . '[25]

The patterns of Labour's parliamentary response to police actions in the two disputes were very similar. A continuing stream of criticism came from a small number of left Labour MPs but, more crucially, a hostility came from coalfield members irrespective of their normal political position. In 1926, this criticism involved George Spencer; in 1984 it involved especially South Yorkshire members who heard complaints from constituents about police actions when they attempted to picket Nottinghamshire coalfields. Such MPs articulated a bewilderment and an anger that could explode in response to one Conservative's defence of the police: 'the hon. Gentlemen's speech was certainly a load of bullshit.'[26] Yet the implications of these criticisms for the position of the Labour leadership were slight. In 1926, Members who ventilated the grievances of the coalfields at least had a regular opportunity to do so. The coal lock-out was conducted under Emergency Powers' Regulations inherited from the General Strike. The need for monthly renewal provided the chance to ventilate criticisms. 1984 afforded no such predictable spaces. Anger tended to focus on the home secretary's appearances at question time, plus occasional debates initiated by back-benchers. With one early exception,[27] Labour's front-bench made no attempt to make the question of civil liberties a matter of major political controversy. To the increasing numbers of people in the coalfields who had experienced the sharp end of police action, the stance adopted by Kinnock must have seemed even less sensitive than the silence of MacDonald. The Aberavon question becomes more intelligible.

Appraisal

The complexities of the two conflicts lead initially to an emphasis on their distinguishing features. The economic significance of any coal dispute has changed; the Labour Party, so optimistic about eventual success in the 1920s was full of self-doubt in 1984; the party's power structure was far more responsive to the leadership's requirements in 1926; MacDonald and Kinnock brought very different preferences and emotions to the issues raised by a coal strike.

Yet these elements of distinctiveness are accompanied by similarities. Both confrontations raised issues that went far beyond the immediate dispute. They served as foci for grievances central to the societies in which they took place and touched sensitive nerves in ways that few socialists could ignore. Indeed in 1984, the underlying issues — a collective response to unemployment, police powers and the legal attack on the NUM — were, if anything, even more basic than in 1926. One consequence of the earlier dispute had been to shape a harsh environment in which many working people remained trapped until the war years. A similar defeat in contemporary Britain threatened a similar consequence. This challenge to the labour movement was faced by a Labour Party with one feature in common with its 1926 counterpart. Significant individuals within it had developed a view of electoral strategy in which a prolonged industrial dispute could appear as a threat. This distancing was increased by hostility or a lack of understanding between the party leader and the most prominent official of the miners.

An analysis of the two party leaders' responses to the 1926 and 1984 disputes reveals a series of common features: reluctance to get involved in the issue, underpinned by a hope that conflict could be avoided; fundamental doubts about the miners' tactics; a persistent demand that the state could serve as a mediator; a failure for the most part to articulate grievances expressed within mining communities and by some backbenchers about the activities of the police.

The similarities demonstrate certain durable themes within Labour politics that cut across the significant distinctions between 1926 and 1984. On both occasions, leaders attempted to operate a sharp distinction between industrial and political action. This surfaced in MacDonald's dismissal of sympathetic action and in Kinnock's claim that: 'There is no possibility and no justification for bringing down a British government by any means other than the ballot box.'[28] Such pronouncements ignored the political dimensions of the disputes and erected a simplistic dichotomy in which industrial action was either directed to the replacement of the government or was narrowly economic. The refusal to admit any position in between blocked the possibility of developing effective relationships between industrial struggle and political mobilization.

This reluctance has been linked with a concern to play down the centrality of class as a basis for socialist growth. For MacDonald this was part of a wider view that class conflict and class-based organizations offered no route to a socialist community; in Kinnock's case, it was perhaps a more pragmatic claim that changing employment patterns offered diminishing scope for conventional class-based politics. Such emphases have been frequent in commentaries on 1984: 'There are those on the Left who maintain that the miners' strike is a vindication of a class-based politics after decades in which the agenda of the Left was defined by cross-class campaigns like feminism and CND. Yet the strike demonstrates the reverse . . . The miners' strike is not the vindication of class politics, but its death throes.'[29]

Such assessments are presented often as if they are novel. In fact, they read like many of MacDonald's comments on the anachronistic and sectional nature of class-based action. This particular example focuses on the failure of other groups of workers to support the miners in 1984. The implication that this is a recent development is historically fallacious. After the collapse of the General Strike the miners battled on alone. They failed to secure an embargo on the movement of coal. Jimmy Thomas played a role similar to that so eagerly taken by Eric Hammond. It is not just that the implied contrast between past solidarity and a sectionalized present is bad history: it also plays down the extent to which the achievement of any inter-union solidarity is always a demanding task.

Despite the hopes of several Labour politicians and intellectuals, the events of 1984 have demonstrated that class-based conflict remains an integral feature of any capitalist system. As in 1926, many have been politicized within the coalfields. Whilst it can never provide an exclusive basis for a strategy for socialist development, any strategy that ignores or marginalizes such conflict is irrelevant. Since the Old Adam of class conflict looks likely to be around for some time, what prospects are there for its political expression?

This requires a consideration of a final common theme in the Labour response to the two crises. In both case, Labour's leaders continued to see the state as an essentially neutral instrument capable of fulfilling a reconciling role. At one level the state was seen as an essential tool for the settlement of such conflicts; at another, a faith in the underlying liberalism of the British State, helped to ensure that Labour's leaders failed to come to terms with the reality of police actions in the coalfield. Such an approach to the state is not only to be found in Labour's responses to industrial disputes; it has dominated party thinking from the beginning and indicates the debt owed by Labour to nineteenth century Radical Liberalism, and also the traditional tendency to equate collectivism with movement towards socialism. The judgement may have been made before; it has acquired a particular urgency in the light of the Labour leadership's response to the coal dispute.

The urgency can be grasped by noting the political legacies of 1926. Some miners, few in numbers but politically significant, joined the Communist Party. Despite the early imposition of the sectarianism of 'Class against Class', an influential political presence developed in some sections of the Miners' Federation, especially in South Wales and in Fife. The coal crisis also radicalized the ILP. It became more of a focus for left-wing criticism within the Labour Party, but lacking a significant trade union presence, its impact was limited; by 1932 it had left the Labour Party. In fact the Labour Party received the greatest benefit from 1926: more people in the coalfields voted Labour; they did so even in 1931. The MFGB became a by-word for loyal support of the party leadership. Little was secured in return. The 1929 Government disappointed the Federation. Throughout the 1930s, the party's dogged pursuit of a parliamentary majority could do nothing for its supporters in the coalfields. It is a misleading judgement to see Labour abandoning the illusions of 'Direct Action' in 1926 to embark on the long haul that led to victory in 1945. The electoral history of the intervening years is much more complicated than a simple progression. The vital breakthrough came only after 1939. Moreover this austere strategy meant that in the 1930s Labour attempts to defend its supporters were largely abysmal. The human costs were enormous.

These consequences came out of a major defeat. At the time of writing, the outcome of the 1984 struggle is unknown. But some tendencies are clear. The dispute has mobilized many with no previous political involvement — the young miners and the women on the picket lines, raising funds, arguing for support, discovering talents and strengths that had lain dormant. They have become different people; for many the world can never be the same again. Like Will Paynter looking back on 1926, they will reflect that this was 'Year One'. Yet a change in perception necessitates an effective instrument. Paynter after 1926 found his in the Communist Party;

others gave their loyalty to the Labour Party. The modern Labour Party at local level where commitment to the miners' struggle has frequently been unreserved often seems a credible force. But as a national organization, the party has presented a very different image. The uncomfortable parallels with MacDonald's party have been traced. Certainly in several important aspects Kinnock is not MacDonald; but ultimately 'Ramsay MacKinnock' points not to a composite figure, but to a cramping, narrowing set of political assumptions — about class, about industrial action, about the neutrality of the state. Perhaps above all, it represents a disabling capitulation before a particular form of electoral politics. This involves a narrow focus on what appears to be electorally prudent in the short-term: the impact of this preoccupation was all too evident in 1926 and in 1984. It incorporates the expectation that most people will act politically only in the intermittent role of voter; this is a condescending marginalization that has been falsified by the responses of many over the last year. Above all, it is a strategy which supposedly aims at radical change but accepts many existing prejudices as a basis for political argument. Hostages are given to prevailing sentiments about strikes, about pickets and police, about the proper scope for political agitation. Definitions are accepted which disadvantage a socialist case. This capitulation has been made by successive Labour leaderships far too often for any reversal to be easy. But it is a reversal that must be attempted if the creativity and the sacrifices of the men and women of 1984 are to have any worthwhile political outcome. Only then is Labour's pursuit of electoral success likely to have any radical potential. Only then can the ghost of 'Ramsay MacKinnock' be laid.

Notes

All Hansard references House of Commons debates; for 1926 and 1972 refer to 5th Series Volumes; for 1984 to 6th Series.

1. Cited in *The Guardian*, 15 November 1984.
2. *Glasgow Eastern Standard*, 29 May 1926.
3. J. E. Williams, *The Derbyshire Miners*, London, 1962, p. 710, quoting *The Times*, 5 June 1926.
4. *Labour Party Conference Report*, 1926, p. 172.
5. Ramsay MacDonald, 'Socialism and Society' in B. Barker, ed., *Ramsay MacDonald's Political Writings*, London, 1972, pp. 89–90.
6. David Marquand, *Ramsay MacDonald*, London, 1977, p. 146, quoting *Leicester*

Pioneer, 24 February 1912.

7. Marquand, p. 424,quoting *Daily Mail*, 4 August 1925.

8. *Hansard*, 14 February 1972, 831, col. 137.

9. Marquand, p. 448, quoting MacDonald to Cook, 14 January 1927, 'MacDonald Papers'.

10. Cited in Robert Harris, *The Making of Neil Kinnock*, London, 1984, p. 164.

11. Marquand, pp. 435–6, quoting 'MacDonald Diary', 2 May 1926.

12. *Hansard*, 12 April 1984, 57, col. 522.

13. *Hansard*, 29 June 1926, 197, col. 1067.

14. *Hansard*, 31 August 1926, 199, col. 159.

15. *Hansard*, 1 June 1926, 196, col. 610.

16. Speech to TUC cited in *The Guardian*, 5 September 1926.

17. *Socialist Review*, August 1926.

18. At a PLP meeting cited in *The Guardian*, 8 November 1984. Military metaphors were also used by a miners' critic in 1926. Robert Williams after emphasising the futility of the MFGB resistance went on: 'These are the men who were they defending a beleagured Mafeking or Ladysmith or conducting an epic retreat from Mons would win the approval of the entire nation', *Labour Party Conference Report*, 1926, p. 172.

19. *Socialist Review*, August 1926.

20. *Hansard*, 13 May 1984, 56, col. 278.

21. In a Granada Television interview cited in *The Guardian*, 9 August 1984.

22. Letter cited by Sir William Joynson-Hicks, *Hansard*, 26 October 1926, 199, col. 737.

23. *Hansard*, 30 August 1926, 199, col. 29.

24. *Ibid*, 28 September 1926, col. 468.

25. *Ibid*, cols. 458–46. Although the Home Secretary added a rider about 'unnecessary violence', he predictably saw no evidence to its use.

26. Martin Redmond, *Hansard*, 23 July 1984, 64, col. 790, in response to a speech by Eldon Griffiths.

27. The debate of 10 April 1984, initiated by the Labour back-bencher Allen McKay — but note the front-bench contribution of Gerald Kaufman, *Hansard*, 58, cols. 212, 219.

28. Cited in *The Guardian*, 17 May 1984.

29. Michael Ignatieff, 'Strangers and Comrades', in *New Statesman*, 14 December 1984, p. 27.

30. For Will Paynter's comment see the contribution of Leo Price in *Llafur*, 1977, p. 25, and for Paynter's own discussion of the impact of 1926, his *My Generation*, London, 1972, chs 3 and 4.

PART THREE
Power Politics:
Coal, Energy and the Future

11

Why Coal is Under Attack
Nuclear Powers in the Energy Establishment

Colin Sweet

The dispute in the coal industry is not about 'uneconomic pits'. It is demonstrably about this government's determination to gain total control over the industry in order to force down real wages and to 'reorganize' it, a euphemism that almost certainly implies privatization. But it is something more: the policy now being followed relates to strategic questions on Energy Supply which predate the Thatcher Government by many years. The Establishment is exceptionally sensitive on this question: energy is crucial to modern society: nothing and no one could move without it. That was established in the late 1960s when, notwithstanding the high costs involved, the first drive to get out of coal began. For the present government, faced with increasing dependence on coal and a resolute trade union with a militant leadership, breaking the miners has become more than a key issue. It has become an obsession.

What does the Energy Establishment comprise? Firstly the supply side monopolies — in both the public and private sector. The Central Electricity Generating Board is the giant. It is the wealthiest body in the country, with assets of nearly £40 thousand million. It claims to be the largest single electricity utility in the world. Its chairman — appointed personally by Mrs Thatcher — is Sir Walter Marshall, formerly head of the Atomic Energy Authority. He was previously chief scientist at the Department of Energy, but was sacked by the Minister, Tony Benn, when it was discovered that he was promoting sales of the American Pressurized Water Reactor for the Westinghouse Company with the Shah of Iran and other reactionary oil states. Not surprisingly it is this same reactor that the CEGB now wants permission to build in Britain. Linked with the nuclear programme are a clutch of other powerful interests: British Nuclear Fuels, owner of the Sellafield reprocessing complex and also part of the public sector, is closely linked to the

Electricity Council and Area Boards. The private sector includes firms like GEC (Britain's largest electro–engineering firm, and the original contractor with Westinghouse), Northern Engineering Industries, Babcock Power (whose American cousin, Babcock and Wilcox built, own and operate the PWR disaster station at Three Mile Island in the USA), the large civil construction companies — Taylor Woodrow, and Wimpeys, plus a clutch of lesser companies. In the mixed public and private sector is the National Nuclear Corporation owned by the AEA, GEC, Taylor Woodrow and the CEGB. As the CEGB is a monopoly producer of electricity, so the NCB is a monopoly producer and distributor of coal. They have to be bracketed together as the centrepieces of the Electricity Supply Industry. The NCB chairman Ian MacGregor pairs nicely with Walter Marshall: both are protegés of Mrs Thatcher, and both are dedicated to her strategy of placing electricity under strong central control. The run down of coal and the build up of nuclear power is central to this exercise. MacGregor and Marshall are there to deliver, and when they have done that we can imagine that the next stage will be to privatize at least the most profitable parts of both industries and dismantle the respective Boards.

The other part of the Energy Establishment which appropriately fits into this scenario is the oil companies. They are the largest private companies in the UK. Immensely wealthy and powerful, they are also heavily involved in the international coal trade, and through their overseas subsidiaries would be eager to import coal into Britain, once the industry was stripped of the protection which it still enjoys. The oil companies, are closely locked into government, especially through their involvement in the North Sea. They have persuaded the government to make the Gas Corporation yield up the biggest of the onshore oil fields, and they are bidding to break up British Gas so that they can put an end to its effective competition with oil and win even higher profits for themselves.

The Energy Establishment also has a presence in Whitehall. This includes the Department of Energy, but more powerfully, it counts its friends in the Foreign Office, the Department of Industry, the Department of Defence, and the Cabinet Office. Put together the industrial muscle, both private and public on the supply side, and the political coherence given by the very highest Whitehall support, and you have probably the most powerful pressure group in Britain. If one wonders why the struggle over the future of the electricity supply industry engages the immense resources that are being disposed of in the miners' dispute (or the lesser, but very costly, side-shows like the Sizewell Public Inquiry on Nuclear Power), one has only to look down this list of interested parties and estimate what is at stake. Power yes, energy power, political power, but also money — many thousands of millions of pounds are at stake for the Energy Establishment. The risks, both political and economic, may sometimes threaten to get out of hand, but the potential gains are great enough to make not only the risks justifiable, but the thought of not winning impossible to contemplate.

The strike that began in March 1984 is the result of a strategy that has run as a continuous thread in Establishment policy for more than ten years. It was not invented by Mrs Thatcher's Government — but in her and her colleagues it has found a political force that has turned it into a crusade. The consequences for the future of this country, should that strategy prevail, will work like a scourge for the rest of this century.

The presence of the Establishment can be discerned at every level in the operation of the coal industry and in the approach to the strike. The question of 'uneconomic pits' is one clear case. Of course, the rising costs of old pits is an issue, but whether or not the cost of mining coal in one pit is 'uneconomic' must be arbitrary — a line drawn by accountants — because there is no free market in coal prices. Britain's coal industry has only one producer, the NCB, and one very large buyer, the CEGB. As a monopoly producer, the NCB fixes the price — not market forces. It does of course take account of the market but its tests of efficiency are effectively determined by itself, the government and the CEGB. It is a nationally protected industry, and its prices are a result of a policy decision not an economic decision. (If the government wins this strike, it would not be surprising if they went on to sell profitable mines to private companies; nor if 'uneconomic' pits were snapped up and worked for their last few tons of coal.)

For instance, for the last five years, the NCB could have sold coal to the CEGB at a higher price. Contrary to what John Hatch, chairman of the Electricity Consumers' Council, has argued, electricity consumers have not been subsidizing coal, for coal prices to the CEGB have lagged well behind the price of electricity.

If the NCB had not held the price of coal almost constant in real terms it would have been able to show a substantial trading surplus. Had it done so, the disputed 'uneconomic pits' would not have required a £285 million subsidy and the question of peremptorily closing them down — the issue that sparked the strike — would not have arisen.

This is not to suggest that had the artefact of 'uneconomic pits' not been used there would have been no conflict. For the government's argument is merely a rationalization of the built-in conflict between its energy strategy, decided upon long ago, and miners' interests.

The future of Energy Supply is such a highly political issue that governments avoid policy commitments in this area (the last White Paper on Energy Policy was in 1967). Given the complex of very powerful interests on the supply side, governments neither initiate nor encourage public discussion.

At the Sizewell Public Inquiry the government's energy policy has been on trial. A nuclear programme that would cost up to £25 thousand million over fifteen years is a serious matter and can only be judged by reference to a long term policy. However the document they submitted for cross examination was the negation of a policy statement. All it said was that the government was committed to breaking up monopolies and letting the market decide. As two of the principal parties (the CEGB and the NNC) are monopolies, and as the government had already made it plain that it supported their claim and that of other members of the nuclear industrial complex to enjoy the benefits of this lucrative project, it is difficult to award the government any marks for breaking up monopolies. If what was presented at Sizewell is what the government presumes to call an energy policy, then we are back in the Dark Ages.

Recently a *Financial Times* journalist, Ian Hargreaves, wrote in the paper's Lombard column that Nigel Lawson, when he was Energy Secretary 'had a favourite game of turning up at energy conferences to give speeches entitled "UK Energy Policy" and then announcing that energy policy, in any sense that the audience understood the concept, did not exist.' It could not have been better put. If there is a concept to which the government relates it is that of the early economists who argued that all intervention was bad and that it was the 'hidden hand' that governed the operation of society through market forces. In the context of the modern economy this would appear to be obvious nonsense. Be that as it may, the Lawson doctrine is still paraded as a policy.

If the government lacks an energy policy this does not mean that it lacks an objective. That objective is very clear. It is to defeat the miners. There is no conceivable rational energy policy into which that objective can be fitted. It is a political objective, and one that must prove destructive of a major energy resource. Characteristically, this objective is being pursued without regard to the cost to the communities that will be destroyed, or to the future of this country.

But supposing this destructive onslaught against the coal industry is successful? According to the Tory view of things, what follows? Here Mrs Thatcher, normally only too willing to be combative, is curiously reticent. For her, the advantage of not having a stated policy is manifest. To discuss the future of an industry openly, when you are set on decimating it, might cause some concern — even among the government's own supporters. It is better that awkward questions are not ventilated publicly — at least until the government is ready to act; and by then other more sensible courses of action will have been pre-empted. Thus secrecy has become an important part of policy for Mrs Thatcher. Her objectives are first to undermine the coal industry, and to do that she needs to promote the nuclear alternative; then to reorganize it, and that includes breaking up the NCB. But to what end is this strategy directed?

Privatization may well be the name of the game. Certainly there are signs that it is being taken out of wraps. It was Mr Tebbit who first gave voice to the idea. Whitehall played it down as just an off the cuff remark. Then John Moore, in a briefing to a newspaper, repeated it. This was taken a little more seriously. Finally, 'Mr Troubleshooter' himself weighed in: Mr MacGregor, on 5 December 1984 gave the subject the full treatment. Appropriately enough for a man of such humane sentiments he chose the pulpit of a City church to deliver his message. It was intended to leave no doubt in anybody's mind as to what lies ahead if the government has its way. From the pulpit of St Lawrence Jewry, MacGregor 'preached the virtues of privatization' — at least that is how the *Financial Times* described the sermon of this Apostle of the new Jerusalem. Mr MacGregor did not shun the hyperbole. He described the idea of private pits as 'wonderful' — forgetting of course the legacy of misery, death and bitterness that the pit owners left behind them when they were taken over in 1947.

Privatization today has, of course, slightly different connotations. The context is one in which independent trade unions would no longer exist. Without the NUM, but with the EEPTU (and its no strike agreements), with the best parts of the coal industry in the hands of the oil companies and other large-scale capitals, we can perceive the shape of the new corporatist state. For this to be achieved, and Mrs Thatcher's Government has its heart set on it, electricity supply has to be severed from its broad base in the coal industry, and grafted onto a nuclear system. In the nuclear state, control will be central, democratic rights excluded and security will be paramount. When, at the time of the assault on GCHQ, Mrs Thatcher described trade unionism as subversive, she manifested a paranoia which also explains her near-hatred of the mineworkers' union. The syndrome to which she and MacGregor ardently subscribe would render free trade unionism a thing of the past. The *Financial Times*, ever anxious to turn an outdated and reactionary concept into a piece of forward thinking, described MacGregor's sermon on individuals buying up pits as 'radical thinking' and 'a preference shared by the Prime Minister'. This goes some way to explain why Mrs Thatcher appointed Mr MacGregor in the first place.

Coal, formally, does have a national policy — *Plan for Coal*, which was signed (and re-signed as recently as 1980) by the unions, the NCB and the government. It is a planning agreement that could be replicated in other industries and it is easy to believe that the present government is unsympathetic to this kind of commitment.

Why then did Mrs Thatcher put her signature to it? The answer lies in what was agreed in 1974. It was not only the year of the miners' strike and a new Labour Government; it was also the year of the great oil price hike. In a reversal of previous policy, it was decided to return to coal on the basis of a new political concordat. However much the corporate bodies in the Energy Establishment disliked the agreement, they did not want to be seen breaching it.

Until the Plan, the policy had been to have an 'All Electric Economy' based on the promise of abundant cheap energy churned out by nuclear power stations. The Plan gave coal the role of principal source of electric power. It projected an output of 135 million tons of coal by 1985, compared with 117 million in 1974, and 170 million by the year 2000.

It is not surprising the miners felt optimistic. This projection meant a very large programme of investment. On the basis of an average loss of two million tons of capacity per year due to exhaustion, the replacement rate would have to be about four million tons of new capacity a year to keep to the target.

But in 1977 the 1985 target was revised down to 120 million tons in the light of the unexpected fall in demand for energy. The weaknesses in the Plan were beginning to show.

The *investment* and planning implications inherent in such a large increase in output were not well thought out. The 1977 revision raised the investment requirement for the period up to 1985 from £1400 million to £3150 million. But this expenditure has not added to total capacity, merely paid for modernizing existing pits.

The *estimate of demand* used in the Plan was seriously defective. It was based on satisfying the wishes of the producers of coal and electricity, not of consumers. The growth target for the year 2000 was about 200 million tons coal equivalent *above* what is likely to be required. It was not for political reasons and the TUC in particular can be held responsible for perpetuating this piece of nonsense and the miners for being foolish enough to buy it.

No reference is made in the Plan to *nuclear power*. Yet it is readily apparent that if nuclear power is to expand coal has to contract. The NUM, then under a different leadership, was constrained by the enthusiasm of most of the other trade unions in the power supply industry. Largely right-wing and isolated from working-class communities, they were sold on the idea of clean and scientifically advanced nuclear power.

By tradition, the TUC leaves the job of formulating policy of energy to those unions whose members work in energy-related industries. Thus the Fuel and Power Industries Committee of the TUC, which drew up the *Review of Energy Policy*, was chaired by Frank Chapple, then general secretary of the electricians' union, EEPTU. Five out of the six other General Council members on the Committee belong to unions with a considerable number of members working on constructing or operating nuclear power stations. Only four out of the seventeen unions represented on the committee have no involvement in the nuclear industry. Unions involved in health, welfare and education, in clothing, textiles, food and drink, in railways, shipping, media and communication — none of these gets a look in. The fact that all trade unionists consume energy, and that most have children who must live with the consequences of these decisions, is overlooked.

The Committee has defined its tasks in narrow terms. While it gives some consideration to conservation and health and safety, it skirts around questions of ownership and control and concentrates on demand and supply. But since it represents the suppliers first and foremost, the demand side of the equation is subsidiary to the chief question: *how much energy can be produced*? In order to maintain a common front (or at least a truce) between the most powerful interests on the Committee, the miners and the electricians and engineers, demand figures are produced which match supply targets for coal *and* nuclear power, as well as oil and gas. In fact, these industries are in competition, because there is a continuing surplus of energy in the economy. The result is that the TUC's demand estimates bear no relation to reality and exceed the government's wildest dreams. No one has faced up to the incompatibility of the two targets for coal and nuclear power.

Also excluded from the Plan was the other politically loaded question — imported coal. Advocates of cutting coal output have argued for open competition in the world markets. This is linked to their case for removing the present subsidy to coal and the two issues need a co-ordinated response.

The pressure for an open door policy comes from UK multinationals, like BP and Shell, operating from off-shore bases with considerable investment in the coal trade. These and other interests believe that they have everything to gain from breaking up a centrally-controlled, nationally-protected coal industry. Their objectives include the restructuring, and possibly the dismantling, of the NCB. In the last analysis, the NCB and the coal unions have a common interest in the long-term defence of a national industry.

There can be no doubt that since 1974 the trade unions and the Labour Party have been complacent about the *Plan for Coal* and unwilling to face the political choices it involved. In the 1970s a strong *economic* case existed for converting the new giant oil-fired stations along the south coast to dual oil and coal-firing. Instead they were moth-balled, as a strategic reserve, ready to resume oil-fired production. What appeared to be economic incompetence was in fact political expediency. This oil-fired capacity was kept intact in expectation of miners' opposition to pit closures. This policy is now being turned against the miners' union. It is a policy which blunted the power of the NUM and with it the case for coal. It has bolstered the aims and interests of those powerful groupings that wish to dethrone coal. Behind their formal commitment to the 'spirit' of the *Plan for Coal*, the Thatcher Government's view is actually the reverse of the Plan.

The government's plan begins with a severe contraction of the coal industry to perhaps half its present size. The CEGB told the Monopolies Commission in 1980 that it envisaged a fall in coal burn of 50–55 million tons by the end of the century. But size is not the only objective nor even the most important. Reorganization is to accompany the scaling down process to reduce dependence on both the mineworkers and, to a lesser extent, the power workers. Here the private interests of giant corporations mesh with the requirements of the state. These requirements dictate that the state has available: 1) a centrally controlled energy supply that is proof against external forces — be they militant trade unionism, consumer pressures, environmental pressures or whatever; 2) a protected civilian nuclear fuel cycle capable of supplying the nuclear needs of the military.

'Getting out of coal' is therefore not so much an energy strategy as a major political option. It was the objective before 1974. It remains the objective, gathering urgency, as time runs out. The policy is one of diversification, especially into nuclear power, through the agency of the CEGB. But because it is not explicit it has caused confusions in the minds of all but the guiding few — and a desperate conflict with the miners as they dig in and fight back.

This confusion is particularly damaging given the economic *risks* and *costs* involved in the nuclear energy strategy. In his recent book, *How Safe is Nuclear Energy?*, Sir Alan Cottrell has presented a view of the nuclear debate that takes into account the accumulated experience of the nuclear industry. A former chief scientist and a widely respected expert on reactor safety, Cottrell is representative of what may be described as the enlightened and tolerant body of opinion associated with the nuclear interests. His view of the debate is that the heat and fury derives very largely from 'an apprehension about future possibilities'. He accepts that there are foundations for some, if not all, of the fears. There are, he agrees, misconceptions about nuclear power. He does not hesitate to say that a good deal of the responsibility for this lies on the shoulders of his fellow scientists and the nuclear industry, though he does not exempt some of the critics who, he suggests rather darkly, have ulterior motives. Clearly there is a degree of validity in this presentation. As an explanation for the debate over nuclear power it fails however for a number of reasons.

Firstly I believe that the scientists have overstated the factual content of their argument. In particular they have failed to assess adequately the problem of risk. This applies both to safety and to economics. In particular they have neglected the close relation between these factors. While they may legitimately argue that it is not their task to evaluate the costs of safety, it is no less true that they are not free to advocate the *necessity* of nuclear power without being sure that what they regard as satisfactorily safe standards are ones that society thinks it worth paying for. To put it simply, there is no purpose in deciding if the risk to safety is one that should be taken, if the cost of so doing is not acceptable.

The oft-repeated statement that no one in the UK has died as the result of nuclear power may be correct — but only in the legalistic sense. In scientific terms it is not a fact, and scientists should not lend their authority to give it credence. But the matter of safety in the strategic context is very much a matter of the size of nuclear programmes and their time horizons. The facts here are indeterminate, and the outcome is not one of fact in the sense that it can be calculated with any degree of reliability. Yet statements are frequently made to the effect that such calculations are reliable.

Because nuclear programmes have been small and experience has been limited, risk analysis based on that experience is imprecise — more a matter of guesses — which in turn are influenced by value judgements. Any study of the record of risk and safety studies in the nuclear industry can only lead to the conclusion that they are at the best not reliable, and at the worst a case of special pleading. The responsible bodies have repeatedly found it necessary to lower the threshold of danger, which means that present–day or past decisions may be inadequate for the future. This can lead to large economic losses. It is not, therefore, surprising that the understatement of risk on the one side has led to its overstatement on the other. To criticize non-specialists for not appraising the facts, as nuclear scientists often do, is no more than saying that they themselves have failed to distinguish fact from informed guesses. In some cases it would have been better to suspend judgement than give a pretended precision to a probability by using figures which are subject to large margins of error.

The problem of size is also central to problems of appraisal because economic risks, as well as the physical risks of nuclear power over time, depend very much on the size and speed of the construction attached to the nuclear programmes.

In evidence to the Royal Commission on Environmental Pollution, published in 1976, the AEA projected a future of 104 GW of nuclear power by the end of the century, and a further fourfold expansion in the following thirty years. In construction terms this meant one hundred large reactors in the first twenty-five years with all of the supporting industrial infrastructure, transport and waste disposal problems. From a base of only 4 GW in 1975, with no commercial experience of pressurised reactors, or of highly irradiated fuel reprocessing, the AEA wanted to scale up the programme by a factor of twenty-five in twenty years. To many these figures now appear unreal because the demand for energy has fallen. The AEA targeting, however, was typical of the government and the nuclear industry in this country and elsewhere and it remains so. It is not simply the magnitude of the programme, however, that strains credulity — it is the *rate* of the expansion envisaged. How, one may ask, did a body such as the AEA seriously project such a programme? The risk factor is undoubtedly related to the speed of scaling-up and construction.

The AEA presentation was a revealing insight into the states of mind of those who advised government. It should have been the point for the initiation of a critical debate. The critical remarks from the Royal Commission did draw attention to the exaggerated demands of the nuclear industry. It is instructive to recall the demand for further discussion did not come from within the nuclear industry, who it might have been thought were aware of the risks of such a massive programme; it came from outside the industry and from outside the government. The failure of the specialist agencies (of which the most important was the AEA), and the failure of the scientists to expose the irresponsibility implicit in the high nuclear targeting, has been a major factor in undermining public confidence. If the view is to be sustained that the concern about future possibilities arises from misconceptions and misinformation, then it arises from a situation that lies deep within the corps of scientists and engineers who make up the specialist agencies.

The requirement made by Sir Alan Cottrell that there is an ethical obligation 'to inform all the people fully and honestly all the time' is a necessary corollary to his view that an informed debate is necessary to arriving at decisions to build nuclear power stations. That is surely right. However, it is a requirement that is not and cannot be met. It is a requirement that is almost the reverse of the situation that has prevailed since nuclear power was introudced. Unwillingness to disclose information, or a direct refusal to do so by the AEA and CEGB for example, has been commented upon by other writers and is common to the experience of research workers in this field. Secrecy is not an aberration or a quirk; it is deeply imbued. It is an institutional condition which has developed over a long period of time and it is founded on very real needs which are important to the existence of the nuclear-industrial complex. It is not a condition which can be corrected by a better public relations programme. On the contrary, the public relations structure has been created in order that the code of secrecy can be maintained notwithstanding the evident concern of many interested persons that it should be broken down. The problem is not without a solution, but it most certainly is an intractable one, and can be overcome only through a thorough overhaul and restructuring of the industry.

The tradition of secrecy was carried over in the first instance from the military structures associated with nuclear fission. Historically the power reactor programme was a spin-off from the weapons programme. For a considerable time they shared some common technical facilities, and the AEA on its creation was given both a military and a civilian function. Collaboration between the military and the civilian technical programmes remains in some parts of the fuel cycle. There are other and more important reasons for secrecy.

In the mid 1950s, when both the AEA and the CEGB were created, a high degree of centralization was adopted. This centralization brought with it a code of rules and behaviour which required that the entire nuclear complex should speak as one. This single view is determined by a decision-making process in which only a small number of those working inside the industry have any direct participation, and about whose results the majority may sometimes be entirely ignorant. The operation of the Official Secrets Act is backed up by conditions of employment and by other control structures that ensure that dissenting opinions are kept within the organization. What freedom of debate exists is difficult to know with any precision, but it is not allowed to pass beyond the perimeters of the Board. This is the basis of the restrictive attitude to providing information to outside bodies. In France the generating board, the EDF, is known as the 'state within a state'. The situation in the UK is not so different.

The task of the central corps of decision-makers is to maintain the continuity of policy formation inside the organization and to keep it intact in spite of political changes or adverse circumstances that may develop. Public relations provide the public with what the organization believes it to be appropriate to tell them, and with what is compatible, as far as possible, with what the public wants to believe. This applies to the risks of nuclear power and also to the economic costs. In this, economists have not proved themselves to be any more scrupulous in their treatment of fact and uncertainty than the scientists have been.

If the question is asked, as it frequently is in Public Inquiries and of energy ministers in the House of Commons, 'What is the cost of nuclear power generated by the CEGB and the SSEB', the only possible answer that anyone who pretends to a knowledge of economics can give is 'we do not know'. Having made that plain it can then be said, 'We can estimate them for you but the value of such estimates is no better than the assumptions that we make, and some of these assumptions are very weak. So please read the assumptions before you quote the figures.' But economists frequently omit to say such things. They either keep quiet if they doubt the value of hard factual statements, as do large numbers of scientists in similar situations, or they repeat the official figures without the qualifications. Whether they actually believe them or not is something that is normally impossible to know, and in any case it is irrelevant. By repeating them they are supporting the institutional interest with which they are directly or indirectly associated. But there are certain rules that ought to be followed, and if they were, the concept of the 'necessity' of nuclear power would be seen to be untenable.

Nuclear power should be cost competitive. Investment projects should be capable of being tested for measurable opportunity costs. In order to get the optimum use of resources across the economy, public sector projects should realize a real rate of return that should be higher than alternative systems. This should be demonstrated before a project is undertaken, and for this the preferred method is to calculate the net present value using the real rate of return. The electricity supply industry has accepted these rules. However its preference for using historic costs rather than replacement costs, and for using such cost trends in extrapolating future requirements has led to a wide divergence between published costs and real costs. This criticism has been applied with particular force to nuclear power operation by the House of Commons Select Committee on Energy.

The commitment of the CEGB's chairman Sir Walter Marshall to the PWR programme which he pushed through when at the British AEA is proving a costly disaster. And as the failure of the construction industry, nuclear agency and generating boards to deliver new plant to time or costs repeated itself to an intolerable degree, so confidence worldwide in nuclear power has ebbed. The attempt to replace coal by the nuclear option is creating immense problems for the Establishment and is beginning to divide it internally. To some in this élite, *only* their desire to make the switch from coal makes it appear worthwhile.

Time and again in public discussion, questions of 'economics' and 'costs' boil down to issues of 'principle' and often of prejudice. Sir Alan Cottrell, for example, is in favour of nuclear power 'in principle'. Specifically he favours gas-cooled reactors. That is, he prefers gas-cooled technology to water-cooled technology for a number of technical reasons which are undoubtedly derived from long experience and a thorough knowledge of the subject. But preferring the AGR is like preferring the Concorde to a subsonic plane. It may be nice to look at; the engineering may be beautiful and it might even be safer, but no government that had regard for the economic welfare of its citizens would encourage its production. It is a loss maker.

They would probably be right to so do, although in hindsight the decision may result in an increase in the accident rate. When therefore Sir Alan Cottrell says that he is in favour of nuclear power 'in principle', what principle is he appealing to? The fact is that cost and safety trade-off. This trade-off has always existed in decision making. The balance may be tilted on one occasion to give greater weight to safety, and at another time to give greater weight to reduced operating costs. If, however, we want to maximize safety and reduce risks of an accident to as near to zero as possible, then we must be prepared to waive the economic tests as they are normally applied in our society. But the scientist has to face the fact that this is normally never done. In the nuclear industry the economic test has not been applied for a long period — but it is impossible for that to continue any longer. The cost of protection is becoming too high. Therefore the specialist cannot be 'in principle' in favour of one technology rather than another. There is no *a priori* reason why governments should favour nuclear power in preference to any other form of energy production. They are social products being produced for use. It is this end use which is of concern to the society that pays the specialist. He cannot and should not be 'in principle' in favour of one technology over another, for there is no principle at stake. There are only costs and benefits, and trade-offs between the two. As almost all scientists who support nuclear power do so on the basis of what Sir Alan calls 'principle', they have a basis of decision-making which by definition is out of phase with the public interest. They believe, and wrongly, that the interest of the nuclear power industry can be equated with the interest of society. There is, no reason for such an assumption.

Nuclear power has to be demonstrated to be superior, not in terms of its own qualities or in technology, but in terms of the energy form which it is displacing, or which is seeking to displace it. The principle is that the best should be preferred over the better. That will involve a balance of several issues, each of them, to a degree, defined in terms of something else. Cost will be measured in relative terms, but it is the balance which has to be got right at the end of the day. He who is a specialist to the degree that his choice is pre-determined is an obstacle to rational decision-making. It is only because our decision-making is in practice so irrational that the role of the specialist who is committed in principle continues to be carefully cultivated.

Before the chairman of any of the institutions in the nuclear complex says a word we know that he is going to say nuclear power is preferable on economic grounds to coal-fired generation. He may understand nothing about economics and he has probably demonstrated this in public many times. Nevertheless he lacks nothing in certainty when it is a matter of making such pronouncements. Why then trust what he says about any other subject? Equally we know that the specialist economists, employed by the agency, will arrive at the same conclusion as their chairman, although perhaps with a little more sophistication. Therefore why should anyone be surprised at the outcome of such evidence? Equally why should anyone take it seriously?

Decisions about nuclear power, as with many other very important decisions that commit national resources and will have far-reaching political implications, are not taken on social, ethical or economic grounds at all. They are institutionalized. The specialist is only a part of a process and can not be an independent actor. All but a few, including many of those in the industry, are without a voice in the matter. The great mass of the public are kept wholly ignorant. Once the decision is taken the specialist may test its wisdom. He or she may have some room to influence its implementation or even in exceptional circumstances urge a reconsideration. But generally the specialist will support the decision and bend his or her expertise to make it a reality. The notion that the logic of science or the rules of economics determine decision-making is the reverse of what usually happens.

What then of the future for electricity supply? In terms of cost and availability coal is the only safe option. The coal industry and electricity supply ought to be planned very largely as one industry, as they are so interdependent. No doubt Sir Walter Marshall and Mr MacGregor were appointed with the same essential brief — to dismember and shrink the coal industry and diversify electricity supply. They were both personally chosen by Mrs Thatcher to slot in with each other. But they are both a disaster. While MacGregor has, in the government's eyes, badly mishandled the reduction of coal, so Marshall, who staked his reputation on the delivery of the PWR stations, has mishandled the build-up of the alternative source.

In the face of this, the performance of the Labour leadership during the dispute appears increasingly banal. What needs emphasizing is their sheer incompetence. Years in government since 1964 have left them with no policy for energy that meets the needs of the British people. They are doing their best to pass up a clear opportunity to defeat Thatcherism and to expose the enormous risks and waste involved in the way the energy sector is being developed. The miners have been forced to take on the government and the state. The task of any political party allied to the trade unions and the working class should be to demonstrate the extent to which Thatcherism is laying this country open to some devastating risks in the future as well as the wanton destruction of a major national resource.

The Thatcher Government has no *policy*, what it represents is a state-inspired *strategy* for energy. If this strategy succeeds then it will become, *de facto*, the policy. With pits closed and nuclear power stations constructed, any future Labour Government will be stuck with it. These points need to be made clear. If coal is to have a future the next generation of power stations should be coal-fired. Equally, coal — and any rational 'Plan for Coal' — needs to be developed on the basis of an integrated electricity supply industry. This is something that the 1974 Plan never tackled. It laid the basis not for the assured future of the industry but the present crisis.

A new Plan for Coal is urgently required. It is not enough to know what we are against. It is at least as important to know what we are for.

12
Cole and Dole
Employment Policies in the Coalfields

Ray Hudson and David Sadler

Introduction

In the present economic climate it is perhaps salutary to recall that the 1944 White Paper on Employment Policy put particular emphasis upon ensuring that the inter-war problems of unemployment did not recur in the 'special areas'. It argued that: 'The first line of attack on the problem of unemployment in these areas must be to promote the prosperity of the basic industries on which they primarily depend e.g. coal . . . '[1] While certain ambiguities surround the notion of prosperity and how it might be achieved, the war-time coalition government's intentions at least were clear. The Labour Government's subsequent nationalization of the coal industry provided an opportunity to develop strategies that would effectively tackle unemployment in those areas. In fact, NCB policies have had precisely the opposite effect. Thousands of jobs have been lost in the mining industry which regional policies have been unable to replace. In 1984 those same 'special areas' still have high rates of unemployment *and* a continued high dependence upon coal-mining. As such, the prospect of further job losses in the NCB threatens those areas with immediate and long-term increases in the level of unemployment. It is the scale of this which we explore here.

NCB Policies and the Creation of Local and Regional Unemployment Problems

Regional Employment and Unemployment Changes

The regional distribution of the coal industry in 1952 illustrates the vulnerability of certain areas to NCB reductions in employment levels. Five regions (East Midlands; Northern England; Scotland; Wales; Yorkshire and Humberside), accounted for over eighty-two per cent of national coal-mining employment; over twenty-five per cent of all industrial employment in the Northern Region and Wales was in coal-mining, with considerable dependence upon employment in this industry in Scotland, Yorkshire and Humberside and the East Midlands. There were also significant local concentrations of coal-mining employment in other regions (see Tables 1 and 1a). The legacy of the development of the coal-mining industry and its geography meant that NCB policies would inevitably affect some regions much more directly than others.

Table 1
Regional Employment and Unemployment Changes, 1952–81

Standard Region	1952 Employment (thousands)		1952–81 Absolute employment change (thousands)		1952–81 Coal-mining change as percentage total industrial change
	All Industry	Coal-mining	All Industry	Coal-mining	
South East	2,902.2	9.3	−812.9	−5.3	−0.6
East Anglia	190.6	0.0	+42.4	0.0	n.a
South West	471.2	6.8	+23.8	n.a.	n.a.
West Midlands	1,323.7	67.0	−407.7	−47.0	−11.5
East Midlands	752.0	116.0	−74.0	−51.0	−68.9
Yorkshire and Humberside	1,149.2	105.2	−370.2	−72.2	−19.5
North West	1,692.1	59.4	−709.1	−49.4	−7.0
Northern	682.5	171.6	−213.5	−134.6	−63.0
Scotland	1,044.1	94.9	−305.1	−61.9	−20.3
Wales	483.4	127.2	−134.4	−105.2	−78.3
Great Britain		802.4		−532.4	

Sources: Fothergill and Gudgin, 1978; CSO, 1984 (*Regional Trends*, 1983); *Abstract of Labour Statistics (see Ham & Lingo Paper)*.

Between 1952 and 1981 eighty per cent of all national job losses in coal-mining were concentrated in the five main coal-mining regions. The effects of decline were most severely felt in the

Table 1 (cont.)
Regional Employment and Unemployment Changes, 1952–81

Standard Region	Regional decline in coal mining as percentage national decline 1951–81	Coal mining as percentage total industrial regional employment		Registered unemployment absolute numbers (thousands)		Registered unemployment percentage rates	
		1952	1981	1952	1981	1952	1981
South East	1.0	0.3	0.2	86.7	686.5	–	9.1
East Anglia	n.a.	0.0	0.0	7.5	70.1	1.3	9.9
South West	n.a.	1.4	n.a.	17.3	179.8	1.5	10.8
West Midlands	9.0	5.1	2.2	18.0	349.7	0.9	15.3
East Midlands	9.6	15.4	9.6	12.3	177.0	1.5	11.0
Yorkshire and Humberside	13.6	13.1	10.0	36.6	277.4	3.7	13.4
North West	9.3	3.5	1.0	107.3	424.2	2.6	15.1
Northern	25.6	25.1	7.9	32.6	216.2	3.3	16.2
Scotland	11.6	9.1	3.2	69.3	325.4	2.8	14.6
Wales	19.8	26.3	9.5	26.6	170.1	–	16.0

Sources: Central Statistical Office, *Regional Trends*, HMSO, 1984; Department of Employment and Productivity, *British Labour Statistics: Historical Abstract 1886–1968*, HMSO 1971; S. Fothergill and G. Gudgin, 'Regional Employment Statistics on a Comparable Basis', *Occasional Paper No. 5*, Centre for Environmental Research, 1978.

Northern Region and in Wales. These regions not only experienced the greatest absolute losses but coal-mining losses accounted for significant proportions (sixty-three per cent and seventy-eight per cent) of their net loss of industrial employment. Despite these very significant declines, there remains at this broad regional level a continuing dependence on coal-mining for jobs and wages. This measure of the failure of policies to introduce alternative employment is even more acutely evident in the very high levels of registered unemployment recorded in these regions by 1981.

Table 2
Changes in Manufacturing Employment, 1960–75

Region	Manufacturing employment (thousands)		Change (thousands)
	1960	1975	1960–75
Yorkshire and Humberside	907.2	776.6	−130.6
North West	1433.8	1,140.1	−293.7
Northern	453.9	465.2	+11.3
Scotland	765.6	657.5	−108.1
Wales	297.9	326.3	+28.4

Source: Fothergill and Gudgin, 1978.

Sub-regional Employment and Unemployment Change

The consequences of continued dependence on coal-mining for regional employment patterns are all the more powerful for communities which rely on the industry as the major — or sole — source of jobs and wages. Comprehensive and comparable employment and unemployment data for such communities are unavailable. However, it is possible to use statistics drawn from employment exchange areas which although not identical with mining villages, are small enough to allow a closer examination of the pattern of change in mining employment and its relationship to employment. 141 such areas have been selected, on the basis that in 1971 in each one over 4.9 per cent of total employment and/or 99 or more jobs were in coal-mining. These findings have been grouped according to region, enabling the more localized effects of change to be examined region by region. These areas together cover practically all coal-mining employment in Great Britain, accounting for 342,519 jobs (from a national total of 345,960) in 1971, and 258,412 (from 269,785 nationally) in 1981, of which most — eighty-three per cent — are accounted for by the NCB (see Tables 3 and 4).

Table 3
Employment Change by NCB Area, 1981–84

Area	Employment (thousands)		Absolute change (per cent)	
	1981	1984	1981–84	
Scottish	19.8	13.1	−6.7	−33.8
North East	32.0	22.9	−9.1	−28.4
North Yorkshire	15.1	12.9	−2.2	−14.6
Doncaster	16.2	13.4	−2.8	−17.3
Barnsley	15.3	13.7	−1.6	−10.5
South Yorkshire	16.7	14.0	−2.7	−16.2
North Derbyshire	12.2	10.5	−1.7	−13.9
North Nottinghamshire	18.1	16.7	−1.4	−7.7
South Nottinghamshire	15.5	12.6	−2.9	−18.7
South Midlands	16.4	12.9	−3.5	−21.3
Western	22.2	18.5	−3.7	−16.7
South Wales	25.3	20.2	−5.1	−20.6
Total	224.8	181.4	−43.4	−19.3

Source: National Coal Board, *Report and Accounts* London, 1981/2; 1983/4.

Between 1971 and 1981, 85,000 coal-mining jobs were lost in these 141 areas whilst nationally employment declined by 75,000. This difference is due to the emergence of a number of new coal-mining areas in the East Midlands and Yorkshire and Humberside. The greatest absolute employment losses were in Northern England, Scotland and Wales, although no region was immune. After 1981 the rate of job loss accelerated. Data are not available for local areas after 1981, the date of the last Annual Census of Employment, but NCB employment fell overall from 224,800 to 181,400 between 1981 and 1984 with losses most heavily concentrated in absolute forms in the North-East, Scottish and South Wales areas. When we consider these absolute figures of decline in relative terms (i.e. as a percentage of jobs in the industry), the South Midlands joins these regions as an area of high job loss (see Table 3).

One consequence of this round of job losses in local areas which had already suffered from severe cuts in coal-mining employment (and in many cases, reductions in employment in manufacturing industries such as steel and textiles) was further to increase unemployment from the existing and unacceptably high levels of 1981. Between 1981 and 1984, total registered unemployment in these areas rose on average from 14.9 per cent to 15.7 per cent and male unemployment from 17.2 per cent to 18.1 per cent. Over the same three–year period, the proportion of those registered unemployed who had been out of work for a year or more rose from 29.1 per cent to 42.5 per cent; for men, the rise was even steeper — from 32.5 per cent to 47.2 per cent. It is this dramatic and, at least in the post-war period, unprecedented rise in long-term unemployment that most vividly conjures up images of the 1930s being repeated in the 1980s in coal-mining areas. There is a further dimension to this. The increasingly common experience of long-term unemployment for the younger generation reflects the particular problems that this group faces in a period of very limited recruitment. As unemployment figures rose, the proportion of the labour force under twenty-five and registered unemployed for more than a year increased from 7.9 per cent in 1981 to 13.3 per cent in 1984.

In conclusion, however, it has to be emphasized that even figures such as those of the employment exchange areas fail adequately to reveal the degree of dependence of individual communities on coal-mining employment. In Seaham, County Durham, for example, over seventy-five per cent of all male employment is in mining and the economic and social structure of the town revolves around the coalfields. But even in places with a lower, though still very considerable, proportion of employment in coal-mining — Barnsley, for example, with thirty-three per cent of all male employment in mining,[2] the local importance of the coal industry is enormous. Despite the past run down of coal-mining employment, places such as these remain acutely sensitive to levels of employment in NCB collieries. This dependence raises questions as to why alternative employment opportunities are lacking in what remain essentially one-industry communities and, more generally, in regions reliant upon coal-mining.

NCB Policies and Regional Policies: New Jobs for Old?

It is crucial that the relationship between NCB policies to cut coal-mining employment and central government regional policies, supposedly intended to replace jobs lost in coal-mining areas, be properly understood. In the period 1945–58, when priority was given to maximizing coal output, the NCB and the Ministry of Fuel and Power successfully argued that new male-employing manufacturing activities should not be introduced into coal-mining areas because they would cause miners to leave the pits and so reduce coal output. When the NCB rapidly began to reduce coal-mining employment after 1958, as cheap imported oil and nuclear power increasingly replaced coal for electricity generation, this constraint was removed. This led to political pressures for a 'strengthened' and vigorously implemented regional policy, with the intention of transforming the coalfield economies to create a more diverse range of industrial employment. Such pressures came mainly from the labour movement and from those living in areas where coal-mining jobs were shrinking rapidly, but a broader political consensus developed around the politics of 'regional modernization' as some sections of private capital recognized the opportunities that such policies offered to them.

Various estimates have been made of the 'new' jobs created by regional policy in the assisted areas. Perhaps the most widely accepted are those that claim regional policy added 325,000 to 375,000 jobs in all the assisted areas, of which 200,000 to 250,000 were in the four development areas of Northern England, Northern Ireland, Scotland and Wales. But even if one accepts these figures, regional policy incentives could achieve this only because of the substantial pools of unemployed labour that were being re-created directly by NCB policies and indirectly by the downward multipliers that followed, particularly in the service sector. Furthermore, any job gains in 'new' manufacturing have to be set against losses in 'old' manufacturing already established in the assisted areas, losses partly attributable to existing companies, some of which were nationalized, using regional policy aid for restructuring, rationalization investments and so labour shedding. At best, then, in terms of total numbers of manufacturing jobs, regional policy was doing little more than replacing job losses from existing manufacturing activities, and perhaps not even achieving this, *during a period of relatively strong economic growth*. Taking into account the replacement of manufacturing jobs lost, regional policy made no contribution whatsoever to replacing the four hundred thousand jobs lost in coal-mining between 1960 and 1976. If we add to this considerations like the mismatch in skill levels and wages between 'new' and 'old' manufacturing jobs, the situation is even grimmer.

After 1976, with the increasing restrictions on public expenditure, cut-backs in regional policy assistance and the further switch in emphasis in regional policy objectives from employment creation to industrial restructuring *per se*, it is generally acknowledged that the net employment creation effects of that policy have been near to zero. Between 1976 and 1978 in the Northern Region, for example, new manufacturing plants moving in provided 3,300 new jobs while job losses in manufacturing activities existing in 1976 amounted to 64,300 over the same period.[3] Since 1978, this basic pattern of change has continued. In these circumstances, with unemployment rising rapidly, increasing emphasis has been given to various local job-creation initiatives, involving local authorities and/or *ad hoc* agencies such as BSC (Industry) Ltd. and more latterly NCB (Enterprise) Ltd. Characteristically, in tackling unemployment, such locally based projects rely to a great extent on the formation and growth of small businesses, an approach neatly described by Cochrane as 'draining the ocean with a teaspoon'.[4]

Perhaps the best 'model' with which to compare the likely effects of NCB (Enterprise) is the activities of BSC (Industry) and its successor, DIDA (Derwentside Industrial Development Agency), in the steel closure town of Consett. BSC(I) began operations in Consett in 1979, a year before the final closure of the steelworks with the loss of 3,700 jobs. Its activities were later taken over by DIDA, an enterprise trust involving local companies, as one expression of central government concern to introduce private capital into 'reindustrialization' schemes. DIDA aims to provide small firms with a three year business plan and to maximize their take-up of financial assistance available from local and central government and the European Economic Community.

The Agency claims some success for its efforts; indeed, it lays considerable emphasis upon self-promotion. It calculates that two thousand 'new' jobs were created between 1979 and March 1984. Given the range and extent of available incentives and the substantial pools of unemployed labour within the area, it would indeed have been surprising had no investors taken advantage of the situation. Nevertheless, it is debatable whether two thousand 'new' jobs have been created. There seems to be considerable confusion between job commitments and subsequent job creation. Many of these 'new' jobs result from existing companies switching location in Derwentside. Others come from DIDA adding existing companies to its portfolio of projects. Moreover no allowance is made for 'new' jobs that subsequently disappear. In so far as DIDA's activities have created jobs, then these number considerably less than the two thousand it claims. Given its performance to date, there seems little chance of DIDA meeting its own current target of five thousand new job *commitments*, itself a considerable downward revision of the original 1980 target of six thousand new *jobs* by 1985.

Furthermore, the new jobs that have been created in Derwentside since 1979 and the extent of reindustrialization need to be seen in relation to the broader labour market changes in the area since the steelworks closure. Many of the jobs created have not been for ex-steelworkers; nor are ex-steelworkers prominent in founding small businesses in the town. In any case, jobs created since the steelworks closure have to be seen in the context of other closures and job losses elsewhere in the district since 1980. Over two thousand jobs were lost in two branch plants after the steelworks closed and there have been subsequent notified redundancies in the district. These figures suggest that the 'reindustrialization strategy' will barely keep up with ongoing job losses. It has failed to compensate for the catastrophic events which hit the district in the period 1978–81, when thirty three per cent of *all* jobs there disappeared.[5] The inability of DIDA to resolve Consett's problems is reflected in the continuing high rate of registered unemployment — 23.8 per cent in March 1984.

One consequence of DIDA's failure is the increased scale of Manpower Services Commission (MSC) activities. Derwentside has spearheaded the growth of major national schemes. Of the 418 school-leavers in Consett in 1983, 247 were engaged on one-year Youth Training Schemes (YTS) by February 1984; at the same time there were 875 places filled on the Community Programme (CP) in the district. Fundamental criticisms may be levelled at both schemes. In the case of YTS, the most pressing question is 'training for what?'; all too often the answer is a year on supplementary benefit in order to qualify for short-term CP projects which themselves offer only low-skill work experience which should be provided by the conventional public sector. In a more general sense the nature of the MSC's dominance over the unemployed tends to stifle criticism of its work and, indeed, awareness of the depth of problems facing the community; alternative conceptions of what the problems are and how they might be tackled are not encouraged.

Conclusions

It is clear that the implications of any further coal-mining job losses will be extremely serious, particularly for communities that, despite past reductions in NCB employment remain heavily reliant upon jobs and wages from mining. These effects will be felt not only by miners who lose their jobs, and by their families — the impact of their loss of income will spread through local economies as employment in the service sector dependent upon miners' incomes also contracts.

The effect of wages permanently lost through coal-mining redundancies is graphically illustrated by the impact of the strike. A local butcher in Easington, County Durham, reported a decline of £300 in weekly sales while a motor dealer talked of sales reduced by £100,000 during the first nine months of the strike.[6] Within a fifteen mile radius of Barnsley, South Yorkshire, it is estimated that £1,750,000 a week, the post-tax incomes of fifteen thousand striking miners, has been taken from the economy.[7] As a result of such income losses, as many as fifty to eighty jobs will be lost in service sector activities for every hundred jobs lost in coal-mining.

As the great majority of work in the service sector is done by women, further job losses in coal-mining will increase female unemployment. The certain failure of regional development policies to stimulate new sources of employment on a scale commensurate with this predictable rate of job losses points only to growing male and female unemployment in areas where unemployment and particularly long-term unemployment is already unacceptably high. And as job opportunities disappear, employment opportunities for young people leaving school will be even more restricted than they are currently, increasing both youth unemployment and the proportion of the young among the long-term unemployed still further, all the more so as migration away from the coalfields holds little attraction at a time of high national unemployment.

But the impact of further job losses would not be confined to increases in unemployment rates, serious though these would be. With the closure of collieries and disappearance of jobs, the material basis of the cultural and social life of the coal-mining communities would be removed. It is not simply employment that is threatened but a way of life. The attempt to resist further closures and job losses must be understood not just as a protest against a future of life on the dole but as an expression of the value placed on this way of life by those who live, learn and work in such communities. Put another way, the resistance to such closures and job losses must be understood as an attempt to prevent the re-creation of the conditions of the 1930s in the coalmining areas in the 1980s.

227

Table 4a
Coal Employment Total and Percentage of Total Employment within Selected Areas, by Region, 1971 and 1981

	South East	South West	West Midlands	East Midlands	Yorks/Humberside	North West	North	Wales	Scotland	TOTAL
1971										
Coal employment	3911	648	25018	71063	84865	14463	60910	46299	35333	342510
Male coal employment	3825	644	23914	69093	82445	13780	59311	44903	34475	332390
Coal as % of total employment	13.6	6.1	4.8	14.6	10.4	5.4	10.0	9.9	6.6	9.1
Coal as % of male employment	20.3	9.0	7.1	23.1	15.4	8.4	15.5	14.6	10.7	13.9
1981										
Coal employment	2275	4	19162	64174	75581	9532	36548	32093	19043	258412
Male coal employment	2224	4	18154	62198	72418	9125	35487	30988	18535	249133
Coal as % of total employment	11.1	-	4.2	12.9	9.8	3.9	6.7	7.5	3.7	7.4
Coal as % of male employment	12.3	-	6.7	21.1	15.6	6.6	11.5	12.2	6.6	12.2

Table 4b
Unemployment Totals and Rates in Selected Areas, by Region, September 1981 and October 1984

	South East	South West	West Midlands	East Midlands	Yorks/ Humber- side	North West	North	Wales	Scotland	TOTAL
September 1981										
Total unemployed	3116	1443	89816	65514	126375	52084	108173	80391	83218	610230
Male unemployed	2158	1046	61681	47719	87831	34653	76263	55351	56724	423426
Total unemployment rate	13.2	12.4	16.4	11.6	14.1	17.5	16.5	15.8	13.9	14.9
Male unemployment rate	10.7	14.1	18.6	14.0	15.9	20.0	19.6	17.9	16.7	17.2
October 1984										
Total unemployed	3662	1422	86813	71864	140488	57841	117812	79938	89291	649131
Male unemployed	2242	884	58841	49972	96839	39834	84136	57013	61393	451154
Total unemployment rate	15.1	12.3	15.9	12.6	15.4	19.0	17.7	15.7	14.8	15.7
Male unemployment rate	11.1	12.1	17.9	14.5	17.3	22.4	21.2	18.3	17.8	18.1

Table 4c

Long-Term Unemployed and Long-Term Unemployed under 25 as a Percentage of Total Unemployed within Selected Areas, by Region, October 1981 and October 1984

	South East	South West	West Midlands	East Midlands	Yorks Humber-side	North West	North	Wales	Scotland	TOTAL
Long-term unemployed as a % of total unemployed										
October 1981										
Total	22.4	24.4	29.1	29.0	27.4	29.4	30.8	29.8	28.6	29.1
Male	25.9	25.0	31.7	32.7	30.7	33.3	34.8	33.0	32.4	32.5
October 1984										
Total	29.9	34.5	45.7	39.5	41.1	45.8	44.2	42.4	40.3	42.5
Male	35.7	37.3	51.0	44.1	45.5	51.2	48.6	47.0	45.0	47.2
Long-Term Unemployed under 25 as a % of Total Unemployed										
October 1981										
Total	4.8	6.3	7.7	6.7	7.7	8.8	8.0	8.1	8.2	7.9
Male	4.7	5.0	7.1	6.2	7.0	8.6	7.6	7.6	8.0	7.4
October 1984										
Total	8.5	7.7	13.2	11.1	13.5	15.2	13.7	13.5	13.5	13.3
Male	8.5	7.0	12.9	10.5	12.5	15.4	12.8	13.1	13.1	12.8

230

Bibliography

Central Statistical Office, 1984, *Regional Trends* HMSO.
Cochrane, 1983, 'Local Economic Policies: Trying to Drain the Ocean with a Tea-spoon', in Anderson, J., et.al. (eds.), *Redundant Spaces in Cities and Regions*, Academic Press, London.
Department of Employment & Productivity 1971, *British Labour Statistics: Historical Abstract, 1886_1968*, HMSO.
Fothergill, S. and Gudgin, G., 1978, 'Regional Employment Statistics on a Com-parable "Basis" ' *Occasional Paper No. 5*, Centre for Environmental Research.
Gudgin, G., Rhodes, J. and Moore, B., 1982, 'Employment Problems in the Cities and Regions of the UK: Prospects for the 1980's', *Cambridge Economic Policy Review*, 8, 2.
HMSO, 1944, *Employment Policy*, Cmd. 6577
Hudson, R., 1985, 'Nationalised Industry and Regional De-industrialisation: the British Disease', *Society and Space,* forthcoming.
NCB, *Report and Accounts*, 1981/2 and 1983/4, London.
Robinson, F. and Sadler, D., 1984 'Consett after the Closure' Dept. of Geography, *University of Durham Geography Department Occasional Publications*,1984, no. 19.
Robinson, F. and Sadler, D., 'Routine Action, Reproduction of Social Relations and the Place-Market: Consett after the closure', *Society and Space* (forthcoming).

Notes

1. *Employment Policy*, HMSO, 1944, Cmd. 6527.
2. *Financial Times*, 8 August 1984.
3. R. Hudson, 'Nationalized Industry and Regional De-Industrialization: the British Disease', *Society and Space*, forthcoming.
4. Cochrane, 'Local Economic Policies: Trying to Drain the Ocean with a Tea-spoon', in J. Anderson et. al. (eds.), *Redundant Spaces in Cities and Regions*, London, 1983.
5. For detailed accounts see: F. Robinson and D. Sadler, 'Consett after the Closure', *University of Durham Geography Department Occasional Publications*, 1984, no. 19; and 'Routine Action, Reproduction of Social Relations and the Place-Market: Consett after Closure', *Society and Space*, forthcoming.
6. *Newcastle Journal*, 11 December 1984.
7. *Financial Times*, 8 August 1984.

13
Computerized Coal
New Technology in the Mines

Jonathon Winterton

The first two national mining strikes since the 1926 lockout, in 1972 and 1974, occurred after a period of rapid contraction in the coal industry. Between 1958 and 1971 almost half a million jobs, two-thirds of the industry, were lost as oil displaced coal in the UK energy market. Simultaneously, in order to make coal more competitive with oil, the NCB introduced powerloading, the mechanization of face work, and about half of the job losses arose from this.[1] To facilitate powerloading, piecework was abandoned in favour of measured daywork, and bargaining was elevated to the national level. The combination of economic decline and reduced opportunities for local pay bargaining caused miners' earnings to decline in relative, and in some cases absolute, terms. Moreover, the industry became far less strike prone and miners increasingly pursued grievances through the pit conciliation machinery.[2] Paradoxically, the decline in strike frequency was accompanied by a growth of militancy and a politicization of rank and file miners which found expression in the two national strikes in the early 1970s aimed at restoring the miners' position in the earnings league.[3] Powerloading also increased the miners' control over the labour process by requiring new skills and by returning 'responsible autonomy' to face teams.[4]

The coal strikes of 1972 and 1974 had a profound effect upon government and NCB strategies. The Conservatives, defeated in the 1974 election partly because of their handling of the miners' strike, while in opposition developed their strategy for the next confrontation with the miners,[5] and after the 1979 election planned to substitute nuclear energy for coal-fired electricity generation.[6] The Labour Government of 1974 responded to the miners' strike and the oil crisis by establishing the tripartite discussions that led to the *Plan for Coal*. Central to this agreement of expansion for the coal industry was a programme of investment to extend the life of existing collieries and to introduce new capacity.

The NCB sought to avert further national pay strikes by fragmenting the bargaining structure with area incentive schemes.[7] In its implementation of *Plan for Coal* the NCB also developed strategies to reduce the miners' control over the labour process. A Central Planning Unit (CPU) was established to co-ordinate investment projects over twenty years.[8] In conjunction with this activity the Operational Research Executive (ORE) reviewed the NCB's activities and, through the application of systems engineering, established a framework for the automation of production, personnel and materials activity throughout the industry.[9] Because of the historical problems of supervision at the coal-face,[10] one of the key objectives of automation was to increase management control over operations and to minimize human intervention,[11] thereby raising the productivity of labour and capital.[12]

To realize the objectives defined by the ORE, the Mining Research and Development Establishment (MRDE) designed MINOS (Mine Operating System), a computer system for remote control and monitoring of colliery activities. MINOS comprises various subsystems devoted to particular functions such as coal clearance, face delays and coal preparation, all of which are overseen by minicomputers in a surface control room. The VDUs of the control console present mimic displays of the coal face, conveyor systems and other operations, indicating the status of items of plant. When the conveyors are not running, when the shearer is stopped or when ventilation fans have failed, the system alerts control-room operators. Much of the information that is passed to the control room is analysed by a secondary computer accessible only to management, and at the top of the system hierarchy Compower, a wholly-owned NCB subsidiary, collates the information obtained from individual pits to compare performance.[13] Figure 1 gives a schematic view of the system.

The design philosophy of MINOS embodies three principles which have profound implications for the NUM. First, the system is hierarchical and centralized; it mirrors the existing management structure but is designed to bring accurate, detailed information from all areas of the pit to the highest levels of management on a continuous basis. This design feature reflects the objective of increasing managerial control. Second, as many functions as possible are subject to closed-loop automatic control: 'Normally and wherever possible, the control actions are taken automatically by the computer. When

Figure 1.
MINOS Hierarchy

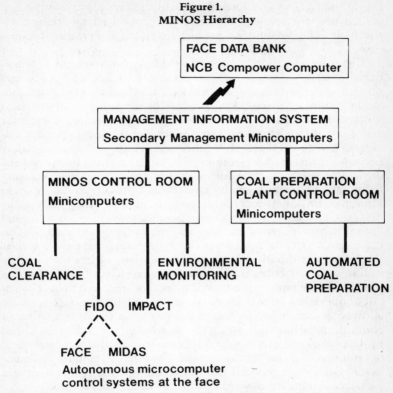

Source: A. Burns *et al*, 'The Miners and New Technology', *Industrial Relations Journal*, 1983, 14.4, p. 13.

an operator needs to change the state of the plant he does so by using simple keyboard procedures.'[14] This feature reflects the objectives of raising productivity through eliminating labour, and of facilitating increased management control through deskilling. The third significant principle of the MINOS design is its modularity. While a modular approach to designing and testing the separate subsystems is a logical consequence of using the systems approach, the piecemeal application of MINOS also obscured the nature of the overall system from the NUM. Before the strike about eighty pits had at least one MINOS facility, but none had the entire system; the first complete MINOS installation was to have been the Woolley complex in Barnsley. Of the 125 MINOS applications identified in 1983, only five were concerned with the ancillary objective of improving the working environment. The remainder were directed towards increasing production.

The colliery activities most affected by MINOS need to be considered briefly before an assessment can be made of the changes occurring in the industry, and it is logical to begin with the coal-face as the origin of production. Because of the complexities of face-work several separate subsystems are being developed to monitor and control face activities. From work measurement the NCB calculated that the available shift time divided into three approximately equal portions: machine-running time, delays caused by operational difficulties such as conveyor or shearer failure, and delays arising from natural breaks taken by face-teams.[15] FIDO (Face Information Digested On-line) was developed to monitor the 'man-made' delays. General purpose monitoring outstations at the coal-face send digital information to the control room computer which indicates on the console VDU the position of the shearer along the face, as well as the cause and duration of any delays. Delays of less than twenty minutes are attributed to the men and adversely affect their bonus pay. Delays of twenty minutes or more that are found to have arisen out of operational difficulties beyond the control of the face-team are allowed as contingencies under the pay scheme. Operating like a continuous tachograph, FIDO, the 'watchdog' as it has been dubbed by face-workers, can distinguish between two successive delays of ten minutes and one continuous delay of twenty minutes. As 'man-made' delays are reduced machine-running time is increased and each face is required to yield a given amount of coal accordingly.

The automation of face activities poses more complex technical problems than does monitoring face-work. An automated system to control the advance of the conveyor and roof supports, FACE (Face Advance Control Equipment), was at the stage of underground trials before the overtime ban. An automatic coal-face surveyor is being developed by MRDE to monitor face alignment. The automation of the shearer itself entails two further subsystems.[16] The subsystem devoted to horizontal guidance of the shearer has passed underground trials[17] and MIDAS (Machine Information Display and Automation System), which controls the vertical guidance of the shearer and monitors the condition of the machine, is already installed on at least twenty faces. At Wath Colliery, a MIDAS prototype (System 70,000) consistently doubled the coal extraction per shift, repaying the investment in microprocessor control equipment in ninety-two machine shifts, or forty working days.[18] As MIDAS increases face output so fewer working faces are required to meet coal demand. The automation of face-work reduces face deployment and deskills the jobs, making face-work more like factory machine minding.

The monitoring of the condition of the shearer via MIDAS is aimed at reducing operational delays at the coal face.[19] A similar facility is offered for all plant and machinery throughout the pit with IMPACT (In-built Machine Performance and Condition Testing). IMPACT reports on breakdowns and, through the monitoring and analysis of information such as oil pressure, bearing temperature and motor torque, can predict failures before they occur. The system specifies the nature of a fault, corrective action to be undertaken and even the personnel requirement.[20] In removing the diagnostic elements of craftsmen's work, MIDAS and IMPACT not only deskill craft jobs but also reduce the number of craftsmen required. Craftsmen increased to twenty per cent of the work-force because of powerloading but in the two years before the strike colliery managers were putting pressure on young craftsmen to retrain as deputies or machine men and encouraging older craftsmen to volunteer for redundancy. In reply to recommendation 9 of the Monopolies and Mergers Commission Report on the NCB that 'priority . . . should be given to developing targets for reduction in the numbers of craftsmen',[21] the NCB argued that remote monitoring systems would substantially reduce the need for craftsmen.

Whether output from the face can be increased depends upon the capacity limitations of the conveyors and bunkers that comprise the coal transport system. MINOS coal clearance has therefore generally been installed before changes are made at the face, and such systems are known to have been introduced to at least forty-four collieries, where a ninety-five per cent availability of clearance to the face is claimed. From the MINOS control room conveyors can be started or stopped and bunkers loaded or discharged, these activities being monitored by the system and displayed in mimic form on the control console VDU. Automatic sequence starting of conveyors prevents overruns and chute blockages at transfer points, while conveyors are automatically stopped if overheating or a torn belt is detected. In North Derbyshire, deployment to conveying systems was halved last year owing to MINOS coal clearance.[22]

In addition to coal clearance, early MINOS applications were concerned with controlling fixed plant — ventilation fans, pumps, and other equipment — and with monitoring the working environment. The environmental monitoring subsystem continuously measures atmospheric pressure and methane concentration, and analyses mine air. The surface control room is alerted of any abnormal conditions, while continuous monitoring provides early warning of methane concentrations building up.[23] There have been relatively few instances of the installation of environmental monitoring facilities despite the recommendation of the Inspectorate of Mines and Quarries in their report on the Cardowan disaster that 'urgent attention' be given to the installation of such systems.[24] The subsystem eliminates entirely the work of individuals deployed to methane and dust sampling, but since they are few in number the manpower savings to the NCB are not so significant, which perhaps explains the limited application of the system.

Like coal clearance, coal preparation was an early automation objective of the MINOS programme because surface facilities have to be able to cope with any increase in face output. Automated coal preparation plants exist at sixteen locations, mostly serving multi-colliery complexes. Microprocessor control of washing, sizing and blending gives a more consistent product than from manually operated plants, while plant monitoring ensures more continuous performance.[25] Besides the economies of scale associated with concentrating surface-production facilities for several pits, the automated plants effectively reduce manning by about thirty-four per cent. Because the work is less skilled and the environment cleaner, the NCB attempted to employ workers on the lowest surface grade, which prompted the first dispute over new technology at South Kirkby, Barnsley, in 1979. A Joint Committee on Grading and Technology was established in response to the action of the South Kirkby branch in boycotting the plant for two years.

The separate MINOS subsystems are linked together in the colliery control room where changes in the operations of one subsystem are made automatically in response to conditions monitored by another subsystem. Beyond the level of day to day operations, the secondary computer collates and analyses information of interest to management. The MIS (Management Information System) comprises software to analyse summary data relating to shift performance, machine availability, maintenance, absence, etc., as well as to make comparisons over time and between shift teams. Performance data for particular faces increases management control at pit level and is passed to Compower's computer at Cannock where the national Face Data Bank is maintained. The information from the Face Data Bank is used in the NCB strategic model developed by ORE for the

CPU to determine the mix of different types of capacity to meet future demand.[26]

The application of new technology in coal-mining reflects the CPU objective of restructuring the industry. *Plan for Coal* envisaged the introduction of new capacity to compensate for that lost through exhaustion. The exercise has been continued even though the demand projections of *Plan for Coal* have proved optimistic. With static or falling demand for coal the introduction of new capacity requires the elimination of corresponding capacity, not through exhaustion but because it becomes *surplus capacity*. The restructuring has led to the closure of surplus capacity which the NCB describes as 'uneconomic pits'.

The restructuring entails a massive loss of jobs deriving from three processes. First, new capacity is being introduced from the development and reorganization of existing collieries. In the Barnsley area sixteen pits have been grouped into three complexes centred on automated coal preparation plants at Woolley, Grimethorpe and South Kirkby. The reorganization enables an optimization of resources so that output is to be increased by twenty-one per cent and manpower reduced by twenty per cent according to the chief mining engineer,[27] although media reports based on NCB press releases have indicated productivity levels that suggest job losses of the order of thirty per cent.[28] The second process entailing job loss is the elimination of human activity through automation. The planned manning levels for fully-integrated MINOS pits are fifty-three per cent of existing levels. Job losses could be even greater depending upon the outcome of the Advanced Technology Mining programme which has the 'objective of a two-man face line in 1987'.[29]

The third process leading to job losses arises with the increased production from the first two changes. It is this process that has led to the closure, and threatened closure, of pits representing surplus capacity. Although 41,000 jobs had already disappeared from the industry between March 1981 and the onset of the strike, the enormity of the crisis has only emerged as the pit-closure programme has unfolded.[30] In February 1981 the NCB issued a list of twenty-three collieries it planned to close but withdrew this after the threat of a national strike. Later that year the NCB undertook an 'intensive review' of about twenty pits and by October 1981 had implemented half of the closure programme withdrawn earlier. In July 1982 the NCB admitted to a 'searching financial review' of some thirty pits, having by then closed or merged fifteen of the twenty-three pits on the original list through the local joint review procedure. In

November 1982, documents leaked from the NCB suggested that seventy-five 'short-life pits', employing fifty thousand miners, could close in the next decade. In June 1983, after the Monopolies and Mergers Commission Report defined 141 of the 198 pits then operating as unprofitable, the NCB announced plans to axe up to seventy thousand jobs over the next five years. On 30 September 1983 the NCB reply to the 1983 pay claim referred to the need to eliminate 'uneconomic pits'.

On 6 March 1984 the NCB told the NUM that 25 million tonnes of new capacity was to be introduced by the end of March 1988, 12.5 million tonnes from Selby and 12.5 million tonnes from the reorganization of existing collieries. The introduction of this new capacity will be associated with the elimination of corresponding capacity from high-cost pits. The scale of job loss with this substitution can be appreciated from the operating statistics for Selby compared with those for South Wales and Scotland. Selby will produce 12.5 million tonnes per annum with a work-force of 3,500 while the two areas together produce 13.5 million tonnes with a work-force of 39,000. As the automation programme increases output from MINOS pits, so more high-cost pits become classified as surplus capacity.

The combined effect of the restructuring announced on 6 March with the continued application of MINOS has been calculated to be the loss of 100,000 jobs by the end of March 1988.[31] The coal industry would consist of 79,000 miners working 93 pits plus Selby to produce 93.4 million tonnes of coal per annum. If the restructuring continues no NCB area will be free from job losses, but pit closures will be most widespread in what the NCB regard as 'peripheral' areas.[32] The application of MINOS is heavily concentrated in the central coalfield: while Scotland, Durham, South Wales and Kent comprise thirty-five per cent of NCB collieries, only twelve per cent of MINOS applications are found there. In the last financial year NCB expenditure per capita on major capital projects in South Wales was under three per cent of the figure for Doncaster and less than one per cent of the figure for North Yorkshire which includes the Selby development.[33] If the pits in the peripheral areas are in any sense 'uneconomic', then this is a direct consequence of NCB investment strategy. Schumacher, when economic adviser to the NCB, warned against describing high-cost pits as 'uneconomic': 'we must recognize that the concepts of "economic" and "uneconomic" cannot be applied to the extraction of non-renewable resources without very great caution . . . To eliminate the losing factory means the elimination of waste. But to close the losing colliery means merely to change the time sequence in which finite resources are being used.'

The concentration of capacity in the central coalfield has serious strategic implications that transcend even the miners' fight for jobs and communities. If the pits in the peripheral areas are closed then the enormous reserves of coal there will be sterilized; even when it is technically possible to reopen a colliery, the associated costs or dangers are usually prohibitive. Concentration of production and sterilization of reserves has been condemned in the past: 'It is a policy of doubtful wisdom and questionable morality for this generation to take all the best resources and leave for its children only the worst. But it is surely a criminal policy if, in addition, we wilfully sterilize, abandon, and thereby ruin such inferior resources as we ourselves have opened up but do not care to utilize. This is like the spiteful burglar who does not merely pinch the valuables but in addition destroys everything he cannot take.'[34] Concentrating capacity not only sterilizes peripheral reserves, it also exhausts central reserves sooner than would otherwise be the case. Selby's 240 million tonnes of winnable reserves will be gone in twenty years at the NCB's rate of extraction, while the rest of the central area's reserves might only last fifty years. This is in contrast with total national coal reserves of about three hundred years if existing collieries are maintained.

The present restructuring, developed to meet an expansion of coal demand under *Plan for Coal*, is therefore an inappropriate strategy for present demand conditions. As Glyn has noted: 'there is no basis whatever under present conditions for using the development of new lower-cost capacity as a justification for premature closing of older pits'.[35] Unless long-term economic interests are to be subordinated to short-term financial objectives, the introduction of new capacity should be delayed to coincide with the exhaustion of high-cost capacity, and sufficient investment made in peripheral areas to extend the life of these pits.

The debate concerning the use of new technology in the mines should not be confined to the strategic question of how the country's reserves of coal are best exploited. A motion from South Kirkby branch, passed at Yorkshire Area Council before the strike, called for a technology agreement to be negotiated between the NUM and the NCB. The NCB has refused to discuss a draft technology agreement; R. Dunn, Director General of Mining, described discussion over new technology as 'inappropriate'.[36] The NUM draft technology agreement seeks to establish a procedure for negotiating technological change with the status quo prevailing until agreement is reached. The agreement would preserve jobs through reductions in working time: a four-day, twenty-eight hour working week; early retirement at fifty-five; and longer holidays. Moreover, it would eliminate computer-based work monitoring systems like FIDO that would be unlawful in Scandinavia.

Rank and file support for the new technology agreement grew out of management's response to the overtime ban. FIDO reports were seen as a crucial weapon for management attempting to maintain production, and IMPACT was used to alter the work of craftsmen who were most affected by the ban. As maintenance work was undertaken on Mondays and, by the fourth week, Tuesdays, miners began to experience a *de facto* three or four-day working week. This experience also demonstrated the inadequacy of basic pay and the importance of the bonus scheme that had fragmented national pay bargaining. Early in the strike a rank and file miners' group, 'Miners for the New Technology Agreement', published their case for the four-day week, arguing that the strike against pit closures: 'should not be squandered on some compromise that gives us nothing but a stay of execution . . . Any return to work following this dispute must involve the ratification and signing of that agreement — otherwise we may well win this battle against job losses but lose the war . . . If we are fighting for jobs let's make them jobs worth having.'

The miners' case for shorter working time does not rest solely upon the vast increases in productivity associated with MINOS and the need to preserve communities. Health is the ultimate legitimization of the miners' case. That miners head the list of occupational mortality for every major cause of death is well known. So, too, is the fact that miners are more likely to suffer pneumoconiosis, bronchitis or cardiovascular diseases than they are to have a serious accident at work, even though the accident rate of coal-mining is higher than that of any industry except fishing.

The NCB's restructuring programme will, unless altered, cause a deterioration of health on three counts. First, exposure to existing hazards, particularly dust, is increased along with machine-cutting time. Even if statutory dust levels are not exceeded, face-workers would inhale a greater volume of dust and suffer a higher incidence of pneumoconiosis and bronchitis unless working time is reduced. Second, work surveillance, increased management control, deskilling and social isolation are all factors likely to increase occupational stress and stress-related illness like cardiovascular diseases and gastro-intestinal disorders. Third, unemployment in mining communities in the 1930s was associated with a deterioration in the health of miners, ex-miners and their families.[37] Unlike the job losses of the 1958–71 period when unemployment was relatively low, the loss of mining jobs in the present recession could have a similarly dramatic effect upon the health of mining communities. The simplistic notion that new technology should be used to eliminate hazardous manual labour like mining ignores the health effects of unemployment and of the deterioration of working conditions for those that remain in the industry.

That new technology is used to serve the objectives of the NCB alone is only inevitable so long as these objectives are determined by managerial prerogative instead of negotiation. Once negotiation proceeds beyond the issue of the distribution of benefits from new technology, miners themselves can influence design strategies to maintain skills and increase their control over the labour process as well as prioritizing the improvement of the working environment.[38] The need for such a strategy is particularly great in the peripheral areas because MINOS has been designed for the relatively stable conditions of the central coalfield. In addition to more investment in the peripheral areas, appropriate technologies need to be developed for the faulted seams of South Wales and for Scotland's steeply-inclined faces.

The questions surrounding the use of new technology have submerged for the present because the strike is a response to pit closures. Pit closures have so dramatic an effect upon mining communities that attention is diverted even from the NCB's restructuring programme that has brought them about; the effect is so blinding that the cause escapes unseen. The NCB's pursuit of policies that are to the detriment of the long-term interests of the industry is the result of political objectives declared in the Ridley Report and the cabinet minute of October 1979, and personified in the appointment of Ian MacGregor as NCB chairman. Dissenting voices within the NCB, like that of Geoffrey Kirk, who edited a book of Schumacher's writings[39] before 'retirement' as NCB director of public relations, have been silenced.

Notes

1. Monopolies and Mergers Commission, *National Coal Board*, HMSO, 1983, Cmnd. 8920.

2. J. Winterton, 'The Trend of Strikes in British Coal Mining', *Industrial Relations Journal*, 1981, 12, 6, 10–20.

242

3. V. L. Allen, *The Militancy of British Miners*, Shipley, 1981.

4. A. Burns, M. Newby and J. Winterton, 'New Technology and the Restructuring of Work in British Coal Mining', paper given at British Sociological Association Conference, University of Bradford, 2–5 April 1984.

5. *Economist*, 27 May 1978, on the Ridley Report.

6. Cabinet minute, October 1979.

7. J. L. Handy, *Wages Policy in the British Coal Mining Industry*, Cambridge, 1981.

8. R. Ormerod, 'Corporate Planning and its use of Operational Research in the NCB: a personal view', *Journal of the Operational Research Society*, 1983, 34, 6, 461–7.

9. A. Burns, D. Feickert, M. Newby and J. Winterton, *An Interim Assessment of* MINOS, University of Bradford, 1982, Working Environment Research Group Report no. 4.

10. C. Goodrich, *The Frontier of Control*, London, 1920; R. H. Heath, 'The National Power Loading Agreement in the Coal Industry and some aspects of Workers' Control', *Trade Union Register*, 1969, 185–200.

11. K. W. Chandler, 'MINOS — A Computer System for Control at Collieries', Second International Conference on Centralized Control Systems, London, March 1978.

12. C. C. Cooper, 'Improving Machine Utilization and Reliability', COMMIT 82, Computer-based Mine Management Information Technology Exhibition and Symposium, Harrogate, 8–10 December 1982; E. Horton, 'Mining Techniques in the 1980s', *Mining Engineer*, February 1983, 451–5.

13. Burns, Feickert, Newby and Winterton, 'The Miners and New Technology', *Industrial Relations Journal*, 1983, 14, 4, 7–20.

14. Chandler.

15. J. Cleary, 'FIDO at Bold Colliery', *The Mining Engineer*, November 1981, 281–89.

16. D. K. Barham and P. Tregelles, 'Progress with the guidance of Anderton shearer loaders in the UK', 108th AIME Annual Meeting, New Orleans, 1979.

17. D. Hartley and J.R. Wolfenden, 'Horizon control system designs for longwall face machines', International Conference on Remote Control and Monitoring in Mining, NCB, 1977, vol. 1.

18. Mining Research and Development Establishment, *Coalface Automation*, NCB, 1983.

19. F. Fennelly, 'Coalface Machine Health', COMMIT 82.

20. J. J. Bates, 'Inbuilt Machine Performance and Condition Testing — IMPACT', *Mining Engineer*, July 1981, 31–7.

21. Monopolies and Mergers Commission, NCB.

22. Mining Department, *Production and Productivity Bulletin*, NCB, September 1983, no. 15.

23. G. W. Gray and I. H. Morris, 'Environmental monitoring in the United Kingdom', International Conference on Remote Control and Monitoring in Mining, 1977.

24. HMI Mines and Quarries, *The Explosion at Cardowan Colliery Stepps, Strathclyde Region, 27 January 1982*, HMSO, 1982.

25. C. T. Massey, 'Opportunities for microelectronics in mining', *Mining Engineer*, February 1983, 451–5.

26. R. J. Ormerod, M. W. Plackett and F. J. Toft, 'The NCB Strategic Model', *European Journal of Operational Research*, 1982, 10, 351–60.

27. C. Shepherd, 'The reconstruction of the Barnsley area of the NCB', Midlands Institute of Mining Engineers, January 1984.

28. *Barnsley Chronicle*, 30 December 1983.

29. Mining Department, *Bulletin*, March 1984, no. 16.

30. Winterton, 'The Crisis in British Coal Mining', *Insurgent Sociologist*, no. 12, forthcoming.

31. Burns, Newby, Winterton, *Second Report on* MINOS, University of Bradford, 1984 WERG Report no. 6.

32. Ibid., 'The Restructuring of the British Coal Industry', *Cambridge Journal of Economics*, forthcoming.

33. NCB, *Report and Accounts 1983/4*, 1984.

34. E. F. Schumacher, 'Coal — the next fifty years', *Britain's Coal*, NUM Study Conference, 25–6 March 1960.

35. A. Glyn, 'The Economic Case against Pit Closures', Report to the NUM, mimeo, 1984.

36. BBC Newsnight, 16 February 1984.

37. J. L. Halliday, *Psychosocial Medicine*, London, 1948.

38. F. Heising, 'The Haus Aden Project', International Conference on Remote Control in Mining, 1977.

39. G. Kirk, *Schumacher on Energy*, London, 1982.

14
Towards a New Future:
Campaigning for Coal

Dave Feickert

In 1974, in the wake of a historic strike by the mineworkers, the NCB agreed with the newly-elected Labour Government and the trade unions a long-term strategy for the coal industry. This became known as the *Plan for Coal*. It was signed in 1974 and reaffirmed in a progress report in 1977 and again in 1981. The *Plan for Coal* was a plan for investment and for growth in production. However it had a number of flaws, both in its construction (see chapter 11) and its implementation.

Take the question of investment: there has been major investment in the infrastructure of some existing pits, for example on roadways and mechanical equipment, as well as the construction of new collieries. There has also been considerable investment in computer technology to operate and control automatically mechanical and electrical equipment. In terms of productivity it is this second type of investment which seems likely to be crucial. In 1974, microchips were not readily available, and at that time the employment effects of this new technology were little understood. However micro-electronics has made possible the development of a new breed of coal-mines with advanced, computer-production techniques. These are the 'super pits' like Selby and the multi-pit complexes now under construction in the Barnsley area (see chapter 13). The effects of this new technology are dramatic. They are a major threat to miners' jobs. They also present a major opportunity for the NCB to increase its profits substantially. At 1983 prices, the NCB expects to make £17 profit on every tonne mined at Selby. This would amount to an annual net profit of at least £170 million — enough to pay the wages of the twenty thousand miners in high-cost pits whose jobs will disappear as the 'superpits' come on stream. The possibility of this happening is, however, somewhat remote under the existing arrangements. More likely is a government-led attempt to sell off the high technology pits to the private sector at a juicy profit. The smaller low technology pits, with poor wages and working conditions, would be left in the hands of the NCB.

Benefits of Technology

But there are two sides to the coin of new technology. The vastly increased productivity it makes possible can certainly fuel large profits and job cutting. But it could just as easily fund cuts in hours worked. Unfortunately, to date, nearly all of its benefits have been enjoyed, exclusively, by the NCB. The miners have gained little: there has been no reduction in working hours in the mining industry since surface workers achieved a forty-hour week in 1969. In this respect, coal–miners have fared badly in relation to workers in other sectors like engineering and chemicals.

For many years the NUM has been attempting to win a four-day week, with pay for five days, and this demand is now central to the Draft New Technology Agreement that the union presented to the NCB in 1983. To date the NCB has refused this draft as a basis for negotiation. But there are signs that the board might introduce its own pet version of the four-day week when the strike ends. This would involve the extension of shift lengths, presently limited by law at 7½ hours, to as much as 8½ or 9 hours. The intention of such a move would be to cut down the amount of time spent travelling to the face as a percentage of the working week, thereby improving productivity and shedding jobs. The prospect of nine hour shifts in 1985 is put into perspective by the promise of the 1919 Coal Mines Act for a *six* hour shift for mineworkers.

On a MIDAS equipped coal-face (see chapter 13) — one with an electronically controlled cutting machine — the NCB has shown that productivity can be doubled. Even without automation, productivity has been soaring in the industry in recent years. In the three years to June 1983 output per man-shift rose by 21.3 per cent, from 8.88 tonnes to 10.77. Figures like these could point the way to a shortening of the working week, earlier retirement, longer holidays, and more time off for education and training. Instead the NCB plans longer hours and redundancies.

Deskilling

New technology presents another hazard. The replacement of human skills with high technology systems can deskill jobs so that although physical conditions of work may be improved, boredom, isolation and stress are increased. People in deskilled jobs find that they have less immediate control over their working environment. Rather than determining the pace of their activity themselves they have to work at the speed dictated by the system. Often they find themselves working alone as other workers are replaced by automatic equipment. The consequences are not hard to predict: high levels of mental stress and fatigue are experienced in the new computerized control rooms. Even the NCB recognizes this:

> 'Operators in computerized colliery control rooms considered their jobs to have been reduced in perceived utility to the rest of the colliery. — The variety of skills required for the job of control room operator was also perceived as being less by operators in computerized collieries. — Autonomy was found to be more a function of managerial policy than the introduction of newer technologies.'[1]

The tendency towards deskilling that computerization brings has been accelerated by restrictions imposed by the NCB on the NUM after the management unions (NACODS and BACM) lost the battle to run the control rooms. This has had an important knock-on effect in negotiations surrounding the regrading of new jobs. Once a job has been established as belonging to the NUM, it is nearly always downgraded, often to a level comparable to the lowest surface grade. Consequently very few grades for new technology jobs have been agreed and NUM officials involved in the negotiations have become increasingly bitter about the board's unrelenting attitude. The national executive committee of the NUM reflected this frustration at its meeting on 9 February 1984 when it not only endorsed the actions of the grading and technology committee but also agreed that 'further consideration will be given to the banning of all new technology in the absence of a new technology agreement'. Like the pit closure issue, the argument over the role of new technology in the mines is still to be resolved.

Markets Present and Future

An expanding market is one of the guiding principles of the *Plan for Coal*. The aim in 1974 was for a total market of deep-mined and surface coal of 135 million tonnes, with the possibility that this could be even higher. But little effort has been put into achieving this target. Under the 'marketing expertise' of Ian MacGregor the concept of the market has been reduced to a simple question of corner shop economics. If supply and demand fail to meet, supply must be reduced.

However, it is increasingly obvious that the energy market has never been reducible to the norms of accountancy — political calculations are also centrally involved. It was a political decision of the government to adopt policies that cut manufacturing output and consequently the demand for coal. Political considerations are also behind Thatcher's commitment, since she came to office in 1979, to favour an expanding nuclear power industry.

Nuclear Energy

The government's pro-nuclear strategy contrasts dramatically with experience in the USA. There, as the *New Scientist* reported: 'The crisis in the American nuclear power industry deepened last week. It was announced that an almost completed nuclear power plant in Ohio is to be converted to run on coal. And another half-completed pressurized-water reactor at Marble Hill will be abandoned altogether . . . It is almost a decade since a US utility company last placed an order for a nuclear reactor that it did not later cancel.'[2] Given this, the decision by the CEGB to build a new pressurized-water reactor at Sizewell is perplexing to say the least. Sizewell is part of a project which, on Whitehall figures, will see an increase of electricity supplied by nuclear power stations from the current equivalent of 18 million tonnes of coal per year to between 38 and 73 million tonnes in the year 2000 and between 69 and 155 million tonnes in 2010. The upper limit of these figures would assume that no coal at all was being used to generate electricity. At present, the construction of only one coal-fired power station is projected.

The Politics of Marketing Coal

Despite the euphoric reception of miners' leaders at the 1984 Labour Party conference, the party has done little at a local level to expand the market for coal. But Labour local authorities could achieve a great deal. If, for example, they were to re-think the use of energy in their council buildings and homes by deciding in favour of coal-firing, the market for coal could be increased substantially. At present, few local authorities can boast even a five per cent share for coal in their overall energy requirement.

One easily achievable measure of support, on the part of local authorities, would be a commitment to building chimneys in all new council houses and the serious investigation of coal-fired district heating schemes for blocks of flats. In addition many councils could profitably convert or replace boilers using gas and oil to coal. In this they could be helped by an extension of the coal-firing scheme. This scheme provides a twenty-five per cent grant from the Department of Industry and a cheap loan of up to fifty per cent from the EEC to cover the capital costs of boiler conversion. At present, however, the scheme only operates in the private sector. Its extension to local authorities and health authorities, which would require amendment to the Department of Industry rules of guidance for local authorities, should be an important focus for campaigning by those who support the case for coal.

There are several reasons, over and above support for the coal industry, why Labour authorities would do well to consider changing the type of energy they use. In the first place there is the simple fact that coal is currently fifty per cent cheaper than oil. In the past year the price of heavy fuel oil (the type burned in large boilers) has risen by some thirty per cent. Furthermore, one of coal's most attractive features, particularly for councils with large housing stocks, is that an open flue in houses burning coal allows air circulation which in turn helps to solve the widespread and costly problem of condensation.

The sad truth is, however, that the Marketing Department of the NCB and the Solid Fuel Advisory Service seems to have relinquished the public sector to the advertising hype of the rival Gas and Electricity Boards. A housing committee chairman in a big northern city described the current situation: 'The Gas and Electricity Boards are practically kerb-crawling members of the housing committee, but I've yet to hear from the Solid Fuel Advisory Service'.

Pollution-Free Coal Burning

The days of coal fires producing smog are over. Much of the credit for this must go to the path-breaking work of scientists and engineers at the NCB's Coal Research Establishment. They have developed a technology called Fluidized Bed Combustion that has revolutionized the potential for coal. The system has many advantages: it enables superior heat transfer so that the same heat can be provided by smaller, cheaper boilers; it allows the use of a wider variety of coal, including low grade fuels; it reduces the corrosive deposits in boiler tubes; above all it eliminates nitrogen oxide and sulphur dioxide — the gases that form 'acid rain'.

This technology is available now and is currently being marketed by foreign companies throughout the world. In Sweden, after a referendum, the decision was taken to close all nuclear power stations by the year 2010 and change to Fluidized Bed Combustion of coal. Sweden has no coal deposits of its own so the Swedes will import the fuel they require. This could provide a lucrative market for the British coal industry — provided, of course, it is then able to meet the demand.

Combined Heat and Power

Sweden provides another example of a progressive and positive use of coal. The *Financial Times* of 21 June 1984 reported that Sodertalje, a large industrial town south of Stockholm, had decided to replace its oil-fired boilers and expand its district heating scheme with a scheme burning British coal. The system adopted supplies hot water for heating through seventy-five kilometres of underground pipes to twenty-thousand homes and several large industrial plants. Two suburbs of Stockholm have now also joined the scheme.

The Sodertalje system highlights the potential for a cost-effective and highly efficient energy option for the United Kingdom — the expansion of district heating with Combined Heat and Power (CHP). CHP power stations convert the heat that normally goes to waste through cooling towers into hot water which is piped to housing estates, schools, offices and factories for use in central heating. The savings that can be made are dramatic. Engineering consultants W.S. Atkins reported to the Department of Energy that CHP is eighty per cent fuel efficient compared to only thirty-five per cent for conventional power stations. Moreover, the technology is tried and tested. Denmark already heats forty per cent of its housing stock by CHP, and Finland and Sweden are not far behind.

In Britain, a Department of Energy consultants' report recommended the widespread adoption of CHP and district heating. Nine cities were studied and it was discovered that CHP schemes would be profitable even when the heat they supplied was marketed at ten per cent less than the cheapest alternative. There is strong support for adoption of the system on a cross party basis. Tory MP Peter Rost, who is certainly no friend of the NUM, has written: 'Why is it that in Western Europe there are already over two thousand urban district heating schemes, most of which use reject hot water from power stations that is piped into houses, while here, millions who need cheaper heating are denied the choice? Why are other countries expanding heat grids, providing cheaper heat than that available from other fuels, while we still argue about it? Why are we still the only country in Europe whose citizens look out of the windows of their freezing homes, often within sight of power stations, to see the stations discharging their hot water into the atmosphere or using it to warm fish?'[3]

Despite such widespread support, the government has allocated only £750,000 for pilot projects in only three of the nine cities that their consultants recommended. Compared with the huge sums involved on the nuclear programme, and even on other alternatives — £14.25 million is being spent on solar and wind power for instance — this is a remarkably meagre commitment.

The CEGB's attitude seems to be that if local authorities want the heat that escapes through the cooling towers of their power stations, then they should come and get it themselves. They ignore the fact that the heat from most of the stations is of too low a temperature to be of any use. Most of the district heating in Europe is derived from highly efficient purpose-built CHP schemes or from existing power stations converted to produce useful heat.

In spite of the fact that recent revision of energy legislation has amended the 1974 Electricity Act so that it is now 'the duty of every Electricity Board to adopt and support schemes for the use of heat produced in combination with electricity, or incidentally from its generation, for the heating of buildings or for other useful purposes', the CEGB's determination to follow a nuclear strategy makes any extension of the CHP programme much more difficult. Although CHP can theoretically operate from nuclear stations the fact that the buildings using the heat produced have to be in fairly close proximity makes its use too dangerous to be acceptable.

The Cabinet, it seems clear, is opposed to CHP for political reasons. Partly this is because the full implementation of the scheme would use up to 20 million tonnes of coal annually. On top of this it is probable that the government does not want to commit itself to an investment that would result in the creation of thousands of jobs in the construction, steel and boiler-making industries. The government's consultants estimated that the local on-site labour would total approximately 6,300 person-years. This figure excludes the jobs involved in producing equipment and components such as boilers and steel piping to carry the hot water underground.

In the light of all this, the desirability of a broad campaign for CHP schemes in the cities recommended by the government's consultants should be obvious. Most of the cities specified — Glasgow, Edinburgh, Belfast, Newcastle, Manchester, Sheffield, London, Leicester and Liverpool — have Labour councils. By joining forces with the construction, steel, boiler-makers' and transport unions they could develop a wide-ranging movement for CHP district heating schemes as an alternative to the environmental threat posed by nuclear power.

With a publicly declared commitment on the part of the Association of Metropolitan Authorities to the increased use of coal and persistent argument on local authority committees to counter the powerful lobbies for other competing fuels, the foundations of a rational and co-ordinated national energy policy can be laid. The time to act is now.

Notes

1. M. Best, *Human Aspects of Computer-Based Monitoring and Coal Mining Operations*, NCB , 1984.
2. *New Scientist*, 26 January 1984.
3. P. Rost, 'The Case for CHP', *Coal and Energy Quarterly*, no. 36, 1983.